C0-DKL-580

BUDDY, CAN YOU SPARE A DIME?

The Great Depression in the Illinois Valley 1929-1941

By R.G.Bluemer

Published by Grand Village Press
134 Cleveland Circle
Granville, IL 61326
© 2008
Printing - MCS Advertising - Peru, IL
ISBN 0-9673680-9-X

No part of this book may be reprinted without the permission of the author or an authorized representative.

A careful effort was made to trace the ownership of material used in this work and to give credit to copyright owners or other contributors. If an error or omission was made, it is completely inadvertent. The publisher will make any correction in future editions provided written notification is sent to the publisher.

The material found in this work was primarily derived from over 50,000 pages of microfilm information found in the LaSalle *Post-Tribune*, the Ottawa *Republican-Times*, the Morris *Herald,* the Bureau County *Republican,* and the Putnam County *Record.* Additional information was obtained from personal interviews with individuals who experienced the events and relatives of those individuals. The author would like to express his appreciation to the employees of the Illinois Department of Natural Resources and local librarians, who assisted in the research for this work.

1929
STOCK MARKET JITTERS

In 1929, Wall Street's financial transactions were of little concern to residents of the Illinois Valley. There were, no doubt, some local bankers and stockbrokers, who watched the ticker tape with growing interest. After all, the stocks of major companies had exhibited a remarkable growth during the 1920's.

On Thursday, Oct. 24, 1929, a brief news item from New York regarding the stock market appeared at the bottom of page one in the LaSalle *Daily Post Tribune*. At the beginning of trading, a block of 150,000 shares of Cities Service Co. stock was traded, breaking the record of 100,000 shares of Commonwealth and Southern Power. By 12:45 p.m., the trading in Cities Service had skyrocketed to over one million shares. Another major company, Simms Petroleum, had also shared the spotlight with a block of 100,000 shares.

Another story was of more interest to those dealing in wheat futures. At the Chicago exchange, pessimism pervaded the pit when December wheat dropped 11¢ a bushel in a single day. Millions of bushels of grain were offered, but there were few buyers. Each transaction drove the price lower.

The editors of the *Post* felt that stories about President Herbert Hoover's plans for Mississippi waterway development and the results of the bribery trial involving former Secretary of Interior Albert Fall and the Elk Hills oil reserve rated more coverage that day. Certainly local farmers and inland shippers would be more elated with Hoover's attempt to reduce the country's battleship fleet at the forthcoming London Naval Conference, which would possibly provide $30 million annually for navigation improvements on the tributaries of the Mississippi River. "It will cost one half one battleship," Hoover said as he promoted his plan.

Local economic news was reflected in the ads of the day. The J.C. Penny store at Second and Marquette in LaSalle was featuring great opportunities to buy cold weather clothes. Work pants were on sale for $1.98, and overalls were a bargain at only 89¢. Gordon's on First Street competed with their sale of overcoats for $23.50. Klein's grocery store at Second and Gooding encouraged shoppers to stock up on canned fruit from California. Peaches were on sale for 20¢, and Bartlett pears were only 33¢ for a large can. Other shoppers scanning the weekend ads would read how they could purchase a new Crosley radio for as little as $67 at Wernsmans Paint Store in LaSalle, W. H. Kays in Tonica, and J. E. Comiskey's in Lostant. At Hummer Furniture, home of WJBC radio, on the corner of Second and Joliet, a person could walk out of the store with a brand new Majestic radio for only $10 down. The purchase price of the sets ran from $137 to $167, but that did not include the price of the tubes.

The closeout sale at the Wonder Store next to Clancy's Drug Store in LaSalle appeared ominous, but in reality a new tenant, the S.S. Kresge store, was moving into the First Street location. Ad reprinted from the *Post-Tribune* on Oct. 24, 1929.

Local gridiron fans anxiously read the interview with Howard Fellows, director of athletics at LaSalle-Peru H.S. He said that John Samolitis, the team captain, would probably sit the bench due to an injured shoulder. It was troubling news for L-P supporters since the Illinois Valley conference title against Streator was scheduled for the weekend. Streator was 4-0 for the season, but both teams were undefeated in the conference.

HERE'S NEWS!

Of Mighty Importance

The Wonder Store

643 First St.   La Salle
is

GOING OUT OF BUSINESS

Lost Our Lease—Must Vacate

Entire Stock and Fixtures must be sold regardless of cost

A Gigantic Sale

that has no parallel in mercantile history of La Salle County will start

Saturday, October 26th
At 8A. M.

SEE THIS PAPER TOMORROW
For Full Particulars

NOTICE

Store closed all day Friday to remark and rearrange entire stock

Extra Salesladies Wanted, Apply Fri. Morning

Other towns had their own news to tell. The Oglesby city council finally opened bids on a new well estimated to cost $25,000. The Princeton American Legion post returned with a silver cup for its locomotive parade entry in a national competition in Louisville.

Nobody seemed to care about the national economic news. The weekend was coming up, and it was time to take in a movie. It was inexpensive, only 25¢ for adults and 10¢ for kids. The LaSalle Theater was showing "Fast Life," a story of "flaming youth" starring Douglas Fairbanks Jr. and Loretta Young. For those who preferred a romantic comedy, Colleen Moore was starring in "Smiling Irish Eyes" at the Majestic. After the movie, moviegoers might stop by Kelly and Cawley's luncheonette for a malted milk. The Peru Theater was featuring a western film, "Smilin' Guns," with Hoot Gibson. Janet Gaynor was featured at the Valley Theater in "Lucky Star," her first talking picture.

However, the news from New York continued to concern investors. As stock prices continued to drop, the leading bankers in

New York tried to rally the market with their moral support. A protection committee, consisting of bankers from J.P. Morgan and Company, Chase National Bank, Guaranty Trust Co., Bankers Trust, and First National Bank, organized in response to the freefall selling on Oct. 24. However, they only promised to commit a small portion of their financial resources to reassure the panicky stockholders.

The stock exchange was open on Saturday, Oct. 26, for a short two-hour session. The attitude was one of caution; the worst was over and no "fireworks" were expected. Everyone from the president on down in the administration together with business leaders tried to assure the trading public that the economy was basically sound. However, nobody was predicting an exuberant upturn in the market.

"Black Thursday," as October 24th was described, was not perceived by all as the end of the long bull market. To some investors, the bottom had been reached. Bargain hunters were bidding up the price on sound companies in the oversold market. Odd lot sales from small investors began coming in to the brokerage houses, but the big name investors were missing from the rebound.

The following week, the fluctuations in stock prices were looked upon as a temporary, albeit painful, decline that would end soon. Even though there had been substantial losses for ten days, the attitude on the part of the government in Washington was that it was better to have a short period of rapidly falling prices rather than a prolonged, gradual decline. If money was taken out of the market, it was assumed that funds would simply be shifted to other investment opportunities in businesses and industry. Democratic Senator King from Utah called for a congressional investigation to explain the market decline during the opening session of Congress in January. However, Hoover had nothing to say about the situation at the regular Tuesday press conference.

On Oct. 30, Richard Whitney, vice president of the board of governors at the New York Stock Exchange, announced that trading would not open until noon on Thursday. The Exchange would be closed on Friday and Saturday simply to allow the workers to catch up on the huge numbers of transactions in the previous week. The market was up 1 to 27 points over Tuesday's close and was described as "a splendid come back." Employees at the brokerage houses needed a break. Traders were characterized as having gone without sleep for as much as 72 hours and nearing complete physical exhaustion. The long weekend holiday was needed in order to effectively handle the trading at the exchange, according to Whitney.

The break in trading did not stem the tide of sell orders. On Monday afternoon, traders were overwhelmed with sell orders ranging from blocks of 5,000 to 50,000 shares. During the first 30 minutes of the session, over $2 million shares were traded. Blue chip stocks such as U.S. Steel, AT&T, Westinghouse, General Electric,

Johns Manville, and National Cash Register, were all dropping in price. In spite of the downturn, the news in New York was that the "Big Six" bankers were not meeting on Monday. Apparently, market conditions were of no concern to them.

This cartoon in the *Post-Tribune* captured the sentiment of the day on Nov. 4, 1929. Wall Street speculators were looking for a bailout from Congress.

One stock closely watched was U.S. Steel. On Nov. 7, a rally boosted its price from $162 to $175. The morning trading more than doubled the previous day's orders. Prices began to rise especially for the major companies, such as American Can, Johns Manville, Montgomery Ward, and American and Foreign Power. It was still not a significant rally compared to the millions that had been lost by speculators in the previous weeks, but it gave a sense of hope to worried investors.

Locally, the events on Wall Street were overshadowed by a celebration in the Illinois Valley. The long-awaited dedication of the Shippingsport Bridge was slated for Thursday, Nov. 7, 1929.

Road crews work on the approaches to the new bridge in 1928. (IDOT file)

5

The Shippingsport Bridge was still under construction on May 31, 1928. (Oglesby Library)

On Wednesday, Nov. 6, 1929, the lift section of the bridge had been given a final test in preparation for the opening of the new span the following day. Flags, bunting, and shields emblazoned with the word "Welcome" hung along the buildings leading to the bridge. The *Post* described the main portion of the bridge as "almost a solid mass of red, white, and blue." City officials closed the municipal offices in LaSalle and Oglesby at noon so that employees could attend the historic event.

A blast of factory whistles and the pealing of church bells in LaSalle and Oglesby heralded the one o'clock event at the south approach to the bridge. The Marquette band provided the musical entertainment. In the absence of Stuart Duncan, chairman of the bridge committee, John Young of Oglesby presided over the event. Other dignitaries included Rev. William Kelly, pastor of St. Patrick's in LaSalle; Rev. Theodore Wujek, pastor of Sacred Heart Church in Oglesby; and Rev. Moses Gunn, a Baptist minister and oldest native son of LaSalle Township. Sponsors were Miss Idalette Campbell, daughter of the first mayor of LaSalle; Alexander Campbell, and Mrs. Allie Jones, daughter of the first mayor of Oglesby, Thomas Watson.

As part of the ceremonies, Mrs. W. S. Mason, acting mayor of LaSalle, and Charles Spurr, mayor of Oglesby, untied the ribbon to allow traffic across the bridge. George McClary, pastor of the First Congregational Church of Oglesby, then gave the benediction. Everyone joined in singing "Illinois," which was followed with a musical selection by the band.

6

The $550,000 Shippingsport Bridge linking LaSalle and Oglesby took more than two years to complete. The concrete roadway was 24 feet wide, adequate at that time for the passage of three automobiles. (Oglesby Library)

Everyone joined in a grand march across the bridge and a motorcade to Matthiessen Memorial Auditorium, where the Marquette and LaSalle-Peru High School bands performed. J. E. Malone presided over the dedication, which included addresses by numerous federal, state, and local government officials. A luncheon was held at the Illinois Valley Manufactures' Club for the dignitaries following the dedication.

Matthiessen Memorial Auditorium at LaSalle-Peru H. S. was used for part of the dedication ceremonies for the opening of the Shippingsport Bridge. (1929 LaSalle-Peru High School yearbook)

7

Traffic traveled over the 1,679-foot bridge for the remainder of the afternoon and evening, but a closing was put into effect for the next ten days to make final adjustments and tests. In the meantime, local residents had to use the older bridge to the west. From that vantage point, they could watch the lift span being raised and lowered for testing.

The lift span, operated from the Shippingsport bridgetender's cabin, looked much the same as this one in Florence, IL.
(Oglesby Library)

In the days that followed, more attention was focused on events in New York. At the stock exchange, almost $3 million in sell orders flooded the market creating a drop of 10-22 points in the industrial blue chip stocks. U.S. Steel closed on Nov. 10 at $159.50, only $2 above its lowest price for the year. Other blue chips followed that same pattern. GE hit its lowest price of the year, $193, and American Can dropped below $100. Those declines and the corresponding financial loses were still not reflected in the daily lives of most Illinois Valley residents.

Impoverishment was not only felt by those who had lost money in the stock market, but also by a growing number of local residents, who had little to begin with. The approaching Christmas season inspired many civic organizations to help those less fortunate individuals. One of the groups participating in charitable work was the Romulus Meehan post of the American Legion in LaSalle. During the week of Nov. 11-18, the post supported the Big Heart Fund, which had been organized in 1928 by the Tri-City Family Welfare Society, the Chamber of Commerce, the Boy Scouts, the Majestic Theater, and the *Post-Tribune*. Their goal was to collect clothing, food, and fuel for destitute families in the Illinois Valley.

Demand for blue chip stocks rebounded on Nov. 14. Economists attributed the 1-17 point gains to optimism growing out of Secretary of the Treasury Andrew Mellon's call for a tax reduction. Among the big movers were Standard Oil of New Jersey –

8

responding to one order of a million shares at $50, General Electric, and U.S. Steel, all up 17. It seemed that the bear market had run its course, and the bulls were regaining strength on Wall Street.

The LaSalle State Bank, directed by President Stuart Duncan, apparently was caught up in the enthusiasm of an expanding market. Duncan urged the directors to increase the capital stock in the bank from $100,000 to $150,000. Mr. Duncan said the move should be taken "in order that the bank can keep up with the increase in business and in keeping with future progress." The capitalization would be accomplished by issuing another 500 shares of stock.

The farm report issued by both the Illinois and U.S. Departments of Agriculture also buoyed spirits. Yields had improved. Statewide corn averaged over 34 bushels per acre, and soybeans were at 17 bushels per acre. The fall harvest of soybeans was even higher than the record-breaking crop of 1928. Much of the gain was attributed to improved weather conditions in October. Killing frosts were generally not experienced until the third week of October. While the crop report was cheered by farm owners, the report also concluded that "throughout the state (farm hands) are too plentiful."

Moving that grain downriver on barges would soon be improved as a major segment of the Illinois Waterway was nearing completion. At the end of November, Sutton Van Pelt, the civil engineer and contractor for construction of the lock and dam at Starved Rock, announced that the work would be completed on Friday, Nov. 22. It took two years to finish the largest and first lock and dam project on the Illinois River.

Work in progress on the Starved Rock Dam. Date unknown.

9

All of the news in the Illinois Valley wasn't upbeat. In fact, serious crime seemed to be a constant problem. Federal investigators continued to make raids on local saloons. The Nov. 19 federal court docket in Chicago listed prohibition violators Steve Urbanowski, Steve Jozwiak, and Frank Retzel of LaSalle; Jerry O'Conner, S. J. Kammerer of Ottawa; and George Plimmer and Charles Collier of Streator. Their fines ranged from $25 to $100, a small price to pay compared to the profits involved in bootlegging.

Although bootlegging was common enough in the Illinois Valley, it usually did not involve the type of gang violence found in Chicago. However, armed robberies and other forms of larceny were becoming more common. Safe crackers, who broke into the Serena Bank and the J.D. Marshall Department Store, were no doubt disappointed after blowing open the small safe in the department store. After discovering it was empty, they were just as frustrated finding the bank safe was too strong to access its contents.

More disturbing was the robbery at the Hotel Kaskaskia, where two men, each about 25 years old, entered the building at 4:15 a.m. and asked Henry Lehmann, the night clerk, for a room. One man then pulled a revolver and told the clerk to lay on the floor while they stole $150 - $200 from the hotel cash register. To make their getaway, they told Lehmann to take the elevator to the top floor and remain there.

The robbery at LaSalle's Kaskaskia Hotel was only one example of the "crime wave" that spread through the Illinois Valley during the early years of the Depression.

Robberies had become so prevalent in the previous months that the *Post-Tribune* was describing the situation as a "crime wave." Indeed, few people would have predicted the number of bank robbers that would descend on the small town banks of the Illinois Valley as the Depression worsened.

While average citizens became more concerned about these troubling events, they could look forward to the many forms of local entertainment. The Majestic Theater in LaSalle was featuring the "all-talking" comedy "The Cock Eyed World," and the Rexy in

LaSalle was showing "The Broadway Melody." The public was invited to the new Utica auditorium to dance to the music of the Roy Peters' Orchestra for only 75¢. Even less expensive was the dance at the Auditorium Ballroom in LaSalle; admission was only 10¢. The Firemen's Riverside Ballroom in Spring Valley, featuring the Nebes Orchestra, was yet another destination. (*Post-Tribune* ad, Nov 13, 1929)

Alger's REXY Theatre

TODAY
and
THURS.

First
ALL SINGING
ALL TALKING
ALL DANCING
Drama

ANITA PAGE
BESSIE LOVE
CHARLES KING

The BROADWAY MELODY

First Time Shown in La Salle at Our Prices

Also Comedy

Prices:
Children 10¢
Adults 25¢

To the increasing numbers of unemployed – two million jobs had been lost in manufacturing, mining, railroading and agriculture since 1920 – a local building project, such as the proposed post office expansion in Ottawa, was encouraging news.

President Herbert Hoover expressed his optimism in the economy of the nation. Citing the strength and health of the business community, he called upon business leaders to carry on the construction work initiated by the government. "These assurances have been given, and thereby we not only assure the consuming power of the country, but we remove fear from millions of homes," said Hoover.

President Hoover summed up his remedy for the economic ills of the country in a single word, "work."

Work did not always come with a paycheck. With Christmas 1929 approaching quickly, the Granville Chamber of Commerce decided to increase its efforts on its Good Fellow program. Usually, the Granville organization collected candy for needy kids, but the need was much more serious in 1929. Julius Hansen and Edward Hawthorne took charge of the project to collect baskets of food and other useful things to brighten the faces of many families on Christmas morning. The activity was not limited to chamber members. Anyone who wished to participate in the program was invited to contact either man to donate his services.

The Oglesby Junior Women organized a similar program. Under the leadership of Miss Dorothy Moyle, baskets of food would be distributed to help poor families in their town during the holiday season.

11

1930
COPING WITH UNEMPLOYMENT

As the new year began, it was apparent that a major portion of the local work force would soon receive their final paychecks. For decades, mining companies were a major source of employment in the Illinois Valley. When mines played out in Braidwood, Carbon Hill, and Coal City, miners moved west. They found work in the mines at Streator, Standard, Spring Valley, Ladd, Toluca, Granville, and LaSalle-Peru-Oglesby. The major employer in the latter area was the Carbon Coal Co., which owned mines in LaSalle, Peru, and Jonesville. There had been trouble with the mining operations over working conditions until the company and the Northern Illinois Miners Union (NIMU) agreed to a three-year contract. After a year of inactivity, the mines re-opened in April 1928.

In spite of the agreement, pickets from the competing United Mine Workers union, which wanted all miners to join their organization, continued to harass shipments from the Carbon Coal Co. On Jan. 11, 1930, the news was made public that 600 men at Carbon Coal would be idled. "Closing the mines is a hard blow to the hundreds of our members and their families. It leaves them without means for a livelihood in the dead of winter," said James Yearsley, president of the NIMU.

The former LaSalle Carbon Coal Office still stands on the east side of LaSalle. This photo was taken in 1907. (Oglesby Library)

Hope for a re-opening of the mines was dashed when C.C. Swift, general manager of the LaSalle Carbon Coal Co., announced plans to seal the entrances to the mines as soon as the mined coal was hoisted. The company said it might sell the mines. The 16 mules used to pull the underground coal cars were soon brought to the surface.

Miners of the Carbon Coal Co. had been hoisting coal for decades. Unemployment was becoming a significant local concern when the mine closed in 1930. Photo circa 1907. (Oglesby Library)

The Union Coal Mine, operated by the UMW, took over the operations of the Carbon Coal Co. mine in Peru in 1930. (Peru Library)

On Feb. 15, the *Post-Tribune* reported that the LaSalle Carbon Coal mines had been sold to Union Coal, and they would be operated by UMW miners. Men were still not working at the LaSalle mine. The Peru mine had 83 men at work. Future mining operations at Jonesville, however, were doubtful. It was not until March that the company decided to seal the Jonesville mine.

The local press continued to report President Hoover's confidence in the economy. Prosperity was in sight according to the former WWI Food Administrator, but the statistics did not support such a rosy picture. Unemployment had grown by another million over the past year. Acute unemployment was identified in 13 states. Figures for the remaining 35 states were downplayed as "seasonal unemployment."

What little savings most people had was often deposited at the local banks. When rumors began to spread that the Peoples' Trust and Savings Bank in Streator might be out of cash, a run developed. There was cause for alarm by both city and school officials as well as ordinary citizens. The city had on deposit $50,000, and the school fund amounted to $33,000. In an effort to cover the tide of withdrawals, money was brought to the bank from Chicago. However, it wasn't enough, and the bank was closed.

Within a month, it was put in the hands of a receiver, J. Weston Essington of Streator. It would be his job to liquidate the $300,000 in remaining cash and bonds. Nobody knew how much of their money, if any, they would receive.

After the run at the Streator bank, there was also a run on the Granville National Bank. Depositors stood in line at the teller cages to withdraw their savings on Mar. 10, 1930.
(Granville Village Hall)

Rumors, which started in Mark, that the Granville bank was calling in outstanding notes and might be "hard up," panicked scores of depositors, who arrived early in the morning waiting for the bank to open. Bank officers were not alarmed about the scene and paid the depositors, who wanted to close their accounts. Small depositors were paid immediately, but there was concern about the redemption of the larger certificates of deposit. John G. Pletsch, president of the bank, reassured anxious patrons, "There is nothing to worry about. We have the situation well in hand," J. W. Hopkins, the cashier, wasted no time in contacting LaSalle banks for additional funds, which arrived at noon.

Seeing that the run was continuing, bank officials contacted the Federal Reserve Bank in Chicago seeking additional funds. In a dramatic scene at 3 p.m., an armored car arrived at the bank. Four guards were in the vehicle armed with pistols and a machine gun. The agent in charge quickly reassured depositors that the bank was absolutely solvent. Cashier Hopkins continued to close out accounts without hesitation. The panic was soon over, and few depositors were seeking withdrawals on Tuesday. The run was over, and confidence was restored.

A similar situation faced the Putnam County State Bank of Hennepin shortly after the run in Granville. Those officials followed a similar course of action by contacting the larger banks in LaSalle and securing the necessary funds to meet the anticipated demand for withdrawals.

There was another way of making a bank withdrawal – simply steal it. On April 30, two men walked into the First National Bank of Gardner at closing and shouted "Stick 'em up!" A.G. Perry, the bank president; D. O. Jeffers, the cashier; Carl Lutz, and Lizzie Barton, bookkeepers; were promptly tied up with radio wire and forced into a back room. Other customers, walking in at the last minute, were also tied up. After moving the hostages to the basement, one of the robbers forced the cashier to open the safe in the vault. In addition to the money from the safe and the cash drawers, the robbers also emptied a secret drawer, whose location was thought to be known only by bank employees. The loot totaled over $8,300 of which $5,000 was the payroll for the South Wilmington coal miners to be picked up that day. The robbers fled in a car unseen since the streets were relatively empty at 4 p.m. Later, the police determined that the getaway car was a Model A Ford. The Grundy County Bankers Association offered a $1,000 reward for the apprehension of the robbers.

The effects of the Depression were also reflected in the increasing numbers of burglaries. Within 36 hours, thieves broke into the Spiller Drug Store in Gardner and took 15 bottles of perfume and a gallon of alcohol. Over $350 in clothing merchandise was stolen on April 11 at the Dunn and Morrow clothing store in Seneca.

At the end of April, the Barr Drug Store and the Rosslo Grocery Store in Braidwood were robbed. The businesses lost a total of $700 in merchandise and cash. Shortly after the bank robbery in Gardner, the Elgin, Joliet & Eastern railroad storehouse at Minooka was burglarized. Thieves took ten gallons of gasoline and tools. There was no apparent pattern in the string of thefts.

15

Other individuals were still making a living from bootlegging. On April 30, Federal offices raided the Putnam County farm owned by Joe Englehaupt. They found two huge vats, one with a first-run capacity of 2,000 gallons and a second-run vat with a capacity of 1,300 gallons. There were also 11 fermentation vats capable of holding 4,600 gallons. The total amount of finished alcohol was 200 gallons. Four men were arrested in Spring Valley: Tony Barceloni, George Smith, Fred Gualandri, and Cosmo Angelen. A second raid on the farm of Elmer Flaherty of Ladd resulted in the arrest of Joe Viglia and John Greno, who were cooking mash. The operation included six vats with a capacity of 4,300 gallons each. The federal agents destroyed the stills at both locations and took seven men to the Peoria County jail. They would be unemployed for some time.

Most people did not resort to criminal activities to pay their bills. In Putnam County, John R. Cox, president of the Prairie State coal mine in Mark, said he would hire as many as 500 men at the Mark mine. His company had purchased the property from the St. Paul Coal Co. in 1929, and it had not been producing coal for the previous five years. The St. Paul Company found other sources of coal that could be produced at a lower cost.

The St. Paul Coal Co. mine in Mark, IL was purchased by John Cox Sr. and renamed the Prairie State Coal Co. (Putnam County Historical Society)

The new operation in Mark would be managed by the Cox family. His wife, Laura, would serve as secretary-treasurer, and their son, John Cox Jr., filled the roles of vice president and assistant general manager. On May 26, John Cox Sr. was ready to hire about 100 men to clean up and rebuild the works. One of their first jobs was to pump out the water that had seeped into the lower level.

The abandonment of the Jonesville mine made it possible for Cox to purchase that salvaged equipment, including the motors and self-dumping cages, from the Union Coal Co. The Mark mine

16

was to be electrified; the tipple was under construction; and the self-dumping cages still had to be installed. Cox felt that there was a demand for the Mark coal. "We have obtained assurances of a steady market for our coal and everything points to success for our mine," Cox told a reporter from the *Post-Tribune*. He explained that he was going to purchase ten new trucks to ship coal to retail customers within a 20-mile radius of Mark. Other coal would be loaded on his Rutland, Toluca, and Northern RR and transferred to the Chicago, St. Paul, and Milwaukee RR, the Chicago & Alton, and the Santa Fe.

Cox planned to continue a gradual increase in hiring miners at Mark until 500 men were on the payroll by Sept. 15, when the first coal would be hoisted. Production was predicted to reach 1,500 tons a day. Cox promised to give miners in Putnam and Marshall Counties preference in hiring. If there weren't enough local miners, he said he would hire miners from neighboring counties. The pay would be the UMW union scale during the preparation work, but a formal contract would not be drawn up until the mine began hoisting coal in September. On June 2, 380 unemployed miners from Putnam and Marshall Counties applied for jobs in the Mark mine. Everyone was hired. By June 11, much had been accomplished at the Mark mine. New smoke stacks were being built, and a group of men was busy painting all of the buildings. Three railroad cars brought in the fire brick to line the boilers, but it would not be until early August before the boilers were ignited. Cox had hoped to have coal in production by Sept. 15.

The Union Coal Co. in Peru was also ready to go into full production. J. D. Walsh said the operation would be at capacity by the end of August or early September. A hundred miners were already in the colliery hoisting coal, and more would be hired as the demand increased for fuel for the fall-winter season. Prospects were good for hiring an additional 300 miners.

Other industries were also hiring. On July 1, hundreds of men at Alpha Cement in LaSalle (pictured) had been laid-off indefinitely. Only a few men remained to run the office and work in the finishing department. However, an increase in demand prompted company  officials to call back up to 200 men in mid-August. (Photo by author)

17

The Peru city council also acted to hire the unemployed at the end of June. The city had two major sewer projects on the agenda with a price tag of $60,000. One sewer line would run from Pike Street to the Illinois River. The other project involved the "big fill," an open and smelly ravine that was both a nuisance and a health hazard. This project would run from the north end of the ravine to Water Street at the south end. The council anticipated that the two projects would require the hiring of a large number of local men.

Even more hiring seemed likely. Illinois Zinc acquired the manufacturing equipment and all patent rights from the Extruded Metals Corp. in New York. Officials of the Peru company said they would need 100 employees for the production of extruded zinc cups used in manufacturing dry cell batteries for flashlights, telephones, ignition systems, and alarms. Skilled operators were needed to run the equipment. An undisclosed number of females would be hired for the sorting and packing departments. Another project that might generate local employment included the construction of the $70,000 Peru Theater. Yet another construction project for Peru was the proposed Peru post office, estimated to cost $100,000.

While many men sought gainful employment through hard work, others followed a get-rich quick path and engaged in various forms of thievery. Bootlegging continued, but, in the early years of the Depression, local robberies and burglaries grabbed the headlines.

Criminals were not always successful in escaping with large quantities of cash. The investigation of the Troy Grove Bank robbery on July 9 showed how diligent police work usually resulted in the apprehension of criminals. Two career criminals, Sam Bottom and Harry Lee Watson, decided to drive their Chrysler "77" (1930 model pictured) up from Yukon, MO to rob one or more banks in the Illinois

Valley. On the way to LaSalle, they stopped at Tonica for gas and took the opportunity to case the local bank. Apparently, the security was too tight, and they drove north until they spotted a roadside sign, "Troy Grove – pop. 261." While driving through the village, they checked out possible escape routes before heading to what they described as an "easy mark," the Troy Grove State Bank.

In his confession, Watson described how they proceeded. "We pulled up in front of the bank and went inside. A man was sitting at a desk. A woman was back of the cage. I made them put up

18

their hands. Then another man came out from the back, and I made him put up his hands. We put him down with the others. I put the money in a pillowslip. Went back in the vault and got the shotgun that was there. Then we took the young fellow (Harvey Crane) with us when he went out, got into the car, and drove around the corner. We let him out down the road a piece thinking it was near the railroad station. Went back down to Missouri."

At their farm in Yukon, MO, they divided the loot, which amounted to less than $2,000 in cash according to Watson. They also took travelers' checks and post office receipts. The total was actually closer to $3,000. A nationwide manhunt resulted in their capture and incarceration in the Chicago jail.

Not all thefts were as profitable. A case in point was the attack on the Lacon toll-bridge collector, Ray Harvey. At 1 a.m. on Aug. 5, two young men drove a 1929 Chevrolet sedan up to the toll cabin, where Harvey handed the driver a toll ticket. Instead of handing over the toll charge, one of the men stuck a sawed-off shotgun out the window and told Harvey to "reach for the sky." While keeping Harvey covered, the other man searched the toll collector and took his cash and watch. The other man went inside the toll cabin and grabbed a shotgun, rifle, and field glasses. Pocketing only $14, the men returned to their car and drove away. Harvey immediately tried to phone the Marshall County sheriff's office but found the phone wires had been cut. He ran into town to spread the alarm, but the men had made good their escape.

The next day, Aug. 6, another significant theft was discovered. This time, the thieves were not after money but rather copper wire. Five LaSalle boys, Frank Urbanc, Louis Sever, Vincent Kmieciak, Anton Murwaki, and Kenneth Whitsel, were playing along the Rock Island tracks near Joliet Street when an eastbound freight passed them. Suddenly, a 140-pound bundle of interurban trolley wire was tossed out of one of the cars. Two black men then jumped from the passing car. The men asked the boys where they might find a junk dealer who would buy the copper wire. The boys didn't give them the information, so the men hid the wire under some brush along the Illinois Central and Rock Island tracks and went off to find a junk dealer. The boys then took the wire home to cut it up and sell it themselves. The wire was thought to be stolen from an abandoned spur of the Chicago and Illinois RR located west of DePue. A similar incident occurred in Ottawa the day before, resulting in the arrest of two different black men for a similar crime. A stakeout was set up near the railroad in LaSalle hoping the thieves would return for their hidden wire, but it was unsuccessful.

Only two days later, on Aug. 8, there was an even bigger theft of copper wire. During the night, the thieves made off with over 500 pounds of phone wire cut from the telephone poles covering a distance of over a mile along a county road east of Grand Ridge. The loss of the Bell Telephone wire was similar to the theft of several tons of AT&T telephone cable cut from poles west of Ottawa.

Copper wire was a valuable commodity, but its theft brought a stiff sentence to Wilder White and his son, Gerald, and their co-defendant Nathan Luceletti. After being found guilty in a Princeton court in September, all three men were sent to the Joliet penitentiary for terms of one to ten years.

Thieves struck in one community after another in rapid succession. After an unsuccessful attempt to break into the A. C. Woodke grocery store in Tonica earlier in the week, burglars were successful in removing a piece of glass from the front door and unlatching the lock of Jenning's hardware store on Aug. 17. The loot, valued at about $150, included rifles, watches, pocket knives, and a small amount of cash. The next day, Mr. Jenning told a reporter from the *Post-Tribune* the crime must have been committed by someone other than local citizens. "Residents of Tonica know where my stock is kept and they would have taken my stock of knives rather than the display board, which was in the show case," he said.

On Aug. 29, the community of Troy Grove remembered one of its most famous residents, Wild Bill Hickok. A thousand people gathered at the village park for the unveiling of a granite monument and plaque (right) commemorating the achievements of the young man, who grew up in the village and later became one of the most famous lawmen of the American West. Participating in the ceremony was Mrs. Martha Hickok, the widow of the lawman's brother Horace D. Hickok. State Representative R. G. Soderstrom was the principal speaker. The Paw Paw band was on hand to provide musical entertainment. Moses Gunn, 91, told stories of the village's "prairie days." Residents and children dressed as Indians and cowboys participated in a pageant. Certainly, had "Will Bill" been alive, the crime spree in the Illinois Valley would have been short-lived.

Petty thievery hardly compared to some of the ill-gotten fortunes made by bootleggers during Prohibition. Federal agents were constantly searching for Illinois Valley stills that contributed to the profits of the Capone syndicate.

On Sept. 19, 1930, five bootleggers from Mark suddenly found themselves "unemployed" when eight federal prohibition agents under Deputy Administrator James Eaton and his men discovered two huge stills in Mark at 1:30 a.m. Taken into custody were August Guisti, Ray Paganelli, Joseph Tulini, Steve Faletti, and Joseph Bueganelli. Three other men from Rockford were also arrested. The gang was operating two 1,000-gallon stills in different locations in Mark, one in the Co-operative store on Hennepin Street and another in an old house west of the jail. At each location, six vats, each with a total capacity of 30,000 gallons, were uncovered. The men had produced 700 gallons of finished alcohol. There were also large quantities of bottles with labels of brand name whiskeys.

Months of surveillance had discovered daily movements of cars and trucks at the locations. The owner of the co-operative store, Mario Bazzani, a former mayor of Mark, denied any knowledge of the operation. The building was actually owned by John Paneir of Ottawa. Eaton expressed confidence that the raid on Mark would curb the supply of booze being shipped to the Capone syndicate, which was operating through Moline, Rock Island, and other large cities in northern Illinois.

The crime wave continued with another bank robbery in Mazon, IL. At 8 p.m. on Oct. 7, four men kidnapped Gardie Platt, the president of the First National Bank of Mazon, his wife, and their son, Edwin. The family members and a neighbor, Miss Louise Stroull, were bound with their mouths taped shut for over ten hours. At 6 a.m. the next morning, the bandits took Platt to the bank where they forced him to disarm the burglar alarm and open the bank safe. They removed $13,000, and after returning Platt to the family home, they made their getaway heading to Chicago. Platt phoned the Grundy County sheriff, Harry Jones, in Morris to inform him of the armed robbery.

Although most robberies were not as dramatic, they were frequent and often perpetrated by local residents. A spree of robberies at gas stations and stores ended with a gun battle between the police officer in Minooka and four young men from Marseilles. Brothers Clifford and Clarence Peddicord and Tom and Harold Babcock confessed to the string of crimes and were sentenced on Oct. 23 to terms of one to twenty years in the Joliet prison. Another

21

young man, Russell Gumm, who was also connected with the robberies, was still at large when the rest of the gang was arrested. Only a relatively small number of individuals found "employment" in illegal activities. Most men were hard working or anxious to find employment. The problem of local unemployment was finally recognized. On Oct. 30, The *Post-Tribune* admitted it in a front-page editorial article with the following comment. "For several months we have buried our heads – buried like an ostrich. We have tried to say that 'everything was alright!' – when we knew it was not, No one has been fooled."

The LaSalle newspaper then began a campaign to help the unemployed by offering free "jobs wanted" ads in their daily newspaper. The paper printed a coupon so individuals could list their name, address, phone, and type of desired work. Within a short time, the coupons were arriving at the newspaper office, and the information was advertised in the newspaper. Most responses from the unemployed were for any work available. Many asked for $2.50 for a day's labor. While most of the job seekers were men, a few women, such as Mrs. Alma George, who lived at 363 Bucklin, sought work washing, sewing, ironing, or mending.

Local municipalities also worked hard to alleviate the growing unemployment. At the end of October, the Peru city council hoped that the Pike Street sewer project would provide jobs. Commenting to *Post* reporter, Mayor Al Hasse said, "This improvement will give aid to many unemployed persons and will last for at least several weeks. This project is one of Peru's answers to the unemployment situation this year."

On Nov. 11, the Peru mayor described the city's progress. Another 40 men would be added to the 50-60 men working on the Pike Street sewer project. Hasse also pointed out that 27 blocks were paved during the summer months. In addition, the unsightly poles and electrical wiring were removed along Peru's Fourth Street business district. These civic improvements, together with the planned construction of a new movie theater, provided many jobs to local men according to the mayor.

Although Illinois Power Co. wasn't hiring, a "Job Wanted" ad in the LaSalle newspaper caught the attention of the company manager, William Schreiner. "I didn't really need an extra man, but I just wanted to help," he said. The Peru man he hired had worked for a local company for 21 years before being laid off, and he had a family of six to support. Touched by that discouraging situation, and with the approach of winter, Schreiner, gave the man a job with the crew laying a gas line in Oglesby. "We had enough men on our crew, and we really didn't need any more help but we thought we could find room for this man. It will help a little, anyhow," said the manager.

Municipalities and relief groups throughout the Illinois Valley didn't wait for relief from Washington but rather took matters into their own hands to help the unemployed and hungry families. Relief for the needy was on the agenda of the Tri-City Family Welfare Society and the business community. Francis X. Kilduff, a prominent LaSalle business leader, chaired a committee of 80 community leaders, who worked with the welfare society to develop a relief plan for the hundreds of needy families in the Tri-Cities.

Peru's Turn Hall was the location for a Depression benefit dance in November 1930. (Peru Library)

On Nov. 11, the LaSalle American Legion post did its part to both observe Armistice Day and to assist the needy by holding a dance. All proceeds from the event at the Illini Auditorium were turned over to the local relief fund.

Another benefit dance was held later in November at Turn Hall in Peru. The Turner family decided to donate the use of the hall. Between 800 and 900 couples bought tickets for the occasion, which featured the Doodledorfer band. Princeton also had a number of projects underway or in the planning stages to bring relief to the unemployed. A total expenditure of $300,000 would provide jobs for many of the unemployed. The $130,000 new junior high school project had employed as many as 60 men at one time as the brickwork was underway. The school was expected to be finished in March 1931. A $45,000 addition that would add 15 rooms to Perry Memorial Hospital would provide two months of work. The Bureau County highway department was constructing a new $25,000 concrete and brick garage. The Christian Science Church continued to employ men until February 1931 on its $40,000 building opposite Memorial Square.

23

The Apollo Theater in Princeton was being renovated at a cost of $40,000. The work required major changes to exterior walls and the addition of two store fronts with second floor offices on either side of the theater. The theater itself would have an enlarged lobby, new seats, and a renovated balcony. Although the marquee advertises current movies in April 2008, the Apollo Theater retains much of its 1930's character. (Photo by author)

In order to determine the extent of unemployment and dire economic conditions in the Tri-Cities, 40 women from the LaSalle Woman's Club began a week-long, house-to-house canvass on Nov. 10. They divided the city into six zones and assigned a ward captain to each one: J. B. McManus, L. J. Stewart, M. J. Faletti, O. M. Benson, R. L. Wright, and W. J. Aplington. The women expected that the canvass of every home would be completed within a week. Individuals who were unemployed could register at the Washington School in Oglesby, the St. Valentine's Church Hall, and the Peru and LaSalle Chamber of Commerce offices.

Speaking on behalf of the Tri-City Welfare Society, Miss Helen Wolfe described the priority to child welfare she felt was necessary in an interview with a *Post* reporter. "No child must suffer from hunger in the Tri-Cities. Relief to mothers and children must be given in their own homes," she said. Citing previous economic depressions, she said it was the children who suffered the most because of the lack of money to buy milk and food. During the last national panic, she recalled how, in some cases, the milk supply was totally cut off. This resulted in thousands of children being malnourished, and their health was permanently injured.

It wasn't only the lack of milk that concerned Miss Wolfe. Shortages of coal, clothing, and overcrowded housing, combined with growing debts created fear and uncertainty when a father was laid off. When a father was idle due to unemployment and mothers went off to work, it posed great family hardship, and the children suffered depression, according to Miss Wolfe.

Although more men in the Tri-Cities were earning an income from jobs on city and factory payrolls, the registration of jobless men continued. On Nov. 18, Peru officials hired an additional 30 men to clean city streets. Albert Wolf, superintendent of streets, assigned the men to work on First, Second, and Third Streets. It was a small project, only expected to last ten days, but it did provide some income. Another 90 men were working on the Pike Street sewer project. The mild November weather made possible continued progress, and it was anticipated that the entire project would be completed without weather delays.

Local industries in the Tri-Cities also took an active role in providing for the unemployed. Marquette Cement Manufacturing advanced plans for a four-month construction project. "We deemed it possible to go ahead with the work at this time believing that in so doing at least temporary employment would be afforded a number of men. We are overlooking no opportunity to find jobs for additional men," said, Frank Moyle, assistant superintendent at the Marquette plant. Thirty men were employed in the raw grinding department of the mill. Another 20 men were at work cutting a new road from Marquette Hill to the southern approach to Shippingsport Bridge.

On Nov. 19, Emil Gebhardt, Matthiessen and Hegeler Zinc Company's general manager, told the *Post* that he had ordered a survey of the plant foremen to determine which of the laid-off employees could participate in the company's relief program. Those who qualified would receive money to purchase food and clothing as well as free coal for the winter months.

LaSalle Township Road Commissioner Bierborn said that he was trying to find temporary work for as many men as possible. Men were called from a waiting list and allowed to work for six days. After that, another group was hired. Because of the anticipated cold weather, the pouring of concrete for the road at the bridge would likely be delayed and extend into 1931.

The citizens, teachers, and businessmen of DePue responded to the village's needy by establishing a welfare fund. An initial goal of raising $600 a month was soon exceeded by generous contributions. Even a new goal of $1,200 a month was soon realized. For five months, pledges of between $2 and $50 were received. Part

25

of the initial $6,000 in donations was used to purchase a carload of coal that was divided between six needy families. Len Spaulding, head of the DePue relief committee, reported that there were about 15 families in need of immediate assistance; he expected many more with the coming of winter.

A major private renovation of the old Colonial Theater in Oglesby provided more local employment. Former owner, John Clydesdale of Oglesby, sold the property to E. E. Alger, who operated theaters in LaSalle and Peru. Alger's goal was to not only provide jobs but also to offer moderately priced entertainment for those unable to buy tickets to movies in the larger cities

A grand opening was held on Thanksgiving Day. Alger's Peru Theater was almost finished. This drawing was used in dozens of LaSalle *Daily Post-Tribune* ads to feature the opening of the Aida Theater.

Alger decided to invest $12,000 in his new Aida Theater by installing new seating, renovating the stage and walls, and installing a DeForest Phonofilm projection and sound system. (Oglesby Library)

By the end of November, local relief work was well underway in the Tri-Cities. The Commission on Relief and Unemployment drew up a cooperative plan with local dairies to contribute $500 in milk or approximately 3,800 quarts for needy families every month for five months. A clothing depot was opened at the Doorman Garage at Second and Gooding Streets in LaSalle. To fill the store, 20 Boy Scouts set out on Saturday, Nov. 29, seeking donations. In spite of their best efforts and large collection of clothes, the Family Welfare Society reported a severe shortage of children's underwear, coats, and shoes. The society also sought the donation of magazines that they hoped could be re-sold with the profits being used to help the needy. Registration bureaus for employment were set up in three locations in the Tri-Cities: the LaSalle Chamber of Commerce, the Link Variety Store in Peru, and the Fraternity barbershop in Oglesby. The Peru Women's Club took charge of food donations. A food depot was established at the Peru fire station. Families, who were recommended as "needy" by the Family Welfare Society, could stop to pick up food donated by local bakers, grocers, and private individuals on Mondays, Thursdays, and Saturdays. Helen Wolfe implored homemakers, "In dozens of homes much good food is thrown away every day. Housewives would help to a great extent if, instead of throwing this food away, they would wrap it up and send it to our food station."

The American Legion Auxiliary in Oglesby decided to open their own clothes depot at the Mickey Moleski garage. Mrs. Michael Pietrzak, Mrs. Rudolph Farneti, and Mrs. Ida Fiedler would be in charge. Florence Chasteen, president of the auxiliary, and Elsie Rigazio were taking calls from those who wanted to make donations.

The Legion Auxiliary unit in Peru took a similar course of action. Mrs. Clara Lemier took charge of the depot above the Walther Drug Store. Clothes could be picked up three days a week. The Auxiliary would take charge one day; work on the other days would be supervised by the Peru Junior Women's Club and the Peru Women's Club.

Another food and clothing depot was established in LaSalle over the Rexy Theater in the Brenneman building. Most of the depots were open two to three days a week from 2 p.m. until 4 p.m.

Mayor H.J. Hilliard of Ottawa took charge of the relief effort in his city by taking steps to organize the United Charities Association in early November. Representatives of churches, civic organizations, lodges, and labor unions met to address the growing crisis. The executive committee of the association consisted of Mayor Hilliard, president; Dr. J. H. Edgcomb, vice president; and Earl Haeberle of the First National Bank, treasurer. These men and others on the executive committee agreed to serve without pay.

A contribution of $2,300 was made by the county and the cities of Ottawa and South Ottawa to initially finance the organization's welfare fund, Other donations came from the Zonta Club ($60), and the Drama Club, the Catholic Daughters of America, and Delta Theta Tau each donated $100. Fred Scherer, a city commissioner, promised a donation of 50 tons of coal from the Scherer Brothers Coal Co.

Speaking at one of the organizational meetings at the Court House, Supervisor Verner Yockey, who, as poormaster, had years of experience working with needy families in Ottawa Township, said that it would take $20,000 – $25,000 to operate the program for the first six months. The association outlined a number of purposes that the executive committee and advisory board would oversee. These included the distribution of food and clothing to the worthy and unemployed. In addition, they would seek to furnish work for the unemployed and keep records of the applicants and expenditures. A headquarters was established at 600 West Madison St. This location would be the site for all distribution of food. Women in the various clubs would handle the collection and distribution of clothing and shoes.

Calls were quickly pouring into the association headquarters. For the most part, requests were for food, milk, and coal. Requests came from those truly in need. One man said he had not worked more than two hours since March and had not had a real meal for over three months. He only asked for a job. An elderly woman said she had no food or fuel for heat. Her adult daughter and son had abandoned her. Another woman pleaded with the committee that she had no fuel and only enough food for two days to feed her two small children.

Workers at the Ottawa relief station heard numerous cases of need. One 19-year old mother had been thrown out of the house by relatives, leaving her to fend for herself and her baby. She passed out on the steps of the headquarters. Tearfully, she told the volunteers how she had a few pieces of furniture in a three-room apartment but had no food or coal. Before she left, relief workers placed an order for coal on her behalf, and the young mother was given enough food to last the weekend. She was told to come back on Monday for more food.

One of the first major projects to alleviate unemployment in Ottawa was the decision by the Public Service Company of Northern Illinois to move forward with the construction of two pipelines. The projects were scheduled for the company's 1931 budget, but the unemployment crisis was so acute, they decided to act sooner. One of pipelines was a temporary 6-inch main across the Illinois River Bridge. The other project involved laying a 12-inch pipeline in South Ottawa running from Christie Street to Glover Street.

In Marseilles, Mayor George Sterrett directed the United Relief committee to compile a list of genuinely needy families to

28

receive benefits. The Altrua Club of Marseilles agreed to carry out an expanded program of its Christmas donations to include Christmas baskets for those listed. N. R. Thompson and Royal Allen took charge of the canvass on Dec. 17 to collect donations for 60 Christmas baskets.

Fortunately, the National Biscuit Company in Marseilles had returned to 80 percent production by the end of December. This allowed the management to call back the remaining workforce that had been laid off for several months. In an interview with a reporter from the Ottawa *Times-Republican,* Mr. E. F. McMahon, general manager, said that the company was trying to hire back men with families first to avoid hardship on the children. Local men were being given priority in hiring; those not from Marseilles were not hired.

Seneca businessmen and local churches also canvassed their community to determine how many families were in need of relief or could not even provide for a Christmas dinner. By Dec. 18, donations in Seneca amounted to $198.

The Cheer Basket Fund, sponsored by the Ottawa *Times-Republican,* got a boost from the local Kiwanis Club with a $100 donation. Another check for $20 from the Pleasant View Athletic Assoc. on Dec. 19 insured that at least 40 needy families in Ottawa would receive a basket. However, United Relief still hoped to receive enough funds to fill 230 baskets.

Ottawa's New-Way Market featured many Christmas bargains on Dec. 19, 1930. (Ottawa *Times-Republican*)

29

The approaching holidays called for a special appeal on the part of welfare organizations to make sure the children's holidays would be joyful. Mr. and Mrs. Jacob Reith, owners of the "Den o' Sweets" confectionary shop on Eight Street in LaSalle, promised 30 pounds of candy for the annual Big Hearts Christmas party for needy children. Other donations included 60 pounds of candy from the A. F. Candy Co. of LaSalle and the U & J Candy Co. of Peru. Even more candy, nuts, and fruit would be needed to fill the dreams of the 900 children expected to fill the Majestic Theater on Christmas Eve.

Ironically, while local organizations were pleading for donations for the children's party on Dec. 18, other self-serving individuals were simply stealing money. Two well-dressed men, about 23 years old, walked into the Wenona State Bank; stole an estimated $7,000; and took hostage the bank president, Lyon Karr. They released Karr not far from the bank after threatening to kill him if the alarm was sounded during their escape. Walking to their getaway car, they left Karr standing unharmed on the sidewalk just as the alarm sounded. Witnesses said they fled east towards Streator in a black Lincoln or Packard.

A few days later, the Chicago police captured the Wenona robbers, Austin and Herman Corray, with another man and two women. The gang had robbed nine Illinois banks of $500,000 and killed one man. When the gang confessed, they said they had stolen $90,000, a greatly exaggerated figure, from the Wenona Bank. The true amount was estimated to be $35,000 – mostly in U.S. securities. This was the same gang that robbed the Toluca bank of more than $4,000. Capturing the robbers on Christmas Eve brought some sense of satisfaction to the police and the bank employees.

That same day, the Big Hearts party provided a "Merry Christmas" for over 1,000 children in the Tri-Cities as they packed into the Majestic Theater. Donations had amounted to over $171, most of which was spent on candy, nuts, and apples. To entertain the children, the theater manager, Mr. I. Weinsheink, rented "Burning Up" starring Richard Arlen, who played the role of a daring racecar driver. The Oglesby Girl Scouts volunteered to act as ushers and to distribute the treats.

Needy families were not forgotten either. Thanks to generous contributions, $419 was collected. Stacks of food baskets were piled high along the front wall of the West Madison Street headquarters. More than 150 baskets, which contained enough food for a complete Christmas meal, were distributed in Ottawa. They overflowed with canned and fresh vegetables, fruits, meats, cookies, candy, and nuts. The Elks distributed 85 baskets while the women's club and unemployment commission volunteered to distribute the remaining baskets.

Spring Valley held a Christmas party for 1,100 children in the city park. Mrs. Harry Cassidy and Mrs. M. J. Rhoades headed the local relief association, which provided 50 food baskets to deserving families. The Delta Ray Club, a girls' social club, donated another 10 baskets.

Peru sponsored one of the largest parties, treating 2,000 children to a visit with Santa, who was located in his headquarters near a large Christmas tree erected at the corner of on Fourth and West Streets. The two-hour stopover by Santa on Christmas Eve was barely enough time to pass out a half-ton of candy and apples at the event hosted by the Peru Retail Merchants' Association.

Needy Putnam County families also enjoyed a bit of relief during the Yuletide season. Mrs. Robert Bell, Maggie Peterson, Nina Geng, and William and Charles Tyler Jr., stocked food and other donations at the Illinois Power & Light office in Granville. Local farmers provided the chickens. To brighten the faces of the children, the OZO Club of Granville donated toys. Other gifts were still arriving on Christmas Eve. On Christmas Day, Edward Edwards, chairman of Governor Louis Emmerson's committee on unemployment and relief in Chicago, came to Putnam County to distribute baskets, each one containing a chicken, potatoes, corn, peas, coffee, sugar, flour, and oranges. Four trucks were needed to deliver the baskets throughout the county.

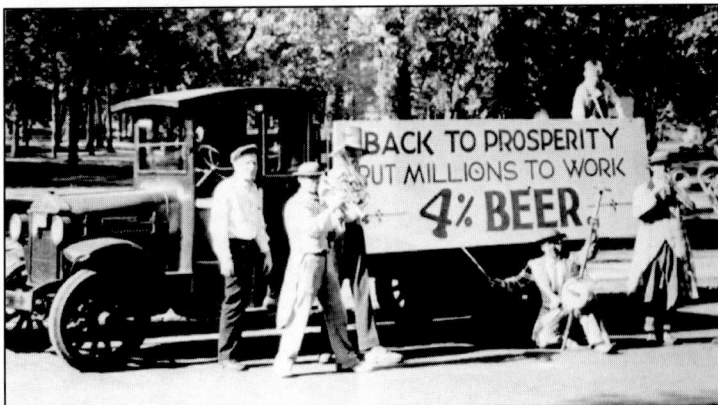

These Streator prohibition protestors may have had ulterior motives besides seeking the return of brewery jobs as they drove their truck around the downtown park in 1930. Both jobs and beer would be important issues in the 1932 presidential race. (Streatorland Historical Society)

31

1931
CHARITY BEGINS AT HOME

After the holidays, the laughter stopped, and hundreds of families with unemployed breadwinners realized that they still faced the economic hardships of a depression. Those having deposits in local banks began to draw out their savings at an alarming rate. On Jan. 20, Mr. O. L. Miller President of the Farmers State Bank of Newark informed the Morris *Herald* the bank's assets had dropped to $89,000. To preserve remaining capital, the bank, which was the only one in town, was forced to close. It was only one of many banks that eventually went out of business.

The downturn in the economy was not felt by all. The majority of the citizens of Peru could still enjoy an inexpensive night out at the movies at their new theater. E. E. Alger renovated the Peru Theater with the latest Deforest Phonofilm equipment. The interior was compared to the Capitol Theater on Chicago's south side with clouds floating overhead and a starlit sky. Upholstered spring seats provided the sensation of "sitting on air" according to Alger. A night at the movies was one escape from the Depression. Alger was committed to providing the latest films at reasonable prices.

The Event of the Season
GRAND OPENING
Thursday January 15th—At 2 P.M.
ALGER'S NEW
PERU THEATRE
One of the Most Beautiful Theatres
In the State of Illinois

"Politics," released by MGM in 1931, packed in the crowds at the Peru Theater in spite of the depressed economy. (Peru Library)

32

Crime continued to persist in the Illinois Valley. On January 22, 1931, a notable Granville businessman, Jack Redshaw was contacted while at the Granville skating rink with his wife and was lured to his downtown shop in the old Granville bank building by a prospective customer.

Above: Jack Redshaw's warehouse in Granville housed thousands of items.

Right: Redshaw shows an assortment of diamond rings to a potential buyer. Although he survived the 1931 mugging, unknown assailants killed "Trader Jack" in front of his vault on Sept. 26, 1955. (John L. Redshaw photos)

The massive steel door in the old Granville State Bank building secured the Redshaw vault, which held untold wealth. The vault is still used to hold Granville Township records. (Photo by author)

Arriving at his office, Redshaw was confronted by four men holding pistols and a sawed-off shotgun. After frisking Jack for weapons, they pulled a $1,000 diamond ring from his hand and took the money from his wallet. Then they demanded that he open his vault, which usually contained valuable gems. Redshaw pleaded poverty due to a previous robbery and was not forced to open the vault. Instead, the robbers hustled him into a waiting car and drove off, followed by two more men in another car. One gunman continued to jab Redshaw in the chest with the shotgun as they fled south in the direction of Peoria. Traveling about three

33

miles, they stopped the car and told Redshaw to get on the ground. "All right, shed the coat buddy," one man ordered. Redshaw dutifully removed his heavy, coonskin coat. "Now start back to town on a dead run or we will shoot you," ordered one of the gunmen. Redshaw walked about 200 yards before one of the bandits shouted, "Hey Redshaw, come back and get your coat." After he returned to the kidnappers to retrieve his coat, the kidnappers fled.

Redshaw hurried into town and contacted the police, who issued an all-points bulletin. No one was apprehended, but the police speculated that the crime might have been members of "Egan's Rats," a notorious gang based in St. Louis, MO.

Redshaw described his ordeal to a reporter and tried to rationalize the kidnappers' actions. He thought his coat was probably just too large for any of the gunmen. He also believed that they let him off without opening the vault or removing any merchandise since it was well-known that he had been robbed a year earlier of several thousand dollars in gemstones. He thought the bandits might have had some sympathy for him since he told them he was still operating at a loss, and there was nothing of value in the vault. The next day, Jack told Ervin, his brother, the gunmen had jabbed him so forcefully that his chest and stomach were covered with bruises.

Criminals continued to sweep through the small towns of the Illinois Valley typically striking at banks and stores thought to be easy marks. On April 22, 1931, bandits looted $20,000 in cash, stocks, and bonds from the Whaples and Farmers Bank of Neponset.

Two middle-aged men walked into the bank at 9:50 a.m. Wednesday morning. Brandishing revolvers, they surprised George Whaples, the cashier, and his brother, L.H. Whaples, the assistant cashier. Neither brother had time to reach for the alarm as one of the men jumped over the counter and forced the men to lay flat on the floor while the thieves emptied the drawers. William Russell and two female customers were told to walk to a room in the back of the bank where they were tied up and left in the locked room.

In spite of a police dragnet, the robbers successfully made their getaway driving through Princeton, Spring Valley, and Webster Park. Three police cars ignored the getaway car since it did not match the description of the robbery vehicle, which was presumed to have been heading to Peru and LaSalle. One report said the car was seen at noon in Wenona.

A week later, one of the robbers, Frank Jordan, 33, was captured by the Chicago police. He was involved in a gun battle on Michigan Avenue in which two officers were shot. During the police interrogation of Jordan, he confessed to the theft of $4,000 from the

Neponset bank and another robbery at an Indiana bank. He also implicated two other men, Arthur Briggs from Rockford and Jack Musen from Joliet. A first-degree murder indictment was handed down against Jordan. Chicago Mayor Anton Cermak promised swift justice for the murderer.

Other local robberies were less dramatic but demonstrated a serious crime problem that continued for a number of years in the Illinois Valley. In one incident in LaSalle, someone threw a brick through the window of the C.A. Jensen Jewelry Store at 709 First St. in LaSalle, and made off with about $500 in watches and rings, a sizeable theft in the Depression. Officers Joseph Klinker and Ed Kasprowicz discovered the robbery at 4 a.m. as they made their rounds in the business district. Mr. Jensen, who lived above the store, was not wakened during the break-in because the store alarm failed to activate. Fortunately, insurance covered all of the stolen merchandise.

While a few individuals resorted to robbery to get rich quickly, most individuals were happy to find even a low paying job. Christmas donations had only a limited impact on the hardship felt by the unemployed and their families. Soon, applicants were again besieging the local relief services. During January and February, the Commission on Unemployment and Relief in LaSalle accepted pledges of financial assistance from individuals and businesses amounting to over $7,000. A generous financial gift from Mrs. Matthiessen allowed the Hygienic Institute to distribute milk to children under two years of age. Other relief funds made possible the distribution of 5,000 gallons of milk to 144 families with children over two years of age. A total of 256 children from 144 families received daily milk thanks to local milk producers.

Requests for assistance came from 103 families in LaSalle, 50 in Peru, and 30 in Oglesby. Altogether 256 families were on the dole in the Tri-Cities area in the early months of 1931. That figure represented about two percent of the population.

On April 7, 1931, news came that a major construction project would soon come through the area. The Ford, Bacon, and Davis Company was building a 155-mile, natural gas pipeline between the Mississippi River and Joliet. The company would need about 500 workers. Of that number, about 250-400 men would be hired within days from workers in the Tri-Cities area. Fifty members of the construction team were already boarding in LaSalle hotels, and another 50 were on the way. The LaSalle Chamber of Commerce quickly went into action seeking large, 4 to 5-room apartments for the construction officials. It was expected that the men would need apartments for the next two months. Ottawa would be the headquarters for the construction project. Nine trucks and other construction machinery needed for the project were stored at the Ottawa fairgrounds.

In May 1931, another project, the manual arts addition at Ottawa H.S., was nearing completion.

The new Ottawa H.S. gym was dedicated in February. (Photos by author)

Local unemployment increased in the summer of 1931. On June 10, the Unemployed Council of Illinois organized a meeting of 300 men at the Riverside Ballroom in Spring Valley. The meeting's speaker, Joe Dallet from Chicago, roused the meeting with his demands, which included immediate relief for unemployed workers and poverty-stricken farmers and the cessation of foreclosures on farms and homes of the unemployed. He also called for a social insurance law that would pay $15 a week for the unemployed and the elderly. Funding would come from an increase of ten percent on corporate taxes. A result of that meeting was the formation of a local 50-man Unemployed Council. From that group, five men were selected to participate in a march to Springfield.

Illini Beach
UNEMPLOYMENT
DANCING
9 TO 12 **Dance** JULY 8TH

ADMISSION . . . . . . 10¢

Free Dancing and Free Parking. Best Music in the World. Come out whether you are employed or not. We want the world to have a good time.

The prospect of having little income did not mean that there was nothing to enjoy during the summer of 1931. An outing to Illini Beach was even less expensive than a night at the movies. This ad appeared in the *Republican-Times* on July 8, 1931.

36

The swings in the stock market affected the businesses in the Illinois Valley according to John O'Kane, secretary of the Ottawa Business Mens' Association. A weeklong upturn in the market in late June inspired hope and confidence. Local purchases were up in anticipation of better times ahead.

The unemployed in Ottawa were gladdened by the news that Libby-Owen-Ford production would be needed by General Motors. However, by Aug. 17, the anticipated demand for plate glass had evaporated. Production had filled the L-O-F warehouse. Only six of the ten furnaces in the casting hall would operate for about ten more days according to J. R. Tyson, factory superintendent. He told a *Republican-Times* reporter, "At this time, nobody can say what the duration of the shut-down will be. It may only be for a few days. It may be much longer." The news was unexpected because, in spite of the Depression, the plant had been producing glass for 18 months. Because of the shutdown, another 200 men were idled.

Another jobs program in mid-August resulted when the Peru city council approved $50,000 to lay water mains in several sections of the city. One of the new 200,000-gallon storage tanks would be constructed at the north end of Pike Street, and the other one would be erected at the north end of Pulaski Street. "The work will do a great deal to relieve unemployment for it will be ten weeks to three months before the work is completed," said Mayor Hasse. "The jobs will be financed entirely from the water and light fund, which at this time has a surplus of approximately $130,000."

Labor Day weekend promised a respite from the worries about jobs. Thousands flocked to the air races and dedication of the airport two miles east of Ottawa. On Saturday night, Sept. 5, two pilots thrilled spectators as they flew over Marseilles, Ottawa, Utica, and LaSalle in their lighted plane.

Ottawa Air Races
AND
Other Spectacular Events
TO CELEBRATE
DEDICATION OF AIRPORT
Sunday, Sept. 6 and Labor Day, starting promptly at 1 p. m. each day. Formation Flight over Ottawa 12 o'clock.

EVENTS

Parachute Jumps by Florence Parker of Minnesota.	Trapeze Act From Ship in Flight By Pat Burns of North Carolina.
Balloon Bursting	Air Races.
Bomb Dropping	Stunt Flying.
Night Flying	Student Events.

| Admission, 25c | Autos Free. | Children Free. |

Don't Miss This Series of Exciting Events

The show continued with the bang of an aerial bomb at noon on Sunday. Planes were flown to the airport from across the state. A formation of 23 planes flew over Ottawa to begin the show. The OX5 race for planes powered by engines of 90 hp or less was the first competition on Sunday afternoon. The planes flew around a five-mile course three times at an average speed of 90 mph. "Slim"

Carstens of Ottawa finished first, and Al Jenkins of Varna finished third in a five-man race. The second race was open to any pilot who could maintain an airspeed of at least 129 mph. Del Koerner from Kankakee was the winner in his 220-hp Travelair plane. Second place went to William McBoyd of Gibson City, who was flying a Waco plane with a 220-hp Wright Whirlwind engine. Joe Kreager of Lostant finished in third place also flying a Waco but with a smaller Warner 120-hp engine. Stunt contests were also flown on Sunday. Marshal Tisler of Marseilles came in second behind McBoyd.

An example of the type of planes used in air races was this WACO-10 with a 30'7" wingspan. It was equipped with an OX-5, V-8 engine and could reach a top speed of 97 mph.

On Labor Day, a free-for-all flying competition was flown around the five-mile circuit. Another local stunt flyer was Harry Hill of Streator. The gaze of the crowd was fixed on the skies as Hill performed rolls, spins, and dives.

Once Labor Day festivities ended, it was time to get back to the serious work of creating local jobs. Ottawa planned several projects. One plan was to fill the hydraulic basin and lateral canal connecting the Illinois-Michigan Canal. Funding would come from a $50,000 bond if voters approved. Failing that, a township tax for pauper relief would be required. In the previous winter, 400 families were on relief in Ottawa. Mayor Hilliard recommended creating jobs rather than subsidizing a welfare program.

This sketch of the proposed Illinois River bridge appeared on Sept. 15 in the Ottawa *Republican-Times*.

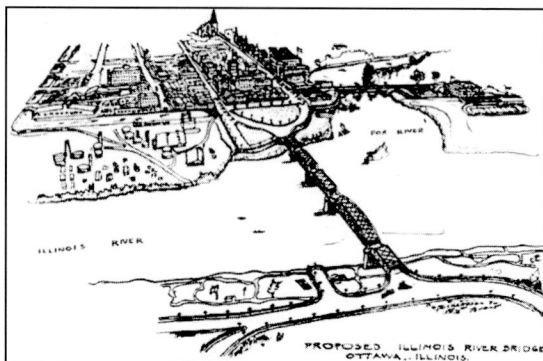

38

On October 27, voters would decide in a special referendum if the $50,000 bond would be issued to fill the lateral canal. The citizens would also vote on a $50,000 bond to build approaches for a new bridge 200-feet east of the existing bridge across the Illinois River. The bridge plan was finally approved by the War Department in Washington and the Department of Waterways in Springfield in mid-September.

While the prospect of additional construction jobs for the bridge sounded promising, various organizations worked diligently to provide basic necessities to families in need, The Altrua club of Marseilles proposed canning fruits and vegetables from the fall harvest. Calls for donations, large or small, were being accepted in September by Mrs. Arthur Lettsome. Only 68 quarts were canned, hardly enough for the demand that would soon become apparent. Mrs. A. P. Gossard, president of the Altrua Club, was joined by a dozen other ladies, who were ready to meet in the Congregational Church on Sept. 18, to can apples and tomatoes. The club promised to continue their canning project as long as food donations continued.

At the end of September, a major banking crisis swept LaSalle County. In rapid succession, a number of financial institutions in Ottawa closed their doors. When The Ottawa Banking and Trust Co., founded in 1903, did not open for business on Wednesday, Sept. 29, a small but calm crowd gathered around the door of the bank at Madison and LaSalle Streets. In a press interview, Henry Arnold, president of the bank, expressed hope that all depositors would be paid in full. In the meantime, Justin Jaeger, a native of Ottawa, was assigned to handle bank affairs by the state auditor. It was the first time in more than 50 years that an Ottawa bank closed its doors.

The next day, National City Bank failed to open. Bank directors said they closed the bank to protect the interests of its depositors. This was a tactful way of saying that they didn't have enough cash on hand to meet the projected demand.

Depositors at Ottawa Banking and Trust, National City, First National, and People's Trust and Savings had been withdrawing funds at a steady pace for the preceding two weeks. The question on everyone's mind was would First National and People's Trust also be forced to close. It was during that time that Peoples' Trust implemented their longstanding, but never used, rule requiring a four-month notice for withdrawals from savings accounts. That restriction limited the potential for a massive run on deposits. First

National sought to head off a run by ordering a substantial amount of cash from its correspondent bank in Chicago.

On Friday morning, depositors' worst fears were realized when Peoples' Trust failed to open. A statement by the bank directors explained that they thought they could have "weathered this storm," but in the interests of the depositors, the bank was closing in order to reorganize.

Three banks had closed in as many days. Now there was only the First National left in operation in Ottawa. Oscar Haeberle, the board chairman, said, "We stand ready at any and all times to pay any depositor. This money belongs to our depositors, and they have a right to ask for it." A large shipment of cash from Chicago made it possible to pay all those who sought a withdrawal.

Would the other banks in the area be able to handle the panic? The Serena State Bank closed, but the banks in Marseilles and Seneca appeared to be functioning normally, at least for the present. A run on the Marseilles bank began late on Thursday afternoon, but S. R. Lewis, the bank president, insisted that the bank remain open for two hours beyond the regular closing time so that all depositors, who wanted to make a withdrawal, could do so.

The LaSalle Savings and Trust also closed their doors on Oct. 1. The following day, panicky investors soon began a run on the LaSalle State Bank and the LaSalle National Bank. When the doors opened at 9 a.m., panicky depositors quickly jammed inside the National Bank and lined up in front of the cashiers' cages waving their passbooks. There was barely standing room in the bank.

At the LaSalle State Bank, the run lasted only an hour. Depositors at the National Bank continued to withdraw their savings through most of the day, but there were fewer withdrawals made in the afternoon. Most of the accounts being closed ranged from a few cents to a few hundred dollars. Large depositors generally left their funds intact.

LaSalle State Bank (Photo by author)

Confidence was largely restored just before 2 p.m. when an armored car carrying over a million dollars arrived from the Federal Reserve Bank of Chicago. Sheriff Welter, bank guards, state troopers, and local police armed with revolvers, rifles, and shotguns protected the million-dollar cargo. Hundreds of people lining the streets watched in awe as the money, guarded by seven police officers, was brought inside the bank. Each guard slung a bag of currency over his shoulder. After each bag was secured, the armored car, still containing hundreds of thousands of dollars, continued its trip to banks in Peru and Spring Valley.

Commenting on the day's events, Bank President Stuart Duncan said, "Cash was our answer to depositors' demands. The LaSalle State Bank has given evidence today of its great strength. We emerge from this public demonstration as strong as ever. Thousands of dollars dispatched from Chicago remains untouched." By Saturday afternoon, the number of deposits actually outnumbered the withdrawals.

Speaking on behalf of the National Bank, President Arnold J. Wilson commented to a *Post* reporter, "We have weathered the storm and have proven our rock-bottom stability. Dollar for dollar, every depositor's demand was met with cash. Our bank stands on a solid foundation, always has and always will." Shoring up that optimistic assessment, T. G. Dickinson, president of Marquette Cement, said that his company was prepared to back up the banks with millions of dollars in company funds "any time they ask for it."

The President of the Oglesby State Bank, Raimund Radcke, expressed his faith in the depositors of his bank. After talking to Oglesby residents, he said he was encouraged by their comments of support. "The bank is solid and has adequate funds to meet the depositors," he said.

The Spring Valley Bank did not experience a similar "run" largely due to the fact that the bank maintained a policy of asking depositors for a 30 to 60-day notice of a withdrawal from savings accounts. The bank's conservative polices and volume of business insured a stable institution.

Looking back on the short-lived run in LaSalle, partial blame was focused on an erroneous radio broadcast, which incorrectly identified the LaSalle State Bank rather than the LaSalle Savings Bank and Trust Company, as the financial instituion closing its doors. Although the radio annoucer corrected the error, the damage had been done, and the run commenced.

Rumors not only affected local banks but also major companies, such as Lehigh Portland Cement in Oglesby. When stories spread that the plant was closing down completely for the rest of the winter months, Superintendent John Young issued a statement clarifying the closing. He explained that the shutdown was temporary, lasting only from Oct. 15 to Dec. 1, at which time,

41

operations would resume. Workers knew the storage facilities were filled to capacity and according to Young, "the manufacturing operations, of necessity, must cease." Since any shutdown resulted in some financial hardships for the plant's workers, Young explained to a *Post* reporter that whatever work was available would be divided among the employees.

The local financial crisis could not overshadow the light-heartedness of hundreds of movie-goers, who were anxious to see Ottawa's newly remodled Roxy Theater. The grand opening of the Roxy was part of a coordinated downtown commercial event sponsored by the Chamber of Commerce. Hoping to stimulate business, the entire commercial district contributed to the gala event by offering special sales. Hentrich's Military Band played stirring martial music for the entertainment of the anxious crowd gathering in front of the theater. On Sept. 30, at 6:30 p.m., with all the business lights extinguished, a series of aerial bombs detonated.

Formal **FALL** *Opening*
and
DEDICATION
OF THE NEW
Roxy Theater

Wednesday, Sept. 30th ∴ Thursday, Oct. 1st
Official Program:

6:30 P. M. Wednesday
Explosion of Aerial Bomb,
Street Illumination and
Window Unveiling.

Roxy Theatre Orchestra
Presentation of Flowers,
Telegrams, Etc.

Address of Welcome
From the management, Mr. Wm. B. Bradley.

Dedication Address
And response from the city, H. J. Hillard, mayor.

Formal Opening
Special Feature—Cutting Ribbon
Miss Catherine Armstrong will dedicate opening
of new theater.

MASTER OF CEREMONIES
L. C. CARROLL
7:00 P. M. STAGE SHOW

Dedication ad heralding the opening of the Roxy on Sept. 30, 1931 reprinted from the Ottawa *Republican-Times*.

The 1,100-seat Roxy replaced the Gayety, an entertainment center which hosted stage shows, vaudeville acts, silent pictures, and talkies, over a span of 20 years. The Gayety was lost in a fire on Dec. 9, 1930.

Standing on a platform erected in front of the theater on LaSalle Street, Lee Carroll, Secretary of the Chamber of Commerce, made a short speech declaring, "The opening of this new

theater is an auspicious and important event for Ottawa. It marks the completion of one of Ottawa's finest and newest enterprises." Miss Catherine Armstrong, a former Miss Ottawa contestant, cut a white ribbon signaling the formal opening of the theater.

Patrons entered the new Roxy Theater under the marquee, illuminated with 2,000 electric lights, and filed into the 30' x 18' lobby and through the three large glass doors of the 45' x 10' foyer. The interior design was decorated in a Spanish motif with canopies supported by spearheads and Spanish tapestries.

The festivities in Ottawa in the fall of 1931 were quickly followed by another huge celebration in LaSalle. After years of planning, a new street lighting system was constructed in the commercial district. The October 15 dedication event was promoted as the Jubilee of Light. An estimated crowd of 25,000 lined First and Second Streets from Tonti to Bucklin Streets to watch the evening celebration. The Spring Valley city band began their musical program at 6 p.m.

The highlight of the ceremony was the arrival of the "Princess of Light," Catherine Orr, the mayor's daughter. She was dressed in a satin gown, wore a jeweled crown, and in her hand, she carried a star-tipped wand. At 7:45 p.m., she turned a switch, and the old street lights were turned off. Simultaneously, "The Great White Way" was illuminated, and the throngs cheered in approval. A parade of over 2,000 participants, including 200 children and delegations of Legion posts from LaSalle, Putnam, and Bureau Counties, marched past the reviewing stand at First and Marquette Streets.

The new lights in downtown LaSalle were the focal point of the "Jubilee of Light."

While the festivities were in progress, desperate individuals took advantage of the situation and robbed the houses of Mayor Orr and his neighbor, Dr. Woods. The thieves made off with $300 of canned goods and preserves.

Celebrations in the Illinois Valley provided only brief diversions from the mundane routine of searching for work, helping others to find work, or providing temporary employment. Ottawa's United Relief found a way to allow some of Ottawa's unemployed to obtain coal for the coming winter.

43

In the early 1920's, Frank Belrose dug thousands of tons of coal from a 36-inch coal vein about five feet deep along the banks of the feeder canal east of Champlain Street and south of the Burlington railroad tracks. When the state took over the property, the director of property and construction gave permission to the city to mine the coal once again.

Taking some of the money donated for relief, the city council rented a power shovel for $40 per day to remove the five feet of overburden to expose the coal seam. A lottery was used to select men on relief, who were given groceries and allowed to dig enough coal to supply their homes for the winter. Supervisors were given coal, food, and $1 a day. Ottawa men were taken to the job site by truck each day. At noon, each man was provided with a hot lunch. Once the men had a sufficient supply of coal for their needs, a different group of men would take their places.

Unemployed men from Ottawa mine coal in the winter of 1931-32 from the banks of the dry Fox River Feeder located on the north side of the I-M Canal directly opposite of the lateral canal. (Lewis University collection)

In Putnam County, coal production at the Prairie State mine was repsonsible for keeping many men off the relief roles. John Cox, the mine superinetendent, told a reporter from the Putnam County *Record* that he had arranged a contract with Republic Steel and Coke to purchase the mine's entire production, about 200-300 tons a day beginning in November. With the installation of a new conveyor belt and other improvements, it was estimated that those figures could reach 1,000 tons a day. The contract was expected to last until 1935.

Edward Edwards, local chairman of the state relief program, recommended consolidation of relief agencies in Putnam

44

County under the auspices of the Red Cross. A headquarters was established in the vacant Kroger Grocery store on McCoy Street. Donations made in other villages in the county could be left at the McNabb bank or the Hennepin bank. Donations were transported to the Red Cross headquarters.

In order to stimulate donations, Granville women were encouraged to participate in a children's shower on Nov. 18 in the Red Cross room at the old store. Baby clothes, blankets, bedding, and clothing for younger children were especially needed. Even slightly worn clothes were accepted; the ladies picked one day to sew and mend. A committee, consisting of two women from each of the Granville churchs, was placed in charge of the "shower."

Meanwhile in Ottawa, voters were preparing to decide on a $50,000 bond referendum for the employment of men to fill in the lateral canal and hydraulic basin and replace bridges. The fill being considered included Madison, Jefferson, Jackson, Lafayette, Superior, and Washington Streets. The basin-fill project would extend from LaSalle to Clinton Street. Mill Street would be widened as well. It was estimated that 150 men would be needed on a daily basis for the hand labor. In order to benefit the greatest number of needy men, each crew was limited to short hours a few days a week.

With the approaching holidays, and little support for the needy from the nation's capital, it was left to the charitable work of local residents to come up with projects to bring a little cheer to the downtrodden. In Oglesby, the women's club planned a tea for Dec. 4 at the home of Mrs. Raimund Radcke on Park Ave. A collection would be taken up to apply to the $1,000 quota set for Oglesby's contribution toward the relief fund. Money was sent to Clancy's Drug Store by various teams and organizations to meet that goal. The congregation of the Union Church in Oglesby agreed to donate food to fill Thanksgiving baskets for the poor.

'Happy Days Are Here Again'

The time of your life awaits you, at the

Knights of Columbus
10th Annual
FALL FESTIVAL
5 Nights—Nov. 25th to 29th
K. of C. Auditorium
Second and Gooding Sts., La Salle

FREE
Entertainment—Music—Vaudeville
Don't let anything stop you—Come every night, a whale of a time for everybody.

FREE PRIZES
Laughter—Fun—Frivolity
What a Time for All.

Admission 5¢
To be donated for work of the Tri-City Welfare Association

Ad from the LaSalle *Post-Tribune*, Nov. 21, 1931.

45

The LaSalle Knights of Columbus planned their five-day Fall Festival to be held at their auditorium on Second and Gooding Streets for the end of November. The 5¢ admission to the 10th Annual Fall Festival was donated to the relief efforts. Every cent of the proceeds was earmarked for the Welfare Association.

Knights of Columbus Hall in LaSalle. (Photo by author)

LaSalle Boy Scouts were also active in helping the poor, especially the children of parents on relief. Meeting at the Herrcke Building in LaSalle, a dozen Scouts repaired or painted donated toys in preparation for the annual Big Hearts Christmas party at the Majestic Theater. The Scouts had served as volunteers in the effort since 1928 when it began. As Thanksgiving approached, the Scouts had 200 toys to refurbish.

Another project sought funds to purchase candy, nuts, and fruit for the children. The goal of the drive was to collect $200.

A similar effort was sponsored by the American Legion Post in Granville. Unused dolls, games, books, and old, discarded toys were soliticited by the Legionnaires to be distributed by Santa Claus when he stopped at the homes of impoverished families on Christmas.

Thanksgiving came and went, but hungry, unemployed men still needed a meal. Taking on that task was the Ladies' Aid Society of St. John's Lutheran Church in Peru. Mrs. Adam Kutter, Mrs. August Hoebeck, Mrs. William Benedix, and Mrs. H.C. Haferman were in charge of the meal. Potato salad, apple sauce, cooked rice, coffeecakes, and jellies were offered to the men at the relief station.

Ladies from St. John's Luthern Church served hot food on Monday, Wednesday, and Friday afternoons at the relief station in the Peru Hotel. (Peru Library)

The L-P-O Commission on Uenployment and Relief would benefit from the proceeds of a charity football game between Welter's All-Stars and the players from Edwards Hall at Notre Dame University at Matthiessen Field on Nov. 29, 1931. It was hoped that it would be a sell-out crowd; 7,500 tickets to "the greatest football spectacle ever witnessed in this section of the state" were offfered to the public. The crowd wasn't disappointed in the 27-0 hometown victory.

Drawing reprinted from the November 27, 1931 edition of the LaSalle *Post-Tribune.*

Local governments made every effort to find at least part-time work for as many men on relief as possible. In Ottawa, an extra $15,000 was allocated for sewerline re-construction. Mayor Hilliard recommended drawing names from the relief roll to give each man a week of steady employment. Beginning on Dec. 21, 150 men went to work for the city. The following week, another 150 men were hired. The project was expected to provide work for 75 to 100 days.

The LaSalle American Legion pleaded with the Army engineers to give preference to veterans for jobs at the Starved Rock pool project. Lt. Col. W.C. Weeks approved the veteran's preference policy and notified the project manager. But, when two LaSalle veterans showed up for work on Dec. 21, they were told there would be no work until after Jan. 1, 1932.

Sometimes local committees simply did not have enough work or money to take care of all those requesting help. In Spring Valley, the relief fund was reduced to less than $300. Rumors that the city was paying cash for temproary work were incorrect. Those who had been unemployed for a very long time were given the opportunity to clean up vacant lots in exchange for food and fuel vouchers – not cash. On Tuesday, Dec. 22, Mrs. R.E. Davis, Mrs. Robert Bradbeer, and Mrs. Andrew Johnson assisted in dispensing food collected by the Spring Valley Women's Club and the Goofus Club, the latter having provided ten bushels of potatoes.

Residents were most generous during the holiday season. The Tri-Cities Family Welfare Society distributed 234 baskets of food and clothing before Christmas. The American Legion and Legion Auxiliaries in LaSalle and Peru filled a total of 42 baskets. Each one included a complete Christmas dinner consisting of a roast, potatoes, vegetables, fruit, cranberries, nuts, and candies. The LaSalle Auxiliary collected toys and gifts for 100 children. Those too old for toys were given gloves or hose. The Peru Legionnaires decided to hold a party for the children rather than putting toys in the 12 baskets going to needy families of veterans. The Elks provided 85 food baskets.

Alger's theaters hosted parties in LaSalle, Peru, and Oglesby. Local Boy Scouts delivered half a ton of candy and over 1,000 toys to the Majestic Theater for the annual Big Hearts event. Two hours before showtime, hundreds of youngsters were pressing close to the doors of the theater. The manager finally opened the doors at 9:15 a.m. for an estimated 1,200 children, who enjoyed a George O'Brien western, "Fair Warning," and a Mickey Rooney comedy, "Mickey's Rebellion." Afterwards, each child received a bag containing an apple, candy, and cookies. The number of children was beyond expectations and exceeded the available gifts so about a hundred children were given vouchers for gift bags at the LaSalle *Post-Tribune* office. The event was described as a "huge success."

Although the children had a chance to temporarily forget their families' need for relief, unemployed fathers had little to cheer about. Some found other ways to make a "fast buck." Merchants had to be watchful for individuals trying to pass counterfeit money or bad checks. On Dec. 19, officers Art Guenther and Ed Kasprowicz picked up a husband and wife team attempting to pass bad checks at Spurgeons Store, Kline's Department Store, and the Diamond Tea Store in LaSalle. Giving their names as Mr. and Mrs. Charles Griffin of Joplin, MO, the pair was arrested and searched. Three checks in the amount of $14.85 were found in their car. Mr. Griffin later confessed, "I don't know why I did it; maybe it was to get some money."

Another incident of larceny was the theft of $1,000 and eight watches by three men at Frank Grennan's book-making establishment at 111 W. Main in Streator on Dec. 24. Two men, one carrying a machine gun and the other a 45 cal. gun, entered the betting parlor and forced 14 patrons to lay on the floor during the robbery. The men fled in a waiting car and escaped on Rt. 17. Sheriff Welter was able to catch one of the suspected robbers, Charles Carona, 28, on the south side of Chicago and return him to the LaSalle County jail.

In spite of these random acts of crime, the prospect of hope for a better year was evident. The LaMoille State Bank (pictured), which had closed on Nov. 28 to protect its depositors, was being reorganized with the intent to open as a national bank.

Numerous construction projects were on the horizon as well. Plans were moving ahead on new post offices in Peru, Mendota, and Spring Valley. Marquette Cement was increasing its kiln facilities in a $250,000 program. LaSalle County road improvements would total $200,000. Peru's expansion of water distribution would account for another $375,000. The Burlington Railroad bridge re-construction project at LaSalle would result in the expenditure of $200,000. These, and a myriad of other projects, large and small, gave hope to the unemployed.

49

1932
READY FOR CHANGE

The new year began with little difference from 1931. Once again, bank robbers thought the small town banks of the Illinois Valley were easy prey. On Monday, January 4, four men tried to hold up the Minonk State Bank. Entering the bank at 9:30 a.m., two men announced their intentions but were unnerved when Miss Margaret Lewis, the 18 year old bookkeeper, set off an automatic tear gas system and the outside alarm. As the bank filled with gas, the robbers fired their guns at the five employees and a lone customer. Two accomplices heard the shots and fled in a Cord or a Chrysler in the direction of Wenona. Within 30 minutes, a hastily formed posse captured two of the gunmen, who were taken to the Woodford County jail in Eureka. Upon interrogation, it was determined that one of the robbers was from California. The other thief had a St. Louis address.

The unemployed men of the Illinois Valley were basically law-abiding and long-suffering. In Ottawa, 100 men had their names drawn in the work lottery for the lateral canal and the sewer outlet projects. In October 1931, voters had approved the $50,000 lateral canal fill project. The removal of the old locks that connected the Illinois-Michigan Canal on Superior Street was the first assignment. Men working on the canal and sewer lines were paid 50¢ an hour and worked a six-hour day. The weekly pay amounted to $15.

Fill was dumped into the lateral canal, which joined the empty I-M Canal.

Another 50 men found employment cleaning the streets of Ottawa. Money was appropriated from the city wheel tax fund to pay the men $1 a day. These men voluntarily worked at the coal mine to compensate the United Relief program for the food, fuel, and clothing the organization provided to their families.

50

Coal for the needy was a major expense in the Ottawa city budget. About 1,000 families representing 4,000 men, women, and children benefited from the relief program. In the first 21 weeks of the relief effort, over $33,000 was spent from the $40,000 account. The largest amount, over $20,000, was for food. The other large expense, over $7,000, was for coal. Every week, on average, United Relief of Ottawa was spending $1,600.

Smaller towns also had programs to assist the needy. In Ladd, the Beta Phi organization organized a fund-raiser with the assistance of the Ladd Theater. Anton Degregoreo, the theater manager, and his film agent agreed to donate the use of the theater and the proceeds from the mid-week showing of "Dixiana" to Ladd relief. Beta Phi's participation also included the presentation of musical numbers and a one-act comedy, "One Way Out," between showings of the movie.

Another act of generosity came from a local farmer, Ray Eiten, who had been donating five gallons of milk each week to needy families with children in Ladd. He decided in February to increase that donation to 15 gallons a week.

In contrast, there were continuing acts of theft in the area. In Mendota on Feb. 23, three young men stole $925 in furs from the storeroom in the second story of the Surl Koopersmith home on the east side of the city at about 1 a.m. The hundreds of furs, including muskrat and mink pelts, were ready for delivery to a dealer. Alerted to the break-in, Koopersmith saw one of the men climb down a ladder and make a hasty getaway in a waiting car.

Four burglaries were reported on March 4 in Utica. The Utica elevator office and company store, the Illinois Grain Co. and the Kleinhaus electric shop were burglarized during the night. This was probably the work of amateurs since the loot consisted of such items as a roll of pennies, a shotgun and shells, radio tubes, and electric lights. The thieves managed to open one small safe but took nothing since it only contained old documents. A larger safe was unopened. The owners placed a value of about $100 on the items taken. George Lewis discovered the ransacked elevator office at 7 a.m., when he came to work. The thieves in Utica went undetected by the night marshal, John Gilchrist

The next morning, a young man was spotted trying to steal a sack of potatoes from the back of a truck parked in an alley near First and Wright Streets in LaSalle. The 18 year old had barely slung the sack of potatoes over his shoulder when the driver spotted him and gave pursuit. Dropping the sack, the boy escaped by running down to Canal Street. The driver was satisfied and gave up the

51

chase. Incidents like this were a reflection of the hard times and desperation due to unemployment.

The apparent solution was to provide more jobs. Good news came on March 25, when John Largura announced that his Gary, Indiana construction company had won the contract to build a post office in Peru. "It has always been our policy to use local labor insofar as possible," Largura told a reporter from the *Post-Tribune*. He anticipated hiring as many as 80 men from the area and pay union scale. However, the awarding of a government contract and the actual hiring of men might be months apart.

In the meantime, relief committees throughout the Illinois Valley continued to seek funds and supplies. At the end of March, the local chairman of the American Red Cross applied for 78,000 pounds of flour from the national headquarters. Eventually, the area received 350 barrels of flour amounting to only 68,100 pounds. That allotment was calculated based on the need to provide one barrel per family for three months.

Relief from the state level was another possibility. The Illinois General Assembly passed a bill for $20 million in pauper relief. A web of bureaucratic red tape, however, prevented the immediate dissemination of the funds to the individual counties. Local commissions would be appointed in each county to assess the needs of the residents and determine how monies would be spent; and decide which townships within the county were most deserving.

At the end of March, 250 unemployed men in Morris were ready to organize a group to petition for jobs. They demanded the hiring of local unemployed men for any Grundy County project. Few local men had been hired so far for the clearing project on the Illinois Waterway at the Dresden Heights Dam. To help the unemployed in Morris, each man was given two days of work at $3 a day, barely enough to provide food for a family. Since city relief funds were down to $6,000, little more could be done.

A meeting of 170 men was held in the Empire Theater in Morris on April 7 to register more men for the Grundy County unemployed organization. Each man was issued a numbered identification card, which could be used like a lottery for the draft. One of the topics at the meeting centered on the use of the $30,000 gas tax refund, which might be forthcoming from the state.

In the spring, the Ottawa Chamber of Commerce organized a "prosperity" parade to highlight the plight of the unemployed. With L. C. Carroll, as parade marshal, the event, led by a police escort and Hentrich's Military Band, began at Washington Park. An estimated crowd of 5,000 residents lined the streets from LaSalle to

Main Street and from there to Columbus Street and back to the park. Stretched out over eight city blocks, more than 2,000 children dressed in various costumes carried placards and posters urging work for the unemployed. The Ottawa H. S. drum and bugle corps also participated.

Bank robbers didn't need a parade and posters to solve their employment situation. A tip to Sheriff William Neill likely prevented thieves from a planned robbery at one of the banks in Princeton, but the warning didn't stop criminals from a holdup at the Spring Valley Bank on April 15. Four men entered the bank with automatic weapons and forced a lone customer, Miss Mary Abraham, and the employees to lie face down on the floor or be killed. After cleaning out the cash drawers, one of the robbers hit Peter Hollerich, the cashier, on the head with his gun when the cashier tried to explain that the vault was controlled by a time-lock and couldn't be opened until noon. The assistant cashier, L. H. Luther, was kicked repeatedly while lying face down on the floor. The bank robbers walked calmly out of the bank to their Buick sedan, the driver of which had been calmly talking to Mr. George Dyer, owner of the soda plant, three doors east of the bank. Dyer had no suspicion of the robbery in progress. The car sped out of town toward Arlington. Within minutes, a dragnet was initiated throughout the area. Two of the robbers were caught in Taylorville, IL on May 2. Both men were from Girard, IL.

Shortly after the Spring Valley bank holdup, the Union National Bank in Streator was robbed on May 14. A gang of five masked men invaded the home of T. E. McNamara at 204 E. Court St. Four of the men took Mr. McNamara, the assistant cashier, to the bank, while the fifth gunmen held the rest of the family hostage. At the bank, the robbers took about $52,000 and made their getaway, meeting the fifth man on a country road northeast of Streator.

Robbers took over $50,000 from the Union National Bank in Streator. Photo taken in 1938. (Streatorland Hist. Soc.)

The search for the bandits resulted in four arrests in Streator two days later. Two of the plotters included Streator's Assistant Police Chief Clarence Goss and Patrolman George Kmetz. The other Streator men were "Steamboat Joe" Casmanio and Frank Cinerani, thought to be local bootleggers. As the investigation unfolded, it was determined that the gang actually consisted of 12 members.

Other members of the gang were gradually hunted down. In June, Sheriff Welter caught one robber in Minneapolis and another one in Boston. The Streator police officers, implicated in the robbery, were tried for their roles in the crime and sentenced to terms of 1-20 years in the Joliet penitentiary.

During the Depression, Sheriff Ed Welter pursued criminals across the country to bring the accused back to Ottawa to stand trial.

That wasn't the end of the case. On June 15, three men came to the Ottawa jail on visitors' day and asked to speak to the Union bank robbers. Suddenly, two of the men released tear gas bombs and walked to the kitchen area where they forced George Mosley, the jailer, to turn over his keys to release three of the inmates connected with the Union Bank robbery. Mosley was locked in the bullpen. Racing out of the jail, the gang got into a Nash only to abandon it a few minutes later on Norris Street. There the eight men fled in a Graham-Paige auto.

This 1932 Graham "Blue Streak" was similar to the getaway vehicle used by the bank robbers in the Ottawa jailbreak.

Robberies were not limited to bank heists. According to the Morris *Herald*, railroad theft was "assuming alarming proportions" for the Rock Island RR. On May 4, the paper reported that a shipment of butter was dumped east of the Morris coal chutes. Fortunately, a brakeman on an eastbound train spotted the package containing 24 one-pound bricks of butter valued at 25¢ each and took the carton to the Ottawa police. Railroad detectives believed that an organized gang was receiving tips on shipments of valuable merchandise and the locations where the loot could be easily stolen. It may have appeared to be petty theft, but the problem was becoming habitual in the eyes of the railroad.

While robberies continued to dominate the headlines, there was other news of interest regarding economic conditions in the Valley. For months, construction had been progressing on federal projects to construct local post offices. On June 4, it was announced that the Spring Valley facility would be finished, and residents were invited to an open house on Sunday afternoon, June 5. Spring Valley Postmaster Anton Faletti was ready to move into the new post office in the summer of 1932.

The Spring Valley post office was one of many federal public works projects that provided jobs in local communities during the Depression.

(Photos by author)

The Mendota post office was completed in summer of 1932. The $72,000 project was made possible through the efforts of Congressman John Buckbee.

While stately new federal buildings began springing up in the area, there was also a buildup of structures of a less attractive style. Along the banks of the Illinois River, 40-50 shelters of a shantytown or "Hooverville" dotted the landscape on the south side of LaSalle. While most of the shanties were barely large enough for a single person to stand in, one larger shelter, made from tin sheeting, housed several men. These rickety structures had become homes for needy individuals and families, many of whom had

55

planted gardens with the free vegetable seeds supplied by the Tri-City Family Welfare Society. The land had not been cultivated for years and was described as "ideal" by the inhabitants, some of whom anticipated selling their excess produce in the fall to local merchants to pay for necessities.

Along the Illinois River bottoms, numerous communities offered plots for private gardening. George Dellos, a truck gardener near the Aux Sable canal locks offered equipment to anyone who needed it. In mid-May, the Morris city council donated $100 to the United Relief Commission, but twice that amount was needed. A community garden was begun in the spring on the Ed Cryder farm on Route 7 northeast of the city. Cryder plowed and prepared the 12-acre parcel for planting. The plan was to plant a variety of crops – an acre each of carrots, beets, parsnips, turnips, and onions, three acres of tomatoes, and three acres of cabbage. A representative of the University of Illinois Extension Service estimated that the Morris garden would produce 21 tons of tomatoes, 4 tons of turnips, and 300 bushels of the carrots, beets and parsnips.

At harvest time, LaSalle County bottomland production amounted to over 3,000 heads of cabbage in addition to bushels of tomatoes and beans. Mrs. Helen Wolfe Penhale, executive secretary of the Family Welfare Society, asked for assistance in making sauerkraut and safely canning the products. Although the welfare recipients were willing to do the work at the society's offices, they still needed supervision.

The Public Loan Corp. of LaSalle ran this ad in the *Post-Tribune* in the spring of 1932.

Help to Relieve Unemployment

Clean Up
Paint Up
Modernize &
Repair-*NOW*

Issued by the National Clean Up and Paint Up Campaign Bureau which is cooperating with the President's Committee on Unemployment Relief

We will supply the
MONEY AND THE **MEN**

FOR THIS WORTHY CAUSE!
● YOU MAY RENEW OR REFINANCE YOUR PRESENT LOAN AND REPAY IT OVER A PERIOD OF 25 MONTHS, HERE IN LA SALLE ●

415 State Bank Building., La Salle, Ill.
PHONE: 611
We Make Loans in Nearby Towns

PUBLIC LOAN *Corporation*

Public works projects were especially important in providing additional jobs. On June 4, 1932, the Morris *Herald* published a sketch (below) of the proposed federal post office. The $100,000 building, constructed of terra cotta and brick, would be "one of the most beautiful and modern post offices in this section of the state when completed," according to the Morris *Herald.* Other major construction projects in the Valley included the Fox River Bridge at Serena, scheduled to open on June 25, and a new $190,000 canal bridge at Marseilles.

That good news was tempered by the announcement that the First National Bank at Gardner was forced to close on June 27. Almost half of the bank's $238,000 cash reserves had been withdrawn since September 1931. The prospect of continued withdrawals, and declining property values forced the directors to cease operations. It was the first bank in Grundy County to close.

On Sunday, July 10, there were two major gatherings in Peru. At 2 p.m., the laying of the cornerstone for the Peru post office drew a crowd of 2,000. That same day, the bicentennial of the birth of George Washington was observed with the dedication of a bronze plaque on a boulder in Washington Park. Everett Dirksen was the main speaker at Peru's Washington Park. Streator had also observed the birthday with a service in Marilla Park on July 4, 1932. Similar civic events tended to distract citizens from economic problems.

Work continued on the "Big Fill" project in Peru. (Peru Library)

57

From May until August, one consistent story in the Illinois Valley newspapers was the report of the progress of local Bonus marchers. One of the first reports of the veterans march to Washington to demand the immediate payment of their WWI bonus appeared in the *Post-Tribune* on May 24, 1932. Desperate for financial assistance and not satisfied to wait until 1945 when the government promised to pay their bonus, small groups of former members of the American Expeditionary Force (AEF) were making their way across the United States. One group came from Ogden, UT, and 50 vets were coming on a freight train from Boone, IA.

Over 300 veterans were camped at Caseyville, IL. There was some excitement in that small southern Illinois town when the men commandeered a B&O freight train and refused to abandon it. Six companies of the Illinois National Guard were sent by train to East St. Louis to maintain order. The AEF vets waved to them as they passed by their freight cars. A peaceful solution to a possible confrontation was worked out when the sheriff of St. Clair County promised truck transportation to Indiana for the Bonus vets if they would give back control of the B&O train to the engineer. That was an agreeable solution for the veterans.

Not every veteran joined the "march," but a small contingent from LaSalle, Peru, and Ottawa decided to go to Washington to appeal for the passage of the Patman-Thomas Bill, which would authorize payment of the bonuses. On June 15, a group of seven men climbed aboard a Rock Island tanker car in the yards behind Westclox. Their leader was Tommy Stankey, a soldier who fought in the battles at Soissons, Saint Mihiel, and the Argonne Forest and was both wounded and gassed. He carried a small suitcase. Written in chalk on the side was the following: "Washington, Here Comes Peru, IL. Now, not '45. Bonus, Beer or Bust!" Assisting Stankey in the organization effort was Stanley Wisgowski, a former sailor in WWI. Others in the group were Guy Gould, Louis Mackowiak, Mike Lipiecki, Frank Masurkewiecz and Steve Cresieleski. Their baggage was meager. One man said he packed a razor, tobacco, and an extra pair of socks. A crowd of about 150 residents cheered them on their way. Ten other young men climbed aboard the train promising to escort them as far as Joliet. Reaching that destination, the veterans decided to board an Elgin, Joliet, and Eastern freight, taking it as far as the Indiana border, where they would continue their journey in Army trucks to Ohio. Two veterans from Ottawa, John Meyers, and Charles Sterling, also joined the "crusade" the same day. A large crowd gathered at the Legion post to see them on their way.

Meanwhile in the nation's capital, some 20,000 veterans had already gathered anxiously waiting for action by Congress. The Patman Bill passed the House 211-176 on June 15, but there was a tough battle ahead in the Senate. Payment of the bonuses would cost the government $2.4 billion, an excessive amount for the Senate.

Periodically, telegrams were sent to the *Post-Tribune* so the paper could inform its readers of the progress of the Peru contingent. One brief message came from Clifton Forge, VA. "Just a day away. Everybody well and happy." From that location, it was assumed that the men would board a C&O freight to continue their journey. Now, their little band had been increased to more than a dozen.

On June 29, another group of veterans met at the LaSalle city hall and marched down to First and Joliet, where a truck, furnished by the city and decked out in patriotic bunting, was waiting to take them to Joliet. A placard on the side of the truck read "LaSalle, IL, Bonus Army, Washington Bound." John Polcyn of Peru shared command with Larry Sonnenberg of LaSalle. The *Post* listed the men from LaSalle as follows: "George Rimmele, Jesse Chambers, John Parel, George Ritchie, Thomas Markiewicz, Anton Kaszynski, Henry Kallner, Stanley and Frank Stelmach, Matt Martin, Frank Kowalski, and John Zimmer." In addition, there were two men from Peru, Henry Dobberstein and Robert Nichols, one man from Oglesby, Vincent Krysiak, and another from Granville, George D. Nichols. Local residents contributed a large quantity of cigarettes and money to pay for their expenses. The Orsinger Bakery and Buehler Brothers Market donated food.

News of their progress came back shortly. After reaching Joliet, they boarded an Elgin, Joliet, and Eastern train with some men from Chicago bound for Hammond, IN. On June 30, a progress message from the men read, "Joined with Reno, NV bunch. 60 fine fellows." The majority of the men moved on, but Larry Sonnenberg was forced to return to LaSalle.

More men were also leaving from Ottawa. A group of 17 men was organized by Jerome Heath, Elmer Walker, and Harry Knutson. Others in the party of WWI veterans were William Scaggs, William Sullivan, Tom Sullivan, John Duffy, Fred Bayers, Mike Fox, Frank Baxley, Max Blue, John Pignatilli, Joe Nevens, Frank Wolfe, Frank Graff, and Ten Zellers.

By the end of June, over 30,000 veterans had arrived in the capital. Congressman John Buckbee's office reported that about 100 more veterans were on the way to Washington. The 11 men, who had arrived from the Illinois Valley, were billeted with a unit from Beaumont, TX. Others who had joined the Illinois Valley group

59

included Rudolph Doll of LaSalle and Charles Sterling of Ottawa. Six men from Morris, William Stimson, Chris Teedall, Robert L. Chrisman, and John Domas occupied rooms provided by Congressman Buckbee (pictured).

Joseph Plumier, commander of the bonus contingent from the 12th Illinois congressional district, reported from Washington that their quarters where the best of any unit in the capital. Their power bill for lighting was paid by the VFW post in Rockford. Their one request was that the people back home would send newspapers and other reading material.

John Polcyn, commander of the LaSalle unit, periodically reported on their status. On July 5, he wrote about the compliments on their marching appearance by a colonel in the regular army. He also said that the men were ready to "stick to the finish." In a letter two days later, Polcyn said that Washington was "just another big city full of shacks and tents of all descriptions. It looks more like a carnival with all its concessions. We have electric lights, water, and gas which we use in preparing our food. 'Corn willie' (corned beef) is kind of forgotten since our army days, but is coming back gradually. We also have 'gold fish' or (canned) salmon, as it is known back home." Polcyn said there were three camps for the Bonus Army. Camp Anacosta with about 18,000 men was the largest. The other two were called Camp Simms and Camp Bartlett. He closed saying, "We're still perched on the capitol steps and it looks like it's going to be a long stay, but the boys have decided to stick to the finish."

Camp Anacosta was located near the nation's capitol. (National Archives)

In spite of the fact that there were reports of veterans leaving the capital, Polcyn wrote to the *Post*, "Our forces are increasing rapidly and the last two nights have paraded the capitol grounds in an orderly manner. They have lined the capitol grounds,

2,000 strong." He asked for donations of food, clothing and money for the LaSalle contingent "at the front." LaSalle veterans wore badges with a ribbon printed with the following: "Bonus Expeditionary Force, France 1917-1918, Washington 1932-? LaSalle, IL."

Capital police fought with the BEF during the summer of 1932. The structure at right was an abandoned government building occupied by the Bonus Marchers. (Herbert Hoover Presidential Library)

Heightened tensions reached a peak on July 29, when Gen. Douglas MacArthur, chief of staff, ordered in regular army units to clear out the veterans' camps after riots broke out the previous day. It was reported that the five men from LaSalle and Peru, George Ritchie, Robert Nichols, Vincent Krysiak, Thomas Stankey, and Guy Gould, who were still in the capital, were uninjured. They were taken by truck through Maryland to a temporary headquarters in Johnstown, PA with about 3,000 other veterans. By Aug. 3, the BEF disbanded, and the men returned home.

Even temporary jobs were difficult to find locally. To alleviate the problem, Peru planned a series of water line extensions. The $15,000 projects would generate jobs for dozens of men. In order to create the greatest number of jobs, Superintendent H.J. Mueller, said crews of 20 men would be hired for three-day periods. Then, another group would be put to work.

The job situation in Mark also looked better. The strike at the Prairie State coal mine, caused by UMW agitators, was finally resolved. The miners went back to work under the assumption that Cox would grant some concessions in their contract. There was still a threat that the UMW would return to Mark if Cox did not allow the unionization of the miners. On Sept. 1, the editor of the Putnam County *Record* wrote, "It may be that a few men who are out of work may pull such a stunt but the home men will be protected, and it is not likely that they can be persuaded to leave their homes and their work until they have something better."

On Aug. 16, bank robbers once again came through the Illinois Valley. Two men walked into the First National Bank of

61

Marseilles at noon and tied up the three women on duty, Miss Edith Covell, cashier; June Parr, assistant cashier; and Anita Nordacci. The bandits grabbed $9,200 in silver and currency. The women sounded the alarm only minutes after the robbers fled in a getaway car, that was last seen passing through Norway, IL. This was the second major robbery at the Marseilles bank. The previous one occurred on Dec. 27, 1926, when bandits looted $8,963.

Two months later on Oct. 25, a gang composed of six men from Chicago and Cicero robbed the First National Bank of Ransom of $2,600 and kidnapped Leo Gondolf, the bank president, and Elma Thompson, the bookkeeper. After releasing the hostages, City Clerk Fred Hart tipped off the deputy sheriff, Andrew McManus, the robbers might be hiding at the home of Mike Martini, an alleged bootlegger, at 1312 S. Illinois St. in Streator. Two hours later, Sheriff Welter, his deputies, and the highway patrol engaged the bandits in a battle involving tear gas bombs, machine guns, sawed-off shotguns, and small arms. The robbers finally surrendered and were taken to the Ottawa jail, where they confessed. A seventh member of the gang, Mike Vito, was traced to a Chicago location. Ironically, Welter's car, which was dropped off in Chicago for repairs while the sheriff searched for Vito, was stolen and stripped of its bulletproof windows, guns, spotlight, and generator. The car was found at 34th and California in Chicago. Supposedly, the theft was in retaliation for capturing the rest of the gang.

More violence occurred two days later on October 27 in Putnam County. This time, it wasn't a bank robbery but rather an explosion three miles south of Magnolia. At about 11 p.m., unknown parties had blown up the 80-foot steel railroad bridge south of the town. The bridge was one of nine crossed by Cox's Rutland, Toluca, and Northern Railroad, a vital component in the operation of his Prairie State coal mine. Replacement of the single-track span was estimated at $5,000. Coal shipments would be delayed about a week.

When a *Post-Tribune* reporter interviewed Cox, he said that enemies were trying to halt his business. Fuse wires found in the wreckage indicated that they were typical of the materials used by miners. On several occasions, Cox had experienced difficulties with the UMW when they tried to unionize his company.

One group trying to organize local farmers was the Farm Holiday Association. Dr. Eddy, the LaMoille chairman, and Fred Nelson of Princeton, who chaired the Bureau County group held a meeting in LaMoille to discuss possible action to stabilize farm prices. So far, there had been no interference with deliveries, but in Whiteside County, livestock and dairy trucks were being stopped.

The movement spread to LaSalle County on Sept. 21, when pickets near Ottawa stopped W. H. Springborn, who operated a slaughterhouse west of Ottawa. He was detained while driving his empty truck to his plant and was told that all shipments would be stopped the following day. This switch to more peaceful confrontations followed violent protests in Iowa and Minnesota the previous week.

For most people, events in the fall of 1932 were far less confrontational. In Mendota, residents had the opportunity to enjoy Alger's renovated Strand Theater, now renamed the State Theater. Alger gave a new look to the exterior with a new marquee and electric sign. The interior now could seat 500 patrons in a modern setting with concealed lighting, new seats, carpeting, and drapes, and the most modern projection system available. The grand opening on Sept. 1 featured George Bancroft in "Lady and Gent."

For Putnam County baseball fans, the 1932 World's Series at Yankee Stadium had special meaning. Charlie "Red" Ruffing, who was born in Granville and later became a pitcher for the New York Yankees, took the mound in the opening game against the Chicago Cubs in New York. Ruffing went the distance. With batting greats, Lou Gehrig and Babe Ruth, the Yankees swept the series 4-0.

On Aug. 13, 1932, "Red" Ruffing threw a shutout and hit a home run in the 10th inning to beat the Washington Senators 1-0, a feat that was never repeated for a Major League pitcher through the 2006 season. During the Depression, he played in seven World Series and won six. In 1967, he was inducted into the baseball Hall of Fame.

The prospect of more jobs also lifted spirits. In Princeton, the city council on Sept. 12 decided to hire about 20 men to take care of small jobs that had previously been eliminated from the city work plan as a cost savings. Rather than paying the men in cash, salaries would be paid in the form of vouchers for food and clothing. The city council knew from the previous year, when 82 families were on relief, they could handle the coming winter without a problem. The Red Cross chapter in Bureau County had stockpiled 4,000 yards of flannel, 750 yards of shirting, and a similar amount of muslin cloth according to the *Post-Tribune*.

More men were hired to resurface Rt. 2 and Rt. 7A near Jonesville. To make sure as many men as possible would have work, the project was divided into two six-hour shifts, and new 11-man crews were hired every two days.

Oglesby's unemployed cement workers were encouraged by the news of the planned resumption of work at Lehigh Portland

Cement. The plant had ceased operations on Feb. 20, 1932, and only 75 men were kept on at the plant to help with shipments from the storage facilities. Managers planned to call back 200 men in November. They said there were enough orders to keep the plant operating for at least three months. About 97 percent of the workers being called back were from Oglesby with the rest coming from LaSalle, Peru, and other nearby communities.

The Conco Crane and Engineering Works in Mendota also announced a call back for 25-50 workers to produce 50,000 ice cream freezers. However, work was not scheduled to resume until Dec. 1. That order would likely keep the men busy for a year. The Conco Press division of the company reported a 50 percent increase in their printing business during the year.

The cold winds of December forced men to accept any kind of assistance to keep their families warm. While men were digging for their coal in Ottawa, others found fuel on the 200-acre farm of Mrs. Windsor near Princeton. She had graciously invited needy men to pick up quantities of dead wood on a large timber tract on her property. Unfortunately, some individuals were overzealous in their wood collection and began cutting down valuable standing timber on the Windsor property.

Seeking re-election in 1932, President Hoover toured the Midwest with brief stops in the Illinois Valley. The whirlwind trip from Washington, D.C. through 8 states with 26 stops provided little time for the president to discuss the issues. Thousands greeted the president at Gary and Joliet. At Morris, the high school band played while the crowd of 5,000 waited for the president's arrival. When the presidential special finally arrived at the Rock Island depot at Morris, the cheering crowd drowned out the President's brief remarks. Within a few minutes, the train pulled out of the station. Due to heavy rains and time constraints, the folks in Marseilles were disappointed when the presidential special failed to stop at their depot. However, Mrs. Hoover was seen waving to the crowd.

Ad from the LaSalle *Post-Tribune.*

PRESIDENT

HOOVER

Comes to La Salle

Friday, Nov. 4

At 12:05 O'clock, Noon

■■

EVERYBODY INVITED

To See and Hear the President in an Important Message to Be Presented from the President's Train at the Rock Island Station.

HEAR HOOVER

A 12-minute stop in Ottawa thrilled the throng estimated to number 10,000. Hoover told his supporters, "I am sure Illinois will continue to give the country the republican leadership that it has in the past."

An even larger crowd of 20,000 awaited the president's arrival in LaSalle. The L-P band arrived only five minutes before the president's train and had time only for one musical selection. As the train rounded the curve east of the Rock Island depot, a great cheer rose from the crowd. When the train came to a stop shortly after noon, the crowd broke through the police lines and rushed to get a better view of Mr. and Mrs. Hoover on the rear platform of their Pullman car. Since he was running late, Hoover made a short speech, barely audible to the people.

Following his visit, support for the Republican candidate continued. Full-page ads with the tag line, "Hold on to Hoover," appeared in the *Post*. The prospect of a Democratic victory prompted Paul Nesbit, manager of the L-O-F plant, to send out a form letter warning the workers at Naplate, "Isn't it plain to see that the Ottawa plant would no doubt definitely and permanently be closed."

The election results reported in the *Post-Tribune* did not reflect the apparent local support for the incumbent president. With the exception of Lee County, which reported a narrow 626-vote margin of victory for Hoover, FDR swept the Illinois Valley. In Putnam County, only Granville and Magnolia gave Hoover a majority vote. Strong support was registered for Hoover in Morris, but the precincts in the eastern part of Grundy County gave FDR a 264-vote margin of victory. In LaSalle County, FDR won by over 8,500 votes.

The New York governor won the presidency with an electoral vote of 472 to Hoover's 59, but it would be a long winter before any of his ideas could be put into place and have an impact on the Illinois Valley. The inauguration would not be held until March.

As Christmas approached, the needy – especially the children – were not forgotten. The Big Hearts party at the Majestic Theater was a great success as 1,200 kids filled the seats waiting for small gifts. The Boy Scouts helped with the distribution of more than 500 toys. The L-P-O area adopted the slogan "A Christmas dinner for everyone" and made good on that promise with the distribution of 300 baskets of food and clothing. The LaSalle Elks and the American Legion post handled the distribution of the gifts. Other groups who participated in collecting the gifts for the needy were the LaSalle and Peru churches, the Intermediate Clubs of the two cities, the Peru Rotary, and the Peru Camp Fire Girls.

1933
THE NEW DEAL IN THE VALLEY

While Hoover and FDR discussed the transition of power, the long winter of 1932-33 dragged on with little improvement in the economy. Unemployed men walked the streets stopping other pedestrians for some change and pestering merchants for food. To alleviate the problem of "moochers," a soup kitchen was opened at the Morris city hall on Jan. 10. The XXX society in town took responsibility for supervision and coordination. In addition to cash donations, grocers were asked for vegetables that couldn't be sold and cheap meats to prepare mulligan stew. Bakers were asked to donate stale bread, biscuits, and cookies. Once the soup kitchen was organized, hungry men were offered two meals a day, breakfast and supper. Local men were given a breakfast and told that if they pestered the merchants or pedestrians they would be ordered to "shake the Morris dust from their feet and never return."

Over the next several months, the program served an average of 25 men a day. Meals consisted of soup, bread, coffee, and sometimes, some fruit. During that time, however, merchants grew weary of the requests, and the XXX society had to ask for monetary as well as food donations to keep the service available.

Transients tended to sleep over night at the railroad station and then come in for breakfast, after which, they were told to get out of town or be arrested. Generally, the program worked out, and the panhandling annoyance was kept to a minimum.

Most men were not freeloaders by choice and were eager to take a job. For those men in Spring Valley there was some good news. In February, the Fleming-Meadows garment company was expanding, thereby creating 100 more jobs.

Attention quickly shifted from jobs to the weather, when on Monday, Feb. 6, a blizzard swept through the Valley. Schools dismissed early as the roads became more treacherous. The Westclox factory, which served as the official weather reporting station since 1919, reported an 11" snowfall accumulation by 9:40 a.m. The bottom road along the Illinois River was covered with several feet of snow. It would take the better part of a day to open the road between Peru and Spring Valley. Local businesses quickly hired a few of the unemployed to clear sidewalks in front of their stores.

Another crisis concerned the entire nation. On Feb. 15, Joe Zanagara, a crazed man, who hated all presidents, tried to assassinate Roosevelt in Miami. His bullet missed its mark and instead mortally wounded the Chicago mayor, Anton Cermak, who was traveling in a car with the president-elect. Newspaper readers followed the story of the mayor's declining health for several weeks until the spreading gangrene finally took the mayor's life. Some months later, the assassin was tried, found guilty, and executed.

While the nation waited for the inauguration of FDR, jobs were still hard to find in the Illinois Valley. There was an effort in LaSalle to make the situation a little less depressing. A degree of levity was planned by the LaSalle Unemployed Council in late February as it organized a "hard times" dance. It was limited to those registered as unemployed. Participants also had to come dressed in a "hard times" costume. In addition to the dance, the Lutheran Church Players organized a play, entitled "School Days," and a boxing match featuring Vince Perino and John Windy. On Mar. 3, the *Post-Tribune* handed out 200 free movie tickets compliments of the Rexy Theater to adults on the relief list. The feature film, "If I had a Million," starred Gary Cooper, George Raft, and Wayne Gibson.

Others had different plans for that day. Three men decided to rob the Farmers' First National Bank of Minooka. Driving up to the bank at 10 a.m. in a Chrysler, two of the bandits walked into the bank with drawn revolvers and shouted, "This is a stick-up. Get back against the wall and elevate your hands." One man went behind the cashier's cage, grabbed the bills, and stuffed them into a bag. Then, they fled in the waiting car. Clark Moore, the bookkeeper, immediately ran to the vault where a rifle was kept and pursued the men outside, firing off a couple of rounds striking the vehicle. The robbery netted the thieves about $2,000.

That same day, FDR was sworn in as the new president. He tackled the banking crisis with swift action. Using 1917 legislation regarding trading with the enemy, FDR declared a four-day bank holiday. In the interim, local banks began preparing scrip to handle transactions since U.S. currency could not be used.

On Mar. 7, the banks in the Illinois Valley were open for limited transactions. Once auditors examined the assets of the nation's banks, licenses could be issued for re-opening. Much to the relief of local depositors, after eleven days, the government authorized the re-opening of the LaSalle State Bank and the LaSalle National Bank and Trust Co. Other banks in nearby towns also received telegrams of approval from Washington. These included the Farmers State Bank of Lostant; the First National Bank

67

in Lacon, Manlius, and Ottawa; the National Bank of Mendota; Citizen's First National Bank in Princeton; Streator's National Bank and First State Bank; and the Citizen's National Bank of Toluca.

This *Post Tribune* ad appeared shortly after the LaSalle State Bank received authorization to reopen.

It took some time before auditors could certify the solvency of some local banks. The Granville National Bank was still being evaluated by federal inspectors on May. 23, 1933. After six weeks, the Farmers State Bank in McNabb received permission to reopen. It was the only bank in Putnam County operating in mid-

The Hoarding Days
Are Over
Confidence
IS HERE

La Salle State Bank

April 1933. The Ladd bank was opened on May 6, and the DePue bank advertised its opening on May 8. The bank in Cherry was scheduled to resume business on May 17. In Grundy County, the First National Bank of Morris announced its re-opening on May. 23. The next day, the Verona Exchange Bank and the First National Banks in Coal City and Dwight were ready for business. The Grundy County Bank opened on Mar. 25.

Another change, legislated by Congress in March, was the passage of the beer and wine act, which allowed the manufacture of 3.2 percent beer and wine. Whiskey manufacturing was still illegal. The Peru Products brewery responded by hiring dozens of men. Andrew Hebel, the owner, said that men would be hired on Monday, April 10, to prepare the facility for beer manufacturing once again. More men would be hired as soon as the plant was ready for full production. The other local Peru brewery, Star Union Products, had still not received a state permit to produce beer.

Tom Cawley placed this April 7 ad in the LaSalle *Post-Tribune* announcing the availability of beer at Kelly and Cawley's in LaSalle.

BEER IS BACK
But better than that—it's a better beer for we are pleased to announce that we are selling

Anheuser-Busch
BUDWEISER BEER
And here's real news

Opening Tonight
Our Second Floor Beer Salon.
Everybody welcome.

Watch for our formal opening next week.

Kelly & Cawley

68

The new legislation would eliminate the need for law enforcement officers to arrest licensed manufacturers of beer and wine. However, Sheriff Welter was facing a new problem during the spring of 1933. For weeks, stories had been in the local papers about thousands of hunger marchers from Rockford and Chicago making their way to Springfield. On April 6, about 1,200 unemployed men and women, led by Karl Lockner, arrived at Marseilles in spite of warnings not to come into LaSalle County. Welter and the state police escorted the group to Twin Hickory Camp five miles east of LaSalle.

A confrontation ensued the next morning when the sheriff decided that the group would have to go back to Chicago. When the crowd refused to disband, tear gas was used to disperse the angry mob. During the fighting, Welter and one officer, Stanley Murray, were injured. Lockner and 36 others were arrested and taken to the Ottawa jail. When the accused were searched, officers found some communist literature, which was confiscated and destroyed. On April 12, Lockner was fined $100. The others were fined $25.

There was also an act of violence in Putnam County. John Cox had problems with miners trying to organize the Progressive Miners of America Union. After the bombing of a railroad bridge on Oct. 27, 1932, Cox had stationed watchmen to guard the bridges used by his Rutland, Toluca and Northern coal trains. On April 10, 1933, believing the danger had passed and another bombing was unlikely, Cox relieved the guards of their duties. Two days later on April 12, a dynamite explosion occurred at one of the bridges used by the RT&N and woke residents in Magnolia. Although, the 150-foot bridge was not seriously damaged, railings and ties were ripped apart at one end. A second explosion three minutes later at the other end of the bridge did little damage. The guards were ordered back to their posts guarding the bridges. For the time being, Cox decided to close the Mark mine. The mules were brought to the surface, and the miners were told to pick up their tools. Cox said he would try to open the mine in July.

Dairymen also faced violent confrontations when some producers tried to establish an embargo to increase prices. In mid-May, a group of six men stopped Everett Jordan of Mazon and James Elam of Goodfarm Township near Braceville as they attempted to make a delivery to the Pure Milk Association plant in Wilmington. Milk cans were taken from the vehicle, and the contents were dumped. Although three of the six men were later identified and brought to trial, the incident was rather tame compared to the violence near Milwaukee, when 1,000 farmers with clubs confronted

15 deputies escorting a milk truck on May 15. In spite of the use of tear gas bombs by the officers, the farmers dragged the men from the truck and drained its contents. It was one more incident in a weekend battle to stop milk shipments in Kenosha County, WI. Similar, but less violent confrontations, would also occur in Illinois.

The spring weather provided an opportunity for the unemployed in the Illinois Valley to begin planning vegetable gardens on plots of public lands. As early as March, certain vacant lots were identified for potential gardens. LaSalle received donations of ten lots generally located between Sixth and Tenth Streets. In Peru, a "garden army," consisting mainly of the unemployed, planned to use the bottomland on the south side of the Illinois River. The Peru American Legion post allocated garden plots in that area and 250 other locations in the city. Alpha Cement donated a four-acre tract east of Oakwood Cemetery on Route 7 for gardening. The company had previously donated another tract from the Little Vermilion River eastward along the highway. A total of 93 lots were made available through the generosity of the company. Free seeds and seed potatoes for the gardens were brought on a Burlington train and ready for distribution to qualified Oglesby residents on April 15. It was estimated that there would be enough vegetable seed packets for 5,000 families in the Tri-County area.

Unemployed workers often fell behind in payments for essential services. In Oglesby, the city council developed a unique method to collect delinquent water and electric bills. In May, Commissioner Ralph Moyle, the head of streets and public improvements, suggested the city hire those unemployed men in arrears and have them work for the city. The excavation of Walnut Street for the inspection of the sewer line and repaving of the street with bricks would provide jobs for at least 30 men. They would receive a salary of $5.20 a day but would sign waivers authorizing the wages to be applied to their unpaid utility bills.

One of FDR's plans to relieve unemployment had a dramatic effect across the nation as hundreds of young men, 18-25, began enrolling in the president's reforestation program. It would take several months before the men would actually be processed for the newly created jobs. An initial quota of 179 men for LaSalle County was soon raised to 192. In Bureau County, 71 men could enroll. Grundy County's quota was set at 34, and Putnam County was allotted 10 spots. Across the state, the new Civilian Conservation Corps had openings for 14,000 men. The "forest army" would be run by the Army, and enrollees would work in the state and national parks. Reforestation would be one of the goals of the CCC.

Robert Kingery, Illinois director of public works and buildings, outlined the general scope of the project in the Illinois Valley. Four camps would be located in LaSalle County near Starved Rock and Utica. As the program developed, consideration was given to the construction of a road along the Illinois-Michigan Canal towpath and the development of a fish preserve at Lock 13.

The goal of turning the I-M Canal into an 81-mile state park began to take shape. One camp was established at the Palos Hills forest preserve near Lemont. Another camp was set up at Romeo near Lockport. Other camps for the canal project were planned for Channahon, Aux Sable, Marseilles, and Lock 13.

A Handbook for Enrollees

Each of the camps would have 212 men; 196 of that number would be engaged in reforestation projects. The remaining men would be regular army officers and civilian supervisors. Cooks would also be assigned to each camp.

Putnam County would also have CCC men working at Coffee Creek bordering the Hennepin conservation district. Because of flooding problems caused by the creek, the CCC would straighten the channel.

On May 31, 1933, a group of nine men from the CCC arrived at Starved Rock. Two days later, a contingent of 209 men arrived from Ft. Sheridan aboard a Rock Island train. Lt. J.T. Taylor, a former resident of Streator, greeted the men as they detrained at Utica and hiked to Dimmick Hill. The camp commander was Capt. E. F. Carey, from Chanute Field near Rantoul.

When they arrived at the state park, the men put up the tents they would occupy during the summer. Instead of using small 8-man tents, the men set up larger rectangular hospital tents that could house 28 men. The first day, the cooks had a warm meal waiting for the hungry men. Beef stew, potatoes, canned fruit, and bread in prodigious quantities were quickly consumed.

Water from the salt well east of Parkman Plain was undrinkable when the CCC arrived in 1933 so a fresh water well was dug closer to the camp.
Note - The water still flows from the salt well and is still undrinkable today.

The *Post-Tribune* sent a reporter to check on the meals at the camp. He reported that food was plentiful. Breakfast included scrambled eggs, bacon, corn flakes, milk, and coffee. For lunch, the cooks served spareribs and sauerkraut with boiled potatoes, rice pudding, canned fruit, bread and butter, coffee. Supper consisted of frankfurters, fried potatoes, bread and butter, jam, and coffee.

In addition to three-square meals a day, clothing, and shoes, the men were also paid. They had one payday at Ft. Sheridan while they were training. It wasn't much, only $5. The rest of their pay, $25, was sent to their families in Chicago. That summer, FDR authorized a 15 percent pay raise for corporals and sergeants in the CCC.

Religious services were also available. For Catholics, Father Jerome Walsh O.S.B. from St. Bede Abbey, who had served as a military chaplain, was assigned to offer the Mass for the next six months at the camp. The Rev. George T. Green, pastor of the Ottawa Methodist Church, held services for the Protestant men. The Salvation Army conducted services on Friday. A gospel team from the LaSalle Baptist Church also came to the camp.

In order to handle any sickness or injuries, Lt. T. F. Mullin was assigned as the camp medical officer. Serious injuries would be treated at the Ryburn-King Hospital in Ottawa.

As the first week progressed at the CCC camp, men were assigned to different projects. These included clearing a parking area; building drives and shelters; thinning out wooded areas to prevent forest fires; and pulling up weeds and other undesirable plants. Although the CCC was really established for reforestation, that would have to wait for cooler weather in the fall. One of the first major projects at Starved Rock was cleaning out poison ivy and poison oak in the canyons and wooded areas.

The camp quickly became more organized. The men used tree limbs for fences and gates and cleared a parking area for visitors. Many of the first enrollees were from Chicago so families or friends could drive down to the park on Sundays to spend the day. Officers' quarters were set apart from the rest of the tents. The fresh water well at the northeast corner of the camp was almost ready.

Young men from LaSalle County were anxious to join the CCC. On Saturday morning, June 3, over 30 young men from

LaSalle, a dozen from Peru, and two from Utica left for training at Jefferson Barracks, MO.

Frank Naujalis, a resident of Spring Valley, got his first taste of a military camp at Jefferson Barracks. He told of the camp routine in a letter to the *Post-Tribune*. After getting his physical and shots, he became a member of Co. 1652. Housing consisted of 38 tents. They slept on straw mattresses on cots with two blankets.

Naujalis said they were up at 6 a.m. to wash and be ready for roll call in 15 minutes. Their hearty breakfast included bacon and eggs, milk and oatmeal, grapefruit, two slices of bread and butter, and coffee. From 8:30 a.m. til 11 a.m., their work consisted of pulling weeds, chopping wood, and generally cleaning up the camp. Lunch at 12:15 consisted of apple butter, bread and butter, lemonade, steak, potatoes, roast, creamed peas, and half an orange. Work in the afternoon only lasted til 3:30 p.m. The men showered and shaved and then had supper. The meal included iced tea, mashed potatoes and gravy, roast, onions, lettuce, celery, beans, bread and butter. For entertainment, the men packed the camp boxing arena, which was large enough to hold 5,000 men. There they watched 20 or more amateur matches after dinner. It was "lights out" at 10 p.m.

Fred Grosso, also from Spring Valley, told how he, John Palmer, and George Vickery were made section leaders in Co. 1652. Others in the group including Mike Bernatovich, R. Michels, J. Taylor, and F. Jeris were appointed squad leaders. Their company also included men from Joliet, Pana, Springfield, and Taylorville, IL.

While most of the men working at Starved Rock were from Illinois, the enrollees from the Illinois Valley were sent to western states to work in one of the national parks or forests. Some men from Spring Valley were sent to Crater Lake, OR. Company 1652 departed from Jefferson Barracks at the end of June, and after a three-day train trip, arrived at Chiloquin, OR. Although it was summer, they found the area deep in snow reminiscent of the big snowfalls in Illinois. Camped at an elevation of 4,525 feet, they slept in their clothes and piled on four blankets trying to keep warm when temperatures dropped to zero. While eating breakfast on a snow bank, Naujalis was amazed when four black bears walked through the area. He said the cook was upset because the bears had gotten into the kitchen during the night and eaten some of the food.

Melvin Johnson from Granville also joined the CCC. After his initial training, he was sent to Crescent City, CA and later to Medford, OR. His company traveled along the Pacific Coast on the Redwood Highway. One of their side trips took them to the Oregon Caves. Writing to his parents from his camp on the Upper Rouge

River in Oregon, he said, "I never imagined I'd get a $1 a day for seeing such sights."

For others, who joined the CCC, the experience wasn't as picturesque. Earl Kooi, an enrollee from Streator, was also sent to Oregon. He was one of the hundreds of CCC men on the fire line trying to stop the Tillamook forest fire in August 1933. Reflecting on the intensity of the fire, Earl said the forest animals raced out of the burning timber, completely ignoring the CCC men trying to move towards the fire, which was one of the worst in American history.

Right: Earl Kooi was 18 when he joined the CCC. The men in his company lived in tents in the CCC camp.
Below: Kooi's CCC camp in Oregon.
(Photos contributed by Dan Head and Myrtle Kooi.)

The Great Tillamook Burn, as it was called, began on Aug. 14, 1933 when a steel cable used in pulling a Douglas fir rubbed against a snag setting it on fire. The estimated loss in 1933 dollars was over $240,000.

Over 3,000 lumbermen, CCC boys, and local volunteers battled the fire that consumed 400 square miles in 11 days.

Back in Illinois, another CCC camp was established at Buffalo Rock. Two hundred men arrived there on June 11 to begin their work for the next six months. Major Moore, a regular army officer, was the commanding officer. In addition to clearing out garbage and trees and landscaping the grounds, their job was to widen the road along the canal.

This green and yellow emblem was worn on the CCC uniform.

Work on the canal was in full stride by mid-June. Four camps were staffed with about 210 men in each location: Willow Springs, Dresden Rock, Marseilles, and Buffalo Rock. Another camp at Romeo was to begin operations in another week. The planned fish preserve and state park west of Channahon required the diversion of the Des Plaines River at Channahon into the canal so fresh water could flow to Buffalo Rock. CCC men worked in groups of 18-20 as they cleared the canal area. At Buffalo Rock, the men widened and leveled the road leading to the top of the rock.

The CCC erected stone and timber shelters, such as this one at Channahon, which has a double-sided interior fireplace. (Photo by author)

75

Along the towpath at Channahon, the WPA built low, stone walls, such as this one, located over a mile west of the park, to mark the locations of turnouts where motorists could safely pass each other as they drove along the canal.

The remains of trail shelters, canal locks, spillways, and towpath turnouts are found between McKinley Woods and Channahon State Park. (Photos by author)

By June 29, 1933, the CCC was also clearing the 16-mile stretch of the canal from LaSalle east to Ottawa. The men from the Marseilles unit were responsible for the next section of the canal.

Enrollment in the CCC was generally limited to young, single men, but others also qualified. The military experience of war veterans filled the need for leadership. In LaSalle during June 12-22, veterans from WWI, the Spanish-American War, the Philippine Insurrection, the Moroccan Expedition, or the Boxer Rebellion were encouraged to register for positions in the CCC. Men with families would get the standard monthly pay of $30. Of that amount, $25 was sent home to their families. Men without families also received $5 on payday. The balance of their $30 would be paid to them at the end of their enlistment.

Other men returned to their jobs with the Rock Island RR. The line announced that some of its laid-off employees would be rehired that summer. The railroad was going to need about 50 men to operate three tie-tapping machines at Ottawa and work westward. Starting at Wyanet, where work had stopped in 1931, another crew would re-lay one mile of rails on concrete ties and finish another 13 miles of track with new steel rails on the westbound main.

The economic news on July 5 was very positive. The Morris *Herald* ran a banner headline proclaiming "Depression Over," basing it on a report from the New York Board of Trade. "The depression is definitely over and the country is well on its way to one of the greatest periods of stabilized prosperity in its history," the story began. "Using every index by which business is measured, the replies (to a survey) indicate substantial progress generally throughout the country." The writer did acknowledge, however, there were some states still suffering economic hardship.

This ad in the July 20, 1933 edition of the Morris *Daily Herald* reflected some of the exuberance of the producer Russ Ferris, who was bringing his "Broadway Vanities of 1934" female troupe to the Morris Theater.

MORRIS THEATRE
COOLEST PLACE IN TOWN

Something New.....
Something Different!

Happy
Days Are
Positively The Most Elaborate Stage Show Ever Seen In Morris!
Here Again
Big Musical Girl Show
Friday and Saturday

Special Midnite Show
Saturday Night
Note—This show will be purely a stage presentation. No picture! Show starts at 11 p. m.
ADM. 10-35 CENTS

Special Matinee
Saturday Afternoon
ADMISSION 10-25c to 6 P. M.
10-35c THEREAFTER

ADMISSION FRIDAY NIGHT WILL BE 10c AND 35c

That optimism was quickly overshadowed by two days of falling market prices. On July 21, the *Herald* headlines announced, "Stock Prices Pounded Down in Selling Wave," and "Suspend Trading in Grain After Two-Day Crash." Indeed, $4 billion had been

77

lost within three days as over 9.5 million shares were traded on the New York exchange, the most since Oct. 30, 1929. The grain market was equally hectic. The Chicago Board of Trade finally closed operations on July 21 when wheat plunged 40¢ a bushel. Restrictions were imposed after 170 million bushels were sold in one day. Trading in rye and wheat was then limited to a range of 8¢ of the previous day's close.

The only ones who seemed to be making any money were bank robbers. The State Bank of Sandwich was robbed of $5,000 on July 10. The five bandits escaped in a hail of bullets as the police attempted to stop the getaway vehicle without success. Bandits, who stole $200 from the Farmers State Bank of Millbrook, were not so lucky. While attempting to flee from the holdup, the three men, traveling at 60-mph in their 1933 Plymouth, only managed to travel south for about two miles before their vehicle failed to negotiate a curve and flipped over. Two of the men from Chicago were still alive when the police converged on the crash site. One of the robbers was killed by a police bullet when he attempted to flee. His body was moved to the Yorkville morgue. The bank robbery business was similar to the traders on Wall Street. There were winners and losers.

The vast majority of people in the Illinois Valley tried to make a living in legitimate pursuits and enjoyed the simple pleasures in life. Occasional celebrations were enough to temporarily forget the concerns of daily life.

After months of delay, the Peru post office opened in July 1933. The building was unique in design. Indiana limestone was used for the exterior walls. Two cast-stone urns were placed on either side of the portico, which was supported by four, square columns.

The setting of the cornerstone for the Peru post office was completed in July 1932. However, the government project, costing over $63,000, was months behind schedule. The contractor said he would finish by February 1933, but the post office did not open until July due to financial difficulties encountered by the construction company. On Sunday, July 2, 1933, an estimated crowd of 4,000 walked up the 25-foot wide gray granite steps; passed through the large oak doors; and entered the lobby, the walls of which were constructed from travertine with a base of Virginia green-stone.

Other than the CCC program, federal projects to hire the unemployed did not immediately affect the Illinois Valley. It was up to local industries to keep men working. Marquette cement workers had been idle for 45 days, but on June 1, the company announced the need for 300 men in anticipation of the state's need for 3.3 billion barrels of concrete for road construction. Marquette hoped to get an order that would require the production of 6,000 barrels a day. Another company, the Medusa plant in Dixon, needed to rehire 250 laid off workers. Lehigh Cement decided to reopen its plant and call back 300 workers in July. A small crew was called in on July 1 to prepare the mill. Others would be needed in less than a week.

The Westclox plant in Peru was not adversely affected to any great extent by the continuing depression. The managers added another 140 men in July to its 1,800-man workforce, which was working 8-hour shifts.

The CCC was involved in much of the initial building construction and trail improvements at Starved Rock. The hotel stands in the foreground in this 1907 postcard. Four cottages are located at the rear of the hotel.

The CCC continued to enroll men from the Tri-Cities. On July 8, seven men from LaSalle, two from Oglesby and one from Ottawa were sent to the Starved Rock camp. Eight more men from

Marseilles, Ottawa, and Streator were sent to the Marseilles camp.

Much work had been accomplished at Starved Rock. Fire lanes were created, and stone steps were laid to Starved Rock. Limestone, supplied by the Utica Hydraulic Cement Co., was used for flooring in shelters. The CCC also cleared poison ivy plants from around the hotel and pool.

Starved Rock bathhouse and pool. (Oglesby Library)

The old Starved Rock hotel. (Oglesby Library)

The CCC completed the cleanup at French Canyon and Whispering Springs. Some of the dead wood was collected for use in the tourist campground stoves. The new well, having reached a depth of 452 feet, was being cased. Drinking water was still being hauled in large tanks to the camp. In Horseshoe Canyon, the men constructed a dam, which resulted in a 6-foot deep, 75'x 40' swimming pool. The men used the natural falls for a shower until a shower house was finished. Lean-tos at either end of the bathhouse would be constructed for tailor and barber shops. The men also completed the construction of a brick oven to bake bread and pies.

80

The CCC removed fallen timber from French Canyon.

Horseshoe Falls provided a natural shower for the CCC men at Starved Rock.

Runoff from Horseshoe Falls creates a natural pond, a perfect swimming hole for the CCC. The vegetation at left hides the waterfall in this view of Horseshoe Canyon.

(Photos by author)

It wasn't all work in the camps. The north end of the camp was cleared for a baseball diamond. Games were scheduled between CCC camps and with teams from Ottawa, Peru, and LaSalle.

Army officers from Washington, D.C. and Ft. Sheridan periodically conducted inspections of the CCC camps. In August, a competition was held in the Sixth Corps Area to determine the most outstanding camps. The commanding officer of the first place camp would be awarded a gold medal. Other officers at the camp would receive silver medals, and the enlisted men would be awarded a bronze button. When the evaluations were completed in September, Company 614 at Starved Rock was rated third best out of the 250 CCC camps spread across Illinois and parts of Indiana, Wisconsin, Iowa, and Michigan.

Action at the national level to establish improved wages and working conditions soon had an impact on local business. The National Recovery Administration (NRA) goals included setting minimum prices and wages and limiting working hours. Businesses were asked to sign pledges of cooperation. The LaSalle postmaster, W. T. Bedford, expected the agreements to arrive on July 26. Carriers would take them to employers the following day. Packages included pledge cards, stickers, and posters. When pledges were returned to the post offices, the names of those enrolled would be added to the "Roll of Honor," which would be hung in each post office for all to see. The Morris *Herald* began publishing an honor roll of local businesses cooperating with the NRA. Small shops with less than three employees did not receive the packets.

Those who participated put the "Blue Eagle" posters in their windows or used the symbol in their advertising. The government hoped that shoppers would patronize stores and businesses displaying the NRA posters and avoid businesses that refused to participate in the program.

The colorful NRA posters depicted a blue thunderbird with the NRA letters and the slogan "We Do Our Part" in red.

82

In order to get everyone behind the NRA pledge registration, local committees were established to canvass every home and business. Harry Debo was the "General" in charge of the effort in Peru. John McCann was named to the NRA advisory board in Oglesby.

Teachers encouraged support for the NRA. Peru's Central School held an essay contest in which pupils were asked to write on the topic, "The NRA and Why Everyone Should Support It." The winning essays submitted by Grace Hoberg (6th grade), Richard Yoder (7th grade), and John Mee, (8th grade) were printed in the *Post-Tribune* on Sept. 18. Washington School in Oglesby also held a similar contest and announced the winners on Oct. 4. Eva Moalli and Betty Williams submitted the best essays in the 8th grade. The 7th grade winners were Ruth Macchi and Dorothy Ferrari.

Six-month enlistments in CCC at Starved Rock were ending in September, but some of the men re-enlisted. The commander of Company 614 said that work would continue during the winter, and the men would have 10-day furloughs. Lt. Ritchie asked for bids from local contractors to construct a number of buildings for CCC winter quarters. These would include a headquarters building, six barracks, a storehouse, a first aid building, a kitchen and mess hall, a bathhouse, two latrines, and a pump and electric building.

If the War Department did not act on Ritchie's request, an alternate plan proposed by the state called for the CCC's use of the Starved Rock Hotel, dance pavilion, and other buildings. If that plan was adopted, then a single rustic barracks would be constructed on top of the hill near the tourist camps. That structure would be converted into a guest hotel when the CCC left the park.

The CCC companies laid drainage tile at the entrance to Starved Rock State Park. (Lewis University)

On Sept. 25, a call was issued for 48 unemployed men from LaSalle County to join the CCC. They would replace some of the original 200 men from the county who did not re-enlist for another six months or who left their units after finding work in their hometowns. There was a steady stream of applicants for the CCC in the Illinois Valley. On Oct. 2, seven men from LaSalle and four more from Oglesby were ready to leave for two weeks of training at Ft. Sheridan.

The number of CCC men at Starved Rock had dropped to 120. Another 24 men would leave at the end of October. A new unit of 200 men, Company 1609 from Reading, WI, was scheduled to arrive at the park and set up camp on Parkman Plain near Dimmick Hill in December.

For other men in the area, the job situation was tenuous at best. Labor disagreements resulted in 600 men walking off the job at the M&H coal company on Sept. 8. On Sept. 28, company officials announced a layoff of 135 men because they decided to close and seal the mine on Sept. 29. The LaSalle County Relief committee immediately appealed to NRA officials to intervene. The committee simply could not cope with more than 600 men on relief. One of the few bright spots at that time was the announcement that Alpha Cement was reopening, and 200 men would be hired to work 6-hour days with 36 hours of work each week.

Miners in the area were never sure if they would have jobs. On Oct. 3, a labor dispute at M&H Zinc over the hiring of three "undesirables" resulted in the firing of 150 men, when the men refused to work. It was a short protest, and the men were back at work on Oct. 4. The next day, Union Coal called back 250 men who had been laid off. The operators obtained their NRA certificates of compliance and were authorized to display the Blue Eagle insignia at the mine. In Putnam County, 420 men went back into the tunnels of the Prairie State mine, which had been closed since April 1, 1933. During that time, Cox spent $40,000 to electrify almost every aspect of the operation. In addition, the owner agreed to abide by the NRA codes for bituminous mining. Miner's wages were set at 97¢ a ton. Laborers working on the surface would be paid $4 a day while common laborers working below ground received $5 a day. The prospects for coal miners in Spring Valley looked better as a new tipple was nearing completion. A small coal mine in Marseilles owned by the former sheriff, Floyd S. Clark, had been closed due to a fire on Sept. 23. However, by October, Clark was ready to hire 63 men and agreed to pay them $1.63 a ton according to NRA codes.

Hungry families on relief heard good news on Nov. 3. Two railroad cars loaded with cured pork arrived and were stored on a switch track of the Illinois Central RR at LaSalle. Five thousand pounds of the canned meat would be distributed to needy residents in Putnam County. Another portion was destined for needy families in Marseilles. A few weeks later, another shipment, consisting of 143,000 pounds of salted pork, arrived in LaSalle. A huge shipment of flour was expected from government supplies as well.

Armistice Day 1933 had special meaning for residents of Ottawa. Not only would the veterans of the World War be remembered, but the day marked the formal dedication of the $350,000 Hilliard Bridge and the opening of the Lakes-to-Gulf waterway. The city was decked out in bunting and American flags.

A parade got underway shortly after 10 a.m. at Washington Park. Parade participants included Spanish-American War veterans, Boy Scouts and Cub Scouts, the Knights Templar of Ottawa, St. Columba's marching band, Ottawa police and firemen, Ottawa H.S.'s drum corps and football team, American Indians, and numerous floats including those from the Ryburn-King and the Ottawa General Hospital. CCC men from Buffalo Rock drove trucks from the Dept. of Interior. Camp Fire Girls and the War Mothers of Ottawa rode in automobiles. The parade down LaSalle Street stopped at 11 a.m. for the playing of taps and the firing of three volleys in remembrance of the fallen soldiers of the World War. After traveling to the north end of the new bridge, where Al Schoch, Frank Sanders, and Fred Scherer Sr. cut a red ribbon, the parade continued across the bridge breaking through a gold ribbon at the south end of the bridge. Speeches by visiting dignitaries and local officials were interspersed with musical entertainment by the Ottawa H.S. Glee Club under the direction of John Hoff.

During the bridge dedication, Frank Sanders unveiled a bronze tablet in honor of Mayor J. J. Hilliard, who led the drive to construct the new bridge. The plaque is now housed in the Reddick Library.

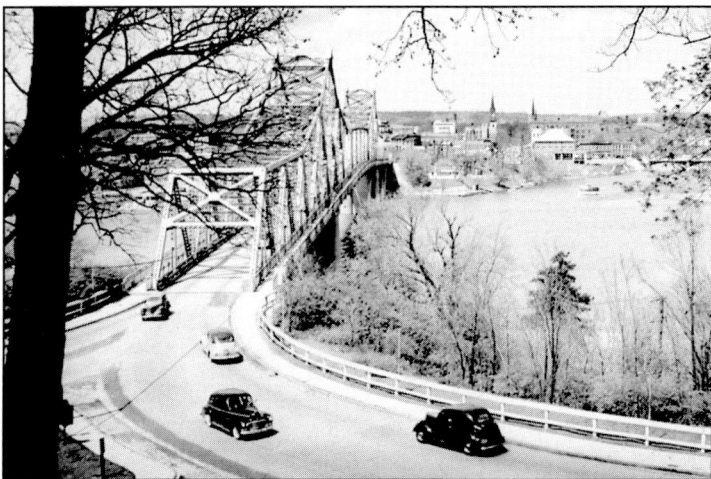

Ottawa's Hilliard Bridge. Circa - late 1930's. (Reddick Library)

After the celebration ended, the reality of widespread unemployment was revealed in the Illinois Valley. The number of men looking for work in LaSalle County had risen to 3,207. LaSalle itself had 750 men looking for jobs. Streator had the second highest number of unemployed men at 672, and Ottawa had 652. Mendota had less of a problem recording only 93 men registered for work.

The only area where there was virtually no unemployment was in Freedom and Waltham Townships, which were mainly agricultural areas of the county. The numbers of those without jobs were soon reduced in LaSalle County by 1,110. On Nov. 17, George W. Sterrett of Marseilles, chairman of county work relief, announced that the Civil Works Administration (CWA) had approved highway repair programs for the county and the hiring of men from Marseilles (90), Streator (350), LaSalle (300), Ottawa (225), Peru (60), Utica (40), Mendota (20) and others from surrounding communities.

Thanksgiving Day 1933 marked the opening of the newly renovated LaSalle Theater. Thousands of children and adults came to see the changes. (*Post-Tribune* ad)

86

Patrons could enjoy a complete Thanksgiving dinner at the Hotel Francis for 65¢. (Peru Library)

PERU

Mat. 5-15c
Eve. 10-25c

LAST TIMES TODAY
NILS   KAY
ASTHER   FRANCIS
In
"STORM AT DAYBREAK"

ALGER'S
NRA

WEDNESDAY Only
Mat. 5-15c; Eve. 10-25c

JIMMIE DUNN
Boots Mallory
In

"HANDLE
WITH
CARE"
A story of the
Whole 'Family!

ALSO

10 TURKEYS
Given Away FREE
After the First Show

"Grown-ups
make me tired
with all this
kissing busi-
ness!"

You must be in the Theatre or in Line with a Paid Admission for the Day.

Alger's Peru Theater ad with the Blue Eagle symbol in the *Post-Tribune* featured free Thanksgiving turkeys for 10 lucky winners.

There was reason to be thankful in the fall of '33. The job situation was improving. The CWA approved 13 projects in Ottawa including street repairs and river front improvements. Peru was approved for $1,949 to clean city sewers. Another $14,000 CWA grant allowed Peru to hire 78 men for three months to relay bricks on Water Street. CWA approved the largest number of projects for Streator. These included grading dirt streets, making repairs at city hall, improving facilities at Marilla Park, and rebuilding the police and fire alarm systems. The CWA also approved a $270 project to clean the ditches and streets in Cedar Point.   .

Some of the jobs paid a good wage. For example, CWA highway workers in LaSalle received $15 a week. Harry Halpin, superintendent of the Illinois Free Employment office, cautioned men if they quit their current job, which paid less than the CWA rates, they would not be considered for a CWA project.

Morris residents had long awaited the opening of their new U.S. post office. On July 29, 1933, a box containing historic photographs including one of the postal employees and one of the Clifton House, which stood on the site previously, was placed in the cornerstone. Other documents placed in the box were lists of members of fraternal and civic organizations, a copy of the 1933 Grundy County Fair premium list, and copies of the Morris *Daily Herald*. Completion of the building was only a few months away.

To mark the official opening of the Morris post office on Dec. 3, 1933, an open house was held that Sunday afternoon. A crowd, estimated at 3,000, toured the $100,000 facility and watched the staff process the mail. (Photo by author)

The employment situation in Grundy County looked promising. One CWA program in Morris provided for an initial hiring of 25 men to begin work on the municipal dock in mid-December. The two-month project, which would be a double-deck structure running 132 feet under the north span of the Illinois River bridge, would eventually employ 75 men. After completion, the riverbanks would be covered with riprap. A 70-foot wide channel in front of the dock would make it possible for barges to tie up there.

Farmers also started to benefit from the New Deal. Those who participated in the Agricultural Adjustment Administration's (AAA) program by reducing acreage by 15 percent started receiving government payments. Farmers, who cut back on wheat in LaSalle County, were paid a total of $9,184. In Grundy County, farmers received $1,181 from the AAA.

Most of the unemployed in the Illinois Valley hoped jobs would be created through CWA programs. On Dec 23, John Lyons presided over a meeting in Granville to discuss the need for repairs on 2½ miles of roads in Hennepin Township. Granville Township needed six miles of road improvements to make rural roads passable all year. The problem facing the group was not the lack of workers but rather the lack of trucks to haul the gravel. "We can't use wheelbarrows," Lyons said.

On Dec. 30, 1933, these men were employed on a WPA project to lay bricks for one of the street projects in Oglesby. (Oglesby Library)

Streator had to cope with thousands of unemployed men and women during the Depression. This was one group of WPA assignees. They posed in front of the Methodist Church on the corner of Bridge and Monroe Streets. No date indicated. (Streatorland Historical Society)

89

1934
BACK ON RELIEF

The new year began with a report from the CCC boys from Spring Valley, who were sent to work in California. MacLain Walloch wrote to the *Post*, describing how they were literally marooned in their camp for a month because of the heavy rains that washed away roads to Santa Barbara. All 26 men were in good health and anticipating a transfer to Oregon or Alaska. Writing from Camp Simi near Santa Susana, CA, John Faletti described in a letter to the *Post* how his company drove through the region around San Fernando with water up to the running boards finding cars buried in mud and bridges and homes washed away. CWA workers were shoveling four-foot high mud drifts from the sidewalks. "It was a pitiful sight," he wrote.

From the CCC camp at Starved Rock came word that a new unit, Co. 1609, would be arriving soon. The new men would establish their camp at Parkman Plain. This photo includes some of the local men in the CCC. (Oglesby Lib.)

In January, local dairy farmers became involved with the regional effort to drive up milk prices. The Pure Milk Association (PMA) organized a milk embargo around Chicago. It soon had repercussions in the Illinois Valley. On Jan. 7, Norman Colby, a young man from Granville, who worked for the Beatrice Cream Co. in Yorkville, tried to deliver 900 gallons of cream to Chicago, where it would be processed into 2,500 pounds of butter. On his way, he was stopped west of Naperville. Dairy strikers dumped the cream on the highway, creating a pool three inches deep. The dairymen prevented Colby from taking down the license numbers on the pickets' trucks, and he was told to forget what happened. The next day, pickets confronted his brother, Theodore Colby, the plant manager in Yorkville, and took his car.

Trying to tighten the embargo on milk headed to the Chicago market, PMA dairy farmers traveled to West Brooklyn and Amboy farms on Jan. 8 to determine the destination of milk shipments. Satisfied with their inspections, the armed dairymen drove to Earlville's Holland-Maid Cheese Factory. With pickets outside the plant, about two dozen farmers kept the plant managers from loading milk on Burlington trains. Their next stop was the Mendota Milk Products Company where a force of 100 farmers charged the company manager with making shipments to the Mid-West Milk Company, described as a 'bootleg dairy," in Oak Park, IL When the farmers inspected the plant, they found 40 milk cans in the cooler. The manager claimed that it was destined for Hines Hospital. In a phone conversation with hospital officials, the strikers learned that the hospital was receiving milk only through authorized channels. With the lie exposed, the farmers took the milk cans and dumped the contents into the plant's cheese vats. It was one way to prevent milk shipments while at the same time being less costly to the Mendota company. In other confrontations, dairymen poured kerosene into milk tanks to punish uncooperative farmers.

Other towns were also under scrutiny by the PMA. Archie McPherson, head of the Oglesby milk producers, said that there would be no interference with the Chicago embargo. Milk would only be shipped to local processors. A group of 40 PMA men drove to Ottawa at 4 a.m. on Jan 10 to guard Norris Drive to check for violations of the embargo. After an hour on guard and finding no milk trucks leaving the city, the men returned to their nearby farms. The confrontations ended shortly after this when an agreement was reached to boost the amount paid to dairymen.

Other men were desperate for any kind of work. On Jan 17, E. A. Leighton, a member of the Board of Education of Hopkins Township, announced the approval of one CWA project in Putnam County. The $5,563 project would involve laying a new gym floor in the high school, repairing the roof, painting the woodwork around the school and pergolas, and repairing the school's concrete driveway, which had "gone to pieces," according to the *Record*.

A grant from the CWA provided for painting the woodwork of the pergolas on the east and west entrances of Hopkins H.S. (Granville Village Hall).

On Jan. 25, there was more good news released from Washington. The Public Works Administration (PWA) had approved a $450,000 grant to build a new bridge on Route 89 to connect Spring Valley with Putnam County. The bridge design would be similar to the one in Seneca but one span longer. It was estimated that 60 men might be employed for the project, which was expected to begin in March 1934.

Not everyone had the skills to work on a bridge so other jobs were created. Ten men were hired for a PWA project to continue the barberry eradication project in Putnam County. The thorny bushes grew to as high as ten feet tall, and the leaves were breeding places for infectious rust. During 1933, over 4,000 bushes were dug up in a 53-square mile area. By the spring of 1934, an additional 15 square miles were cleared of the pest plant.

In spite of the good it was doing by providing temporary jobs, the CWA was frequently charged with political favoritism and incompetence. CWA payrolls were sometimes padded with ineligible workers. To detect any fraud, county paymasters were required to personally deliver paychecks instead of mailing them and have each recipient sign a receipt.

Lawmakers wanted to end the CWA programs quickly because of the rapidly escalating payrolls, but FDR asked Congress for an additional appropriation of $850 million to continue the program. Roosevelt argued that with $350 million the programs could continue until May. By that time, he assumed that the four million men hired for CWA projects would be absorbed back into private industry. If his assumption was incorrect, the remaining $500 million would allow CWA projects to continue until the fall.

On Jan. 20, the CWA ordered an 11 percent workforce reduction in order to cut costs. Furthermore, the workweek for those still on the job was reduced from 30 to 24 hours. Initially, Bureau County laid off 115 men. Of that number, 57 had CWA jobs in Spring Valley. In LaSalle County, 375 men went back on relief.

In February, word came from Washington that the CWA was definitely going to cease operations, and more jobs cuts were necessary. Putnam County lost 21 of its 111 CWA workers. Of the 700 men working on CWA projects in Bureau County, 190 lost their jobs. Sherman Lewis, the CWA administrator in LaSalle County, reported 591 men would lose their jobs. In Ottawa, 25 CWA projects ended. Those remaining on the job would find their wages cut. Unskilled laborers in Ottawa received 40¢ an hour; skilled workers' pay was reduced from $1.20 to $1 an hour.

Other bad news came to Streator. The PWA had rejected the city's application for an $825,000 loan for a new water system. Washington administrators contended that Streator could never pay back the 30-year bonds with its current revenue.

However, officials in Henry were pleased to learn that their application for a bridge, estimated to cost $252,000, was approved. The bridge would link Rt. 29 with Rt. 89c.

Local banks continued to return to normal operations. In March 1934, bank auditors announced that the Granville National Bank could finally reopen. Bank President Edward Barnard and Vice President Victor Hartman assured depositors of the safety of the bank. The Federal Deposit Insurance Corporation (FDIC) now protected accounts up to $2,500.

ANNOUNCEMENT!

FDIC MEMBER

We Are Pleased to Announce that

Deposits in this bank are **Insured** BY THE

Federal Deposit Insurance Corporation

in the amount of

$2500.00

for each depositor under the terms of the Banking Act of 1933

DIRECTORS

Farmers State Bank of McNabb

The Putnam County State Bank in Hennepin and the Farmers State Bank in McNabb (pictured) advertised the safety of funds deposited in their institutions in the Putnam County *Record*. (Photo by author)

Students at L-P-O junior college also benefited from New Deal legislation. In March, a grant from the Federal Emergency Relief Administration (FERA) provided jobs for 22 students. Boys and girls, who maintained at least a "C" average and showed financial need, qualified for a variety of jobs at the college and high school. These included positions as assistants for testing, home-rooms, study halls, the social center, science laboratories, and clerical work in the office. Students were limited to a maximum of 8 hours per day and 30 hours per week. Pay was 30¢ per hour. The total payroll averaged $300 a month. While the college offered similar positions in previous years, the school funds were limited, and the program had been discontinued. The new funding from FERA would make it possible for many students to continue their education.

Those who did not continue their formal schooling received a different type of education by enrolling in the CCC. The Spring Valley boys sent to the Pacific Coast wrote to the *Post* about their experiences. Cyril Foy said that most of the CCC men re-enlisted for six months. They had some time off and took the "Magic Isle" boat to Catalina Island. They also had an opportunity to see the Chicago Cubs in spring training and met Mr. Wrigley and Zane Grey. A little later, Ernest Pautachnik wrote how their company was transferred from Camp Juncal near Santa Barbara to Pierce, ID in April. "We are going to have some new lines of work up here such as building lookout towers, bridges, and roads," wrote Pautachnik. He also commented that they met other boys from Bureau County, and they "enjoyed reading the LaSalle *Post-Tribune* as this is the only way we have of knowing what is happening around home."

In mid-April, 66 more men joined Company 614 at Starved Rock. That company would move to Ava, IL near Murphysboro while Company 1609 continued its work at Starved Rock.

The young men in Co. 1609 at Starved Rock lived in barracks similar to the quarters of men in the regular army. (LaSalle County Historical Society)

For those men, who were too old or could not meet the physical requirements of the CCC, the times were desperate. Jobs were disappearing due to work stoppages and permanent closings in the Illinois Valley. In Mark, John Cox closed his coal mine again in a wage dispute with the miners. He said he just couldn't compete if he abided by NRA codes. Workers at Peru Wheel Co. walked off the job demanding a 20 percent increase. This action idled about 250 men. Although the work stoppage was short, the company lost contracts and did not rehire all of the strikers.

On Mar. 30, the CWA officially ended even though there were still some projects that would be finished after that date. The CWA office in Granville closed on April 26. Since the office was first opened in November 1933, 162 men had found work in the county, mostly graveling township roads.

94

In April, there was a peaceful, but useless, parade organized by the Illinois Workers Alliance (IWA) protesting the closing of CWA projects. Harry Hopkins, CWA administrator in Washington D.C., promised a new work program in the months to follow. In the meantime, many workers, who lost their CWA jobs, went on relief.

Another business closing its operations was the Chicago and Illinois Valley Railway. Earlier known as the Chicago, Ottawa, and Peoria RR, (C.O.& P.) the interurban streetcar line provided service between Joliet and Princeton. The links to Ladd, DePue, and Streator became unprofitable and had shut down in the 1920's.

For many years, the Chicago and Illinois Valley interurban cars provided dependable transportation for Westclox workers. At center is Motor 56 with trailer 155 – the "Westclox Special." This photo was taken in 1930. On March 15, 1934, some workers began riding busses to work after the interurban line ceased operations. (William Raia collection)

Since the depression began in 1929, the interurban line was reportedly losing $4,000 a month. Two employees, Fred Reeve of LaSalle and Charles Werner of Peru, had been with the company since the line started – over 30 years. They and 18-19 other long-time employees had no idea of what would happen to them. In any case, management decided to make the last run to LaSalle shortly before midnight on May 14. The cars would be stored in the Ottawa car barn. About 40 jobs were lost when the line ceased operations.

The next day, the Valley Motor Bus Co. of Ottawa began running one 20-passenger bus five times a day to Utica and LaSalle. Westclox management requested "tripper" service for its employees. A bus would leave Spring Valley at 6:25 a.m. At 4:30 p.m., a bus would take employees back to Spring Valley.

95

Chicago & Illinois Valley Motor 56 was stored next to the Ottawa car barn in January 1934. It was one of the original cars and was still operating when the line closed. (William Raia collection)

The Chicago, Ottawa, and Peoria car barn in Ottawa was photographed by Paul Stringham on Jan. 22, 1934. (William Raia collection)

Railroad transportation was also making news in 1934. Other railroads were developing the concept of a light-weight, high speed passenger train, but Ralph Budd, the genius behind Burlington's new streamliner, was ready to make railroad history. The Century of Progress in Chicago had re-opened for a second season in May 1934, and Budd was about to focus attention on his new *Zephyr* train. Starting in Denver, CO. on May 28, the *Zephyr* would begin a non-stop trip to the World's Fair. For residents of the

Illinois Valley, the view of the new streamliner was anxiously awaited. Visitors came from 75 miles to catch a glimpse of the gleaming passenger train. Bureau County residents jammed the Princeton station platform in anticipation of the historic event. The train only slowed slightly coming around the curve leading to the depot and then quickly increased speed as it sped on to Mendota and Earlville. Local Burlington men were in charge at every crossing to make sure the train could speed along as fast as 112 mph.

The *Zephyr* engineer reduced speed to 45 mph as the train approached the cross-over with the IC tracks in Mendota. (Photo by Leo Muhlach)

The *Zephyr's* engine light grew larger and larger as the train slowed to 45 mph coming into Mendota at dusk. The train completed its historic trip to Chicago in record-breaking time. It took only 13 hours and 5 minutes to cover 1,017 miles, coming to a stop in the middle of the railroad exhibit in Chicago.

Thousands of visitors to the Century of Progress toured the *Pioneer Zephyr* in 1934. (Postcard photo from author's collection)

97

Later in June, the *Zephyr* stopped in Mendota and Earlville to permit local residents the opportunity to tour the train. During the hour-long stopover in Mendota, a crowd of 2,793 marveled as they viewed the interior of the passenger cars. Local businessmen and dignitaries rode the train to Earlville, where the 45-minute stop was barely enough time for the 1,270 people to walk through the short train.

The excitement faded, and conversation turned to the rising temperatures of summer. The Westclox weather station reported 105° on May 31, breaking the all-time record. The following day, the temperature set another record high of 107°. The scorching heat was having a direct effect on the farmers, who had earlier demanded relief from AAA regulations, which prevented them from planting hay or clover. The AAA would not allow farmers under contract to plant a cash crop or even forage for the animals. Instead, they said farmers could plant soybeans and then, without harvesting the beans, plow the entire crop back into the soil to improve it.

The lack of rain also affected Illinois farmers, who faced soaring prices for hay. The crop was so poor that farmers were simply plowing under their sparse wheat fields. According to C. E. Gates, the LaSalle County farm advisor, wells had gone dry and many farmers in the area were hauling water from the city to fill their wells. By June, the drought affecting 31 Illinois counties, including LaSalle, Bureau, and Putnam, finally convinced Washington bureaucrats to revise their rules. The Bureau County farm advisor reported that farmers would be allowed to plant emergency feed crops. These included soybeans, cowpeas, corn, Sudan grain, rye, millet, sorghum, rape, and buckwheat. The rule changes came in late June, and while that was too late to produce a mature crop, there would still be some forage for the animals.

That summer, the federal Surplus Commodity Corporation started shipping both canned and fresh foods for distribution to families on relief. In July, the local relief agencies reported the arrival of 11 railroad cars containing 2,200 barrels of white potatoes from Virginia. A short time later, a Rock Island train arrived with 17,000 1½-pound cans of roast beef and a supply of "milkwheato," a breakfast food. In August, fresh foods arrived. The shipment included a million pounds of beef and veal, 10,000 pounds of cheese, lard, prunes, grapefruit, and rice. However, due to the weather and previous pork contracts, there was no pork or flour available. The beef, that had arrived earlier, was still hanging in refrigerators because the relief agency lacked the proper tools to cut the meat. The following month, 15,000 pounds of butter arrived.

Just as other communities had seen new or renovated movie theaters open during the previous years, residents in Granville also enjoyed films being shown in its new Granada Theater.
Ad from Putnam County *Record*

GRAND OPENING

Granada Theatre

GRANVILLE, ILLINOIS

Friday, August 31

We Know You'll Like this "First Nighter" Picture

Revel in the Romance, Sing with the Songs, Giggle with the Gags in this cheerful chunk of screen enjoyment!... It has its fill of Drama, Romance, Comedy, as well as some of the swellest songs your ears ever thrilled to!

GLORIA STUART
ROGER PRYOR
Marian Marsh
Gloria Shea

A Stanley Bergerman Production. Presented by Carl Laemmle.
A UNIVERSAL PICTURE.

Merna Kennedy,
Noel Madison

I LIKE IT THAT WAY

In August 1934, the Marshall-Putnam Farm Bureau spelled out some of the AAA rules for farmers who had contracted with the government to reduce livestock and grain acreage. The AAA agreed to pay $15 for each animal eliminated. Farmers would be penalized $20 for each hog beyond the contract allocation. Penalties would be waived if the excess animals were donated to local relief agencies. Special rules also applied to farmers signing corn-hog contracts. AAA also placed limits on wheat acreage. No more wheat could be planted than the highest amount planted in 1932 or 1933. AAA contracts encouraged reductions in the 1935 crops. Corn was limited to 90 percent of the 1932-33 base. Farmers would be paid 35¢ per bushel of the estimated corn yield for acres taken out of cultivation. Hog production could increase to 90 percent instead of the 75 percent limit on litters in 1934.

PWA projects and local work relief helped the unemployment situation during the summer of 1934. An $825,000 sewer project in Streator was expected to keep 250-300 men busy for almost two years. The city of Dixon received approval for a $40,000 street-paving program, putting 285 men to work.

However, there were always bureaucratic hurdles to overcome. Peru was having a problem getting its application for a public works project approved. The PWA called one project "a waste of time" because the city was only hiring men for one shift. The government insisted on two crews. Henry lost its PWA funding for the bridge over the Illinois River because city officials didn't follow PWA regulations. Rather than give up on the project, the Illinois highway department stepped in to fund it.

Small towns generally didn't receive PWA grants and had to devise jobs for the needy. For instance, in Cherry two men were employed cutting weeds for the village during August. To help their needy neighbors, residents in Cherry took their home-grown produce and organized a major canning project. That fall, over 2,000 cans of tomatoes, beets, peas, corn, and vegetable soup were available for needy families in Cherry.

For some young men the alternative to a PWA job was enrollment in the CCC. When registration opened on July 18, scores of men jammed the Ottawa armory to register. WWI veterans were encouraged to sign up at the American Legion posts. The Veterans Administration in Washington made the final selections from the list of veterans applying for positions in the CCC.

Starved Rock was the site of many CCC projects. (Oglesby Library)

This building, which still stands in Starved Rock State Park, served as one of the barracks for the CCC. (Photo by author)

At Starved Rock, the CCC completed several projects in the spring. The familiar concession stand and cafeteria, located at the base of the rock near the hotel, were torn down, and a new concession stand was built. Only the hotel and a few cottages remained, and once the new lodge was completed, the park service planned to demolish the old hotel. Trails were re-marked, and wooden bridges were constructed. Company 2601 came down from Ft. Sheridan on August 9, and arrived in Utica. Their barracks and other buildings at Starved Rock would make up Camp LaSalle.

This structure originally served as the day room for the CCC camp at Starved Rock State Park. (Photo by author)

CCC men loading logs for the Starved Rock Lodge. (Lewis Univ. collection)

For Co. 1609 there wasn't much heavy equipment to move dirt. They generally used shovels, wheelbarrows, and a lot of manual labor.

Men of Co. 1609 rest on their wheelbarrows after a hard day's work. (Marseilles Library)

In the fall, numerous projects were underway at Starved Rock. Campground drives were finished for the new tourist camp located between Fox and French Canyons. Fireplaces, tables, and a water supply with stone drinking fountains were added. Using rock from a quarry in Utica, the men were adding riprap to the riverfront. The new lodge under construction by the CCC was a sore point with local carpenters who felt the work should be theirs.

A leisure moment for friends gathered around the flagpole at the center of the CCC camp at Starved Rock. (LaSalle County Historical Soc.)

Life in the CCC camps wasn't constant work. The men often held inter-camp baseball games. During the 1934 season, the Starved Rock camp beat Camp Brandon at Morris 5-2 to become the district champions.

In December 1934, a photographer in the *Pantagraph's* airplane, *Scoop*, took this aerial view of the CCC camp at Starved Rock.

One of the
bridges
constructed by the
CCC. (LaSalle
County Hist.
Soc.)

Work on the I-M Canal by other camps was progressing, but CCC jobs were in jeopardy at Starved Rock. The trade union representative claimed that the CCC men, who were working on a sewer system, were taking jobs rightfully belonging to local union men. The controversy continued until an apparent agreement was reached with the union representatives in Springfield. Robert Kingery, director of the Illinois Department of Public Works and Buildings, recommended work on the lodge "including the walls, windows, comfort facilities, dining room, and kitchen wing" would be completed by local union men. They would also be responsible for the construction of the dock, campground stoves, electrical wiring, and demolition of all buildings abandoned by the CCC. The recommendation still had to be approved by the CCC authorities.

David Latimer, the National Park superintendent at Starved Rock, reported that one-third of the new lodge was completed. While the local unions were going to take over the completion of the work, the two CCC companies had enough work for at least another year. This included the development of a picnic grounds west of the lodge and the construction of an overhead rustic bridge spanning the entrance highway. Other plans called for the construction of shelters, well houses, and toilets near the salt well.

In Oct. 1934, 40 CCC men from Buffalo Rock were landscaping and working on this Ottawa shelter. The 16' x 24' stone structure was located near the entrance to the old lateral canal. It included a fireplace to warm ice skaters using the I-M Canal. The area was to include seven blocks of parking, sunken gardens, trees, shrubs, and rustic benches. Today, because of vandalism and the deteriorating condition of the Ottawa shelter, the windows were barred, and a locked, iron gate prevented entry. A section of the roof collapsed due to rotting timbers. (Photos by author)

The CCC constructed this footbridge at Buffalo Rock. (Lewis University)

104

Many of the CCC enrollees from the Illinois Valley were sent to the West Coast. Letters to families and the newspapers gave the folks back home an idea of the challenges of their work. In a letter to the *Post-Tribune*, Cyril Foy described how he and the other men from Bureau and LaSalle Counties in Company 1651 constructed a 68-foot bridge, firebreaks, roads, and campsites in the Santa Barbara National Forest. The unit was later transferred to the summit of Button Hill in the Lewiston district in Idaho. Foy said the new work involved bridge building and the construction of 100-foot steel lookout towers in the Clear Water National Forest. Some of the men in the outfit, including John Blatnik, Bally Bertrand, Bruno Maggi, and Barto Cioni, were on detached duty at Jaype.

Sometimes the work was dangerous and even deadly. Albert Ricci, a graduate of L-P High School and a former athlete at L-P-O Junior College, described the work of 5,000 CCC men who were fighting the fire on a 45-mile front raging through the Selway National Forest. Sitting with John Kozar at their campsite, Ricci said they could see the smoke rising over Sheep Mountain. The inferno described as the "Red Demon," moved steadily closer to their camp. Company 606, which included men from the Tri-Cities, Streator, Ottawa, and Mendota, finally got a break after working on the fire line 14-18 hours a day for 20 days.

Edward Halliday from LaSalle wrote to the *Post* describing how he and others from the area were engaged in fire fighting. Frank Ritz, Ed Kramarsic, Paul Zawil, Leonard Wasielewski, Frank Strell, Paul Urbanc, Lester Johnson, and Leroy McGinnis of Company 1645 were on the front lines trying to slow the advancing fire. Sadly, the Idaho conflagration claimed the lives of Johnson and McGinnis after two days of fighting the fire. In September, when McGinnis' body was returned to Ottawa for burial, 25 members of the CCC camp at Buffalo Rock and another CCC contingent from Starved Rock honored McGinnis with a military style funeral when he was laid to rest in St. Columba Cemetery.

Some students attending L-P-O Junior College were fortunate to receive government aid through a continuation of the previous year's work-study program. As many as 27 boys and girls were eligible for the program. The government eligibility rules required that the students had to be in the top third of their high school class. Half of those meeting the class rank requirement would be chosen from the college freshman class and half from the sophomore class. The jobs would be divided evenly between males and females. If selected to work, they could expect salaries of about $15 a month.

You Don't Have To Walk a Mile To See Things at DePue; All the Attractions Are Right on the Lake Front

Two Day Celebration
DE PUE, ILL.

Sunday, September 2nd
BIG BASEBALL GAME and CONCERT by DE PUE COMMUNITY BAND

LABOR DAY

Monday, September 3rd
THE FOLLOWING EVENTS TAKE PLACE MONDAY:

Motor BOAT RACES
10:00 a. m. Big Float Parade
12:15 p. m. - CONCERT - 100 PIECE BAND
Combined Walnut Ho Bo, Tiskilwa Municipal. Ohio High School and DePue Bands
V. GALSTER, Director

PROGRAM OF EVENTS

10:00 A. M.—Float Parade.
10:30 A. M.—Baseball Game.
11:00 A. M.—Horseshoe Pitching Contest.
12:15 P. M.—100-Piece Band Concert.
2:00 P. M.—Baseball Game.

1:45 TO 5:00 P. M.—**Boat Races**
5:00 P. M.—Girls' Kitten Ball Game.
SPRING VALLEY vs. DePUE
6:00 P. M.—Kitten Ball Game.
DePUE vs. LA SALLE BUTCHERS
6:30 P. M.—Band Concert.
7:30 P. M.—10 Acts High Class Vaudeville

MERRY-GO-ROUND — FERRIS WHEEL — CONCESSIONS
8:30—FREE DANCE, LAKE SHORE PAVILION

Labor Day provided a break from the stress of work. What a better way to spend it than at the DePue boat races as advertised in the *Post-Tribune*.

After the Labor Day weekend, it was back to work. Illinois Zinc signed a contract with its miners raising their wages to $1.10 per ton, a 3¢ increase. The mules were being lowered into the coal mine, and work would resume on Sept. 25. About the same time, Conco Crane and Engineering Works in Mendota called back a hundred men to begin work on Oct. 1. The timing of the announcement was perfect. Fortunately, when they were laid off in July due to plant expansion work, most of the men were able to find employment at the J. B. Inderrieden Canning Co.

One of the major obstacles to maritime traffic on the Illinois Waterway was the low clearance of the Morris bridge built in 1900. Work on a new bridge began in the fall of 1933.

The Morris *Herald News* described the bridge as "a showcase of modern engineering." The Route 47 Morris bridge lasted almost 70 years. This photo was taken just prior to its demolition in March 2003. (IDOT)

In November 1933, coffer dams were constructed to divert the Illinois River at Morris. By May 29, 1934, concrete was poured for the last pier. The historic opening of the new 1,458-foot bridge took place on Sept. 24, 1934. Costing $232,768, the two-lane span provided many jobs during the Depression. Chuck and Ray Girot, two members of the construction crew, were paid $1 an hour and happy to get it since jobs in the WPA and CCC paid much less.

Bridge construction was one important source of employment, but mining was also important. Due to labor unrest, the Prairie State coal mine had been closed for several months. During the shutdown, a few men were hired to build a new washhouse. Cox also spent $50,000 to build coal yards not only in Mark but also in Joliet, Rockford, Freeport, South Beloit, Janesville, Madison, LaCross, and Minneapolis. He finally reopened his Mark mine in the fall of 1934. On Oct. 4, Cox sent 350 men back to work and predicted as many as 450 men would be needed to produce 1,400 tons a day. However, there was trouble among the miners over which union, if any, would represent them. In a vote taken in November 1934, 180 men backed the Progressive Union while only 80 miners voted for the UMW. More than a third of the men didn't even vote. In spite of the outcome, Cox signed a contract with the UMW. The Progressive Union members immediately set up a picket line in protest. Since only 80 men were willing to cross the picket line after two days, Cox closed the mine and returned the UMW contract. Over 400 men were idle again.

The hot summer had been a major problem for Illinois farmers. The Illinois Department of Agriculture confirmed what area farmers long suspected. The Illinois corn crop was the lowest in 61 years. It was 36 percent below the 1933 harvest and 53 percent below the five-year average (1927-1931). Because of the prolonged drought and damage by chinch bugs and corn earworms, the average yield was down to 20 bushels per acre.

Putting food on the tables of the destitute families was made a little easier with the arrival of government surplus food. Partial carloads of rice and veal arrived in LaSalle along with 4,800 one-pound cans of beef stew. Later, more food in the form of cranberries, popcorn, and nuts was available. The government even sent LaSalle surplus towels to distribute to families on relief.

In spite of relief, workers were frustrated and organized a protest march. On Nov. 24, the Illinois Workers Alliance (IWA) organized 150 marchers at Washington Park. The county relief agency was aware of the impending march and secretly closed all relief offices to prevent a confrontation. Carrying banners reading,

"We Want Cash Relief" and "We Want Work Not Relief," the marchers followed a police car, color guard, and one man with a bass drum in orderly fashion to the unoccupied Ottawa relief agency. The IWA was hoping to draw attention to its goal of a 30-hour week and minimum wage of $1 an hour. They eventually tempered their demands to the AFL standard of a 24-30 hour week with a minimum wage of 65¢ per hour.

More men were forced to go on relief in Ottawa after the Valley Motor Bus Company filed a petition to discontinue service between Ottawa and LaSalle. The company claimed insufficient riders to make the route financially viable.

Panhandling in the Ottawa courthouse became a problem in spite of the "No Loafing" signs posted in the building. Sheriff Ralph Desper ordered his men to charge any violator with vagrancy.

For those who were eligible, the CCC offered three meals a day, a place to sleep, clothing, and steady employment for six months or more. The *Post* continued to publish letters from Bureau County men working in camps in the Pacific Northwest. On Oct. 15, Company 697 was sent to Camp Wilark, located 13 miles from the little town of Houlton, OR, a mile from the town of St. Helens.

The boys had a variety of jobs. Gene Giacomelli from Ladd was promoted to caterpillar driver at Camp Latourelle in Oregon before being reassigned to Camp Wilark. Louis Pecchio from "The Location" (Spring Valley) had the job of head baker. Harold Buchanan (Princeton) was second baker, and Walter Bernatovitch (Location) was second cook. Stan Brussock (Spring Valley) became head clerk, and Steve Bertalot (Location) worked on the telephone lines. Giacomelli wrote to the *Post*, "I sure like this outfit. I think it's the best experience that anyone could have."

Another group of boys from the Illinois Valley were assigned to Company 615, in Estacada, OR. Ross Serrentino of LaSalle sent Christmas greetings, and described the work of Ray Loebach, Louis Hoffman, Cosmo Ganze (LaSalle), Anton Justinato (Peru), Peter Mahalick (Oglesby) and himself in the Mt. Hood National Forest. Since October, the boys removed fallen timbers, cut trails, improved roads, and installed phone lines for lookout towers. Their company spent 26 days planting 550,000 Douglas fir trees in an area covering 1,180 acres.

As the weeks passed, the CCC men at Starved Rock decided to get into the Christmas spirit. They brought a spruce tree into the recreation room and decorated it. Those members of Co. 1609 still in camp on Christmas day enjoyed a traditional turkey dinner and grab bag gift exchange. One group had taken a five-day furlough beginning on Dec. 21; another group left on Jan. 2.

The coming year would mark a reorganization of the CCC as the 20th Forestry District of the Sixth Corps Area. That would include Camp Starved Rock (1609), Camp LaSalle (2601), Camp Buffalo Rock (628), the two camps at Marseilles, and the camps at Joliet, Thornton, and Lemont.

The CCC built this shelter in 1934 at Lockport. The I-M Canal is located in the tree line across the street from the shelter. (Photo by author)

The Big Hearts party was held at the Majestic Theater on Christmas Eve. After watching Randolph Scott in Zane Grey's "Wild Horse Mesa," 1,200 children filed up to the stage to receive a one-pound sack of candy and a Jonathan apple. The LaSalle Boy Scouts, who spent many hours refurbishing old toys, took charge of distributing 1,000 toys to children in needy families. The local Elks lodge also handed out 100 bags of candy, and the American Legion passed out another 51 bags of candy and apples.

Other towns had similar parties. In Oglesby, 800 children packed the Aida Theater. Following the movies, each child received a bag of candy. This was the second time that a party was sponsored by the theater and the Oglesby Women's Club.

The families of the unemployed in Oglesby received food baskets. Donations from the Junior and Senior women's clubs, the Friendly Four Club, the Oglesby Loyalty Club, and others made it possible to fill 25 baskets with canned foods, vegetables, and meat. The Elks prepared 150 baskets containing a roast and all the trimmings for Christmas dinner. The Legion post took 50 baskets of food and toys to families of war veterans in the vicinity of LaSalle.

1935
NEW GOVERNMENT PROGRAMS

In January, more letters arrived from Spring Valley boys, who enrolled in the CCC and were sent to Butte Falls, OR. Ray Wirtz and Herman Urbanski, members of Company 9525, said they were camped at the base of Mt. Pitt. Among their pastimes was catching snowshoe rabbits for dinner. They also enjoyed deer tracking. Their housing consisted of small log cabins for 4-5 men. They were among the fortunate men who had jobs.

For others, it was a difficult time. Harold Moore and Lucian Urbanski of DePue were caught stealing coal by Grover Patterson, an agent for the Chicago, Milwaukee and St. Paul RR. Moore was especially desperate, trying to support a wife and five children. At the Princeton courthouse, the testimony described how the two men had thrown coal from one of the St. Paul gondolas and then were caught bringing back gunny sacks to carry the coal. The judge fined them $5 and sentenced them to one day in jail.

This trial hardly made the front page headlines in January. For weeks, people had been reading about the testimony of Bruno Hauptmann, who was accused of kidnapping and killing the infant son of Charles Lindbergh. The disposition of that case with its many appeals lingered on into the following year.

Even more relevant was a local bank robbery. The rash of bank robberies in the Illinois Valley seemed to disappear in 1934. The bank robberies committed by John Dillinger had been the topic of discussion in small towns in Wisconsin and Indiana, but everything was relatively peaceful in the Illinois Valley until Wed. Jan. 16.

The scene was the State Bank of Leonore. Two hours before the bank opened, four men drove into town in a Willys Knight (similar to the one pictured) and parked behind the bank. One man stayed at the driver's wheel while the other three entered the bank through the coal chute.

According to the *Post*, Wilbur Zimmerman of Leonore was suspicious of the car's location and called the bank cashier, Charles Bundy, who in turn called Sheriff Desper. In spite of the sheriff's warnings not to go to the bank but rather to keep the driver under surveillance until he arrived with deputies, Bundy went to the bank. When he opened the door, the three bandits rushed him, but Bundy

110

slammed the door and escaped. The bandits fled through the back door of the bank and headed to George Yusco's garage, where they stole a Chevrolet. They took Yusco and Norbert Naas, 16, who was waiting to have a car repaired, as hostages. With Yusco at the wheel and Naas forced to ride on the running board as a shield, they first drove north and then turned around heading back into Leonore, to pick up their accomplice. That man had already fled but was quickly captured by Bundy, Charles Seipp, a Leonore supervisor; and some bank guards. As they came out of a field with their captive, they spotted Yusco at the wheel of the Chevrolet and assumed the others in the car were more bank guards. The captured robber made a break for the robbers' stolen vehicle. One of the bandits in the Chevrolet fired his machine gun killing Bundy and mortally wounding Seipp.

Two miles south of Tonica, the fleeing bank robbers stopped a Pontiac sedan driven by Leon C. Vacherant, a salesman from Streator. The bandits left Yusco at the scene with the Chevrolet and forced the salesman to drive them in his Pontiac. They passed the Swaney School and headed toward the Illinois River. After traveling a short distance to the south, they doubled back, heading east towards Magnolia on Route 89C.

Because of the widespread use of telephone party lines, the news spread quickly among the farmers. State, county, and local police were informed of the whereabouts of the fleeing felons by farm families. Marshall County Sheriff Glenn Axline and Renis Brown, a deputy, were soon in pursuit of the Pontiac. As they closed in, they opened fire on the speeding car.

About 10 a.m., the robbers stopped at the north edge of Magnolia. Axline and Brown also stopped their vehicle and approached the Pontiac with weapons drawn. The salesman got out with his hands raised pleading with Axline not to shoot. Just then, one of the bandits in the car broke out the back window and fired, killing the sheriff and wounding Deputy Brown. Approaching the police car, the robbers took the dead sheriff's machine gun and reminded the wounded deputy that they still had the teenager.

Next, the desperate men drove north again and finally took refuge at the Jacob Ioeger farm east of McNabb. Two of the men hid in a corn field while the other two, along with Naas, went into the farmhouse. A state trooper stopped at the house and was tipped off by Mrs. Ioeger that two men were hiding upstairs. The LaSalle county sheriff arrived on the scene. Seeing no hope of escape, the bank robbers in the house surrendered. The men in the cornfield were also trapped. One of the men, Melvin Leist, said to be the ringleader, committed suicide rather than being taken alive. The

111

other man was arrested and was taken to jail along with the other two robbers.

Justice was swift. The bank robbers were indicted by a Putnam County grand jury and shortly thereafter a trial was held in Ottawa. On Mar. 6, the LaSalle County jury returned a guilty verdict against Fred Gerner and Art Theilen. The other bandit, John Hauff, had already pleaded guilty. According to the *Post*, it was the first time in almost 50 years that the death penalty was ordered in LaSalle County. There was no appeal filed. The murderers were executed in the electric chair on Mar. 21, 1935.

George Yusco, owner of the garage and hostage in the failed Leonore Bank robbery, and Norbert Nass, the teenage hostage who was wounded in the arm during the shootouts with police, were photographed at the LaSalle County Court House.

Sheriff Desper is seated at front left, next to John Hauff and Fred Gerner, two of the robbers. In the back row are some of the law enforcement officers who participated in the capture of the Leonore bank robbers.

(Photos reprinted from the *Post-Tribune*, Jan. 7, 1935)

112

jumped into a small boat near the upper face of the dam, causing water to flow over the gunwale and swamp the boat. Robert fell overboard, but managed to get close to a concrete ledge and grabbed a long strap thrown to him by his younger brother, who screamed for help while clinging to a steel-rung ladder near the dam. Al Filipiak of Peru, who was assigned to Co. 1609, heard the cry and helped pull Robert to safety. Filipiak then wrapped the older brother in his own clothes to keep him warm. Their commanding officer regarded Filipiak and two other CCC boys, who assisted in the rescue, as heroes and recommended them for commendations.

The CCC continued to encourage Illinois Valley men to enroll during April. As a result, 138 boys from LaSalle County were sent for training. The month-long dust storms in Kansas, Colorado, Texas, and New Mexico established a new priority for the CCC. Fifty-three of the Illinois Valley boys were assigned to drought relief. Others were sent to Marenisco, WI, Bruel, WI, Danbury, IL, and Carrollton, IL.

Bureau County also had a large contingent sent to camps in Michigan and Illinois. A letter to the *Post* from 15 CCC boys camped at Marenisco, MI. on the upper peninsula was published on May 15. The boys from Spring Valley, Buda, Cherry, Arlington, Wyanet, DePue, Dalzell, and Seatonville wrote about their daily schedules: up with the bugle call at 5:45 a.m., off to work blazing fire roads from 7 a.m. until lunch at 12:30 p.m., followed by more trail work til 4:30 p.m. After dinner at 5 p.m., some of the boys attended classes. The farm boys tended to turn in at 7 p.m., but others stayed up til "lights out" at 10 p.m. The boys marveled at the work of the lumberjacks, who felled trees "like toothpicks." The Bureau County boys together with others from Marseilles, Ottawa, and Peoria were especially eager to read the accounts of what was happening back home in the "good old Daily Post-Tribune". The letter was signed by William Yanish, Ray Wosick, Adolph Lokosis, Anton Marchetti, Ray Yeager, Alex Kinkin, Floyd Davis, Peter Venardi, Stan Katkus, Carl Coss, Marco Parachetti, Henry Roberts, Ed Kwit, Merle Lamkin, Melvin Lampley.

The new NRA regulations caused problems for at least one local businessman. In April, E. E. Alger, the local movie theater entrepreneur, found himself in hot water with the Great Lakes Film distributors, who supplied his movies. They sued him for violating NRA motion picture codes. In his *Post-Tribune* ads for "Gold Diggers of 1935" and other movies, he violated the codes by offering discounts for "Bargain Night" and holding a "Cash Award Night." The bargain ticket prices for matinees were 10¢ for kids and 15¢ for

The slain sheriff was not forgotten. A memorial service was held for Sheriff Axline on May 17, 1935 in Wenona. Hundreds listened to Lacon attorney, R. M. Barnes, deliver a fitting tribute to the Marshall County sheriff, who he described "not as a local hero but as a national hero just as the boys who fall in battle." The crowd stood in the rain as the American Legion men unveiled a bronze plaque mounted on a boulder, and the band played the Star Spangled Banner. Another ceremony was held at the Marshall County courthouse where a large bronze star, inscribed with his name, was displayed.

The memorial to Sheriff Axline is located in Wenona on the corner of 1st North and Walnut Streets. (Photo by author)

IN MEMORY
OF
OUR SHERIFF
GLENN T. "MIKE" AXLINE
BORN AUG. 17, 1901
KILLED BY BANK BANDITS
JAN. 16, 1935

During the winter of 1935, most municipalities and county boards in the Illinois Valley were busy filing applications for PWA and WPA projects. Putnam County sought numerous grants for graveling, bridge repairs, improvements to the building and grounds at the McNabb H.S., conversion of Senachwine Township swamp into a nature preserve, improvements at Magnolia's city park, construction of a community center in Hennepin. LaSalle hoped to have its $1.27 million application approved for a water treatment system, and road and sewer improvements. Streator applied for projects valued at over $2 million for improvements to its sewer system, brick streets, and tennis courts. Oglesby was interested in obtaining a grant for street improvements from Mormon to Crocketsville and Piety Hill.

In February, some of the local CCC men participated in a writing contest based on the theme, "What Being in the CCC Has Meant to Me." The first prize was a suitcase; the runner-up received an athletic shirt. There was also a variety of tournaments: ping pong, checkers, bridge, pool, 500, and other games. The champions in each contest received two packs of cigarettes.

One of Peru's CCC enrollees became something of a hero at Starved Rock in the early spring of 1935. Robert Rexwak, and his brother William, 11, lived with their family east of the dam at Lovers' Leap. On Saturday, Mar. 30, the *Post* described how

113

The slain sheriff was not forgotten. A memorial service was held for Sheriff Axline on May 17, 1935 in Wenona. Hundreds listened to Lacon attorney, R. M. Barnes, deliver a fitting tribute to the Marshall County sheriff, who he described "not as a local hero but as a national hero just as the boys who fall in battle." The crowd stood in the rain as the American Legion men unveiled a bronze plaque mounted on a boulder, and the band played the Star Spangled Banner. Another ceremony was held at the Marshall County courthouse where a large bronze star, inscribed with his name, was displayed.

The memorial to Sheriff Axline is located in Wenona on the corner of 1st North and Walnut Streets.
(Photo by author)

During the winter of 1935, most municipalities and county boards in the Illinois Valley were busy filing applications for PWA and WPA projects. Putnam County sought numerous grants for road graveling, bridge repairs, improvements to the building and grounds at the McNabb H.S., conversion of Senachwine Township swamps into a nature preserve, improvements at Magnolia's city park, and construction of a community center in Hennepin. LaSalle hoped to have its $1.27 million application approved for a water treatment system, and road and sewer improvements. Streator applied for projects valued at over $2 million for improvements to its sewer system, brick streets, and tennis courts. Oglesby was interested in obtaining a grant for street improvements from Mormon St. to Crocketsville and Piety Hill.

In February, some of the local CCC men participated in a writing contest based on the theme, "What Being in the CCC Camp Has Meant to Me." The first prize was a suitcase; the runner-up received an athletic shirt. There was also a variety of tournaments for ping pong, checkers, bridge, pool, 500, and other games. The champions in each contest received two packs of cigarettes.

One of Peru's CCC enrollees became something of a hero at Starved Rock in the early spring of 1935. Robert Rexwak, 14, and his brother William, 11, lived with their family east of the dam near Lovers' Leap. On Saturday, Mar. 30, the *Post* described how Robert

113

jumped into a small boat near the upper face of the dam, causing water to flow over the gunwale and swamp the boat. Robert fell overboard, but managed to get close to a concrete ledge and grabbed a long strap thrown to him by his younger brother, who screamed for help while clinging to a steel-rung ladder near the dam. Al Filipiak of Peru, who was assigned to Co. 1609, heard the cry and helped pull Robert to safety. Filipiak then wrapped the older brother in his own clothes to keep him warm. Their commanding officer regarded Filipiak and two other CCC boys, who assisted in the rescue, as heroes and recommended them for commendations.

The CCC continued to encourage Illinois Valley men to enroll during April. As a result, 138 boys from LaSalle County were sent for training. The month-long dust storms in Kansas, Colorado, Texas, and New Mexico established a new priority for the CCC. Fifty-three of the Illinois Valley boys were assigned to drought relief. Others were sent to Marenisco, WI, Bruel, WI, Danbury, IL, and Carrollton, IL.

Bureau County also had a large contingent sent to camps in Michigan and Illinois. A letter to the *Post* from 15 CCC boys camped at Marenisco, MI. on the upper peninsula was published on May 15. The boys from Spring Valley, Buda, Cherry, Arlington, Wyanet, DePue, Dalzell, and Seatonville wrote about their daily schedules: up with the bugle call at 5:45 a.m., off to work blazing fire roads from 7 a.m. until lunch at 12:30 p.m., followed by more trail work til 4:30 p.m. After dinner at 5 p.m., some of the boys attended classes. The farm boys tended to turn in at 7 p.m., but others stayed up til "lights out" at 10 p.m. The boys marveled at the work of the lumberjacks, who felled trees "like toothpicks." The Bureau County boys together with others from Marseilles, Ottawa, and Peoria were especially eager to read the accounts of what was happening back home in the "good old Daily Post-Tribune". The letter was signed by William Yanish, Ray Wosick, Adolph Lokosis, Anton Marchetti, Ray Yeager, Alex Kinkin, Floyd Davis, Peter Venardi, Stan Katkus, Carl Coss, Marco Parachetti, Henry Roberts, Ed Kwit, Merle Lamkin, Melvin Lampley.

The new NRA regulations caused problems for at least one local businessman. In April, E. E. Alger, the local movie theater entrepreneur, found himself in hot water with the Great Lakes Film distributors, who supplied his movies. They sued him for violating NRA motion picture codes. In his *Post-Tribune* ads for "Gold Diggers of 1935" and other movies, he violated the codes by offering discounts for "Bargain Night" and holding a "Cash Award Night." The bargain ticket prices for matinees were 10¢ for kids and 15¢ for adults. In the evening, adults paid 25¢ for admission. The resolution of the complaint was important since the Alger Amusement Corp. was one of 5,000 independent theaters.

Offering discount tickets to see "Gold Diggers of 1935" was a violation of NRA codes.

Others were also appealing the NRA codes. Several cases were headed to the U.S. Supreme Court. Those trials finally culminated in reversal of charges in the landmark case against the Schechter Live Poultry Market. Chief Justice Hughes said, "The attempt to fix hours and wages was not a valid exercise of federal power." That outcome brought an end to the NRA and wiped out 557 codes regarding the fixing of working hours, setting minimum prices, and banning other business practices that were considered unfair to the competition.

One reaction to the court's decision was voiced by local businessman Oscar Eliel from the LaSalle Buick Co. Eliel, who served as vice chairman of the automobile dealers in LaSalle, Grundy, and Putnam counties, said, "Dealers long ago forgot about code pricing on used automobiles and paid no attention to the code schedule. A number of garages had been complying with a set weekly salary, but I doubt that policy will continue."

Bargain prices at Alger's theaters were hardly a top priority for over 100 destitute families in Granville in May 1935. In Granville Township alone, there were 700 individuals going hungry. Neil Glover, the village clerk, reported that nobody had even notified the village board that the crisis was so acute.

At a May 9 meeting of local businessmen and pastors in the village hall, Granville supervisor A. Piccinelli, admitted that he had been contacted by families "crying for bread." Richard Whitaker from the local relief office told the group that his office had provided families with enough canned milk and meat along with some rice to last for about a week. His supplies were down to 100 cans of milk, 46 pounds of rice and some cans of meat. Glover was also questioned about the availability of relief funds held by the village. He said that some money might be distributed, but a reserve was needed for emergencies, such as medical operations and deaths. Following the meeting, the village decided to appropriate $200 to buy flour for the neediest families. It was a stopgap measure.

Only the federal government had sufficient resources to buy and distribute surplus commodities to help the many families on relief. On April 29, a supply of hamburger, canned milk, apples, and cheese arrived at the LaSalle distribution center. Hardship cases soon faded from the front pages of local newspapers.

For months, Peru was preparing for its five-day Centennial celebration. The much-anticipated event began on Wednesday, May 22. A crowd of over 5,000 in Washington Park witnessed the arrival of a 60-year old stagecoach carrying Mr. and Mrs. Joseph Reinhardt, Mr. and Mrs. James Maze, Mr. and Mrs. Joel Whitaker, Mr. and Mrs. Joel Hopkins, and Miss Wilhemina Whitaker. All were garbed in historic attire. Mayor Al Hasse had the honor of introducing Charles Hobbs, Peru's oldest, native-born, continuous resident. Following Arthur Janz' introduction of the ten young ladies, who were selected as attendants to the Peru queen, Walter Koehler, general chairman of the Centennial, crowned Miss Dorothy Kelsey as Miss Columbia. Next, Peru Mayor Al Hasse had the honor of crowning Miss Ardell Stedman as Miss Peru.

The Pioneer Honor Roll dinner at the Hotel Peru and a historical pageant in Washington Park followed on Thursday night, May 23. Dorothy Blouke Carus conducted the community orchestra. On Friday, a reception was held at the Congregational Church for those on the Pioneer Honor Roll, and there was a repeat performance of the historical pageant featuring over 600 men, women, and children dressed in period costumes, representing ten episodes of the last hundred years. These included stories of early Indians, pioneer settlers, the building of the I-M Canal, the coming of missionaries, incorporation of Peru in 1838, the arrival of Daniel Webster in 1839, early education, incorporation of the Illinois Central RR, Peruvians enlisting for the Civil War, and LaSalle County's participation in the World War. According to the *Post*, about 6,000 spectators braved the frigid weather at Washington Park to watch the event.

On Saturday morning, the celebration officially opened with the detonation of aerial bombs; the ringing of school bells; and the blowing of factory whistles. American flags were then raised, and the L-P High School band played the national anthem in the

116

Fourth St. business district. A children's costume and animal parade marked the first official event of the celebration. The Illinois Central's miniature train was a big hit with the kids. Concerts and sports activities continued throughout the day.

The parade on Sunday featured over 200 units and stretched 34 blocks. R.J. Unzicker, a *Post-Tribune* reporter, provided a detailed account of every unit on May 27. The parade started at 1:45 p.m. lead by Ottawa's Company C of the Illinois National Guard. Additional color guard units of American Legion posts from neighboring towns were interspersed with colorful floats created by local unions, businesses, churches, and civic organizations.

Mrs. Leslie Wixom, 85, from Troy Grove rode in a 1904 Rambler (pictured). She wore the same outfit as the one she wore for the Chicago Columbian Exposition in 1893. The historical entries continued with a covered wagon, a horse and buggy, the IC's train replica, and "Mr. and Mrs. Depression," dressed in tattered clothes.

The city entries followed the Shriners with their Oriental band. In addition to floats carrying Miss Peru, and Miss Columbia and their attendants, the "royalty" riding on their city's floats included Antonette Morandi, Miss Dalzell; Rose Manley, Miss Utica; Angie Pettie, Miss Spring Valley; and Margaret Corso, Miss Ladd. Rochelle, Marseilles, and Mendota were also represented.

The judges at the reviewing stand singled out several entries for special recognition. The First National Bank of LaSalle won first prize for the best commercial float, and the First National Bank of Peru captured first place for the most decorative float. The Peru Women's Club had the outstanding entry in the historical division.

Thanks to E. E. Alger, the 2½-hour Centennial event was captured on film. The movie of the parade was ready for showing the following week at his Peru Theater. This ad appeared in the May 28, 1935 edition of the *Post-Tribune*.

SCOOP!

— Exclusive Showing —

TODAY and WEDNESDAY

Both Theatres (PERU) ★ (REXY) Both Theatres

Official Centennial Motion Pictures

SHOWING SCENES FROM THE

● Doll and Pet Parade.
● School Children's Program.
● Distinguished Visitors.
● Historical Landmarks.
● Centennial Chorus.
● Floats and Musical Units in the Mammoth Parade and Many Other Features.

NOTE: This Film Will Be Shown Exclusively in All Other Alger Theatres Soon!

SCOOP!

Peru's 100th anniversary was one of the largest celebrations in the Illinois Valley, but the euphoria soon faded, and the daily concerns for employment returned. On June 22, it was announced

117

that the construction of a seawall along the Illinois River was planned at Starved Rock. The project included the installation of cabinets with life preservers and the construction of promenade walks along the wall. The controversy continued regarding whether local labor or the CCC men would be involved. A compromise plan called for local men to build the wall itself while the CCC was engaged in leveling the ground around the wall and building cabins near the lodge. Actual construction was not scheduled to start until August. Two of the Oglesby recruits in the CCC, who were sent to the West Coast were quickly recognized for their leadership skills. Ed Pierczynski was promoted to assistant leader and soon after, became leader. Joseph Pocius rose in rank to First Sergeant of his company. The men were working at Emigrant Springs near Pendleton, OR at the summit of the Blue Mountains. Thirty-five more men from the LaSalle-Peru-Oglesby area were sent to Oregon in late June.

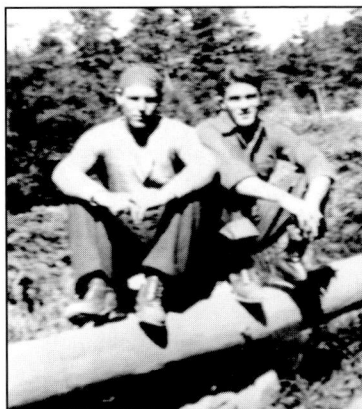

Most of the young men from the Illinois Valley were sent to distant locations. Morgan Vishnausky (at left) was one of the CCC men from Spring Valley, who was sent to the West Coast, where he worked in the national forest around Puget Sound, WA. (Photo contributed by Mary Vishnausky)

Young men from Putnam County were also headed in that direction. Six enrollees from Granville, Myron Brown, Joe Postulka, William Bell, Anton Mishendy, Francis Newbaum, and Pete Usavage, along with Ray Osborn from Hennepin, John Novak from Standard, Gwynne Peterson from McNabb, and Theodore Mills from Magnolia left on June 25 for Ft. Sheridan for their initial training before being sent to the Pacific Coast.

Ray Baxter, one of the Putnam County men who had already been sent to Pineville, OR, wrote to Mr. Hawthorne, editor of the Putnam County *Record*. Baxter described his work in Company 1648, which was digging springs and building water troughs out of pine trees for sheep and cattle. Their camp was located about 30 miles from Mt. Jefferson and the Three Sisters Mountains. He said that the boys took pride in the construction of community kitchens for campers on the Metolius River. They used

118

black lava rock for the fireplaces and cooking ranges. The Forest Service, which supervised the CCC work, also took the boys on a trip to The Cove on Crooked River Gorge. Baxter closed his letter by asking the editor to send the *Record* to Camp Elk Lake at Fort Rock, OR, since he was being transferred to Co. 2637.

This poster from the WPA Federal Art Project in Chicago encouraged young men from Illinois to think about the opportunities for those who joined the CCC.

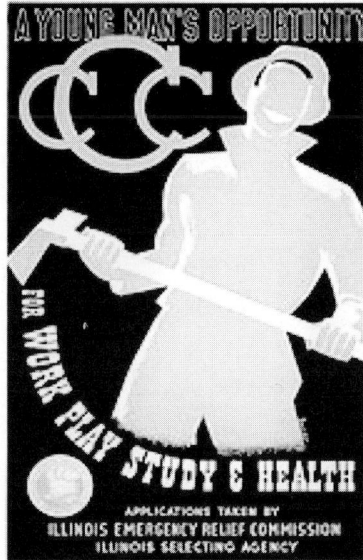

While the CCC boys were busy building new structures, John Cox of Granville was more interested in wrecking a couple of his old railroad engines in a head-on crash near Magnolia as a publicity stunt. With a flair for the dramatic, Cox made the June 30 event into an outing for the entire family. The 25-piece Lostant band was scheduled to offer a concert on the Sunday afternoon. Food and refreshments stands were to be found among the nearby shade trees. Reporters from Peoria and Bloomington were invited as well as film crews from Fox Movie Tone, Paramount, and R.K.O. studios. Sheriff Ellena was in charge of 40 deputies for the expected throng.

The head-on collision of RT&N Engines 50 and 51 took place south of Rt. 18. Both engineers jumped to safety before the impact, but there was no explosion. The cloud of steam hid the fact that only the cowcatchers were damaged.

119

Such theatrics were a temporary diversion from problems being addressed in city council and school board meetings, where administrators tried to find funds for infrastructure improvements. LaSalle found jobs for about 340 men with a payroll of $5,000 in June. The men had been engaged in building fences along Buck and Bluff Streets and cleaning catch basins. Mendota sent 21 men to work for the Henry Zolper & Son construction company on the underpass beneath the Burlington tracks over Rt. 51. All of the men were World War veterans with dependents.

Pictured is one of the Burlington crossings in Mendota before the construction of a subway under the tracks. (Art Kistler – IDOT)

More men found jobs constructing the subway under the CB&Q tracks on Route 51 in Mendota. (Photo by author)

In Bureau County, the Spring Valley school board's hope for a PWA grant for a $130,000 elementary school faded since it couldn't manage the matching funds required by the PWA. In spite of that forecast, the Hall H. S. board of education hoped their application for WPA funds to landscape the school grounds – especially the football field – would be approved since it was a project requiring mostly common labor. By comparison, the elementary school work would require many skilled laborers.

Remodeling the Princeton courthouse with a WPA grant also seemed to have a good chance of approval. Bureau County could come up with $107,000 as its share of the $196,750 project. However, nothing was certain; the application still needed the approval of the WPA engineer in Chicago.

Prospects for students hoping to continue their high school and college education improved in the summer of 1935. FDR launched his National Youth Administration (NYA) with a program to use $50 million to fund jobs for young people 16-25. His idea was to encourage high schools and colleges to hire students for various jobs in the schools and to encourage private industry to create apprenticeship programs. Local municipalities would also receive NYA funds if they hired students on a part-time basis for public works projects and clerical positions. Responding quickly in July, L-P High School sent its list of eligible students to the NYA.

The CCC expanded its program in July to include camps to abate soil erosion. A headquarters was to be set up in Henry, IL so that work in Bureau, Marshall, and Putnam Counties could begin Aug. 1. The Army would build the barracks for the 12 camps across the state. The plan was to send thousands of men to work 40 hours a week on private farms to build terraces and gully dams. The Army would assign regular Army officers to fill the positions of camp commander, medical officer, and education advisor. The Soil Conservation Service would furnish technical support, which included a camp superintendent, an engineer, a forester, an agronomist, a foreman, and his assistants.

FDR's New Deal programs were not without controversy. Farmers in the Illinois Valley were in a state of confusion in July. The Boston Circuit Court of Appeals had ruled that the Agricultural Adjustment Administration had illegally established a processing tax on producers of pork, cotton, tobacco, and grain, resulting in a billion dollars in tax revenues. The U.S. Supreme Court finally ruled that certain aspects of the AAA were unconstitutional. In a 40-38 vote, the U.S. Senate also struck down the price-fixing aspects of the AAA rules.

Agricultural concerns in the Illinois Valley were less focused on the court's decision. Families on relief, who had planted about 50 gardens along the Illinois River bottomlands, were distressed by the week-long rains, which were made worse by a cloud burst over Marseilles in July. The Illinois River rose to almost 16 feet. When the water finally subsided, they saw their sprouting plants had been washed away. Normally, gardens would have been planted earlier in the spring, but the river was too high at that time.

121

To make matters worse, Miss Ethalene Rowland, manager of the Peru unit of the Illinois Relief commission, said that their supply of free seeds was exhausted. Her sad advice for the gardeners was simply to abandon any hope of replanting this season.

For those lucky families who did not plant their gardens on the bottomland on the south side of the river, the Illinois Emergency Relief Commission (IERC) announced the planned opening of canning centers in LaSalle, Ottawa, Streator, and Marseilles. No canning centers existed in LaSalle County in 1934.

Gardens proliferated throughout LaSalle County. Of the 2,223 gardens in LaSalle County, 422 were planted on community property, while 1,801 were found in backyards or isolated fields. As early crops were harvested, families needed to find their own jars since the relief agency would only provide lids and rubbers. The relief commission had already provided insecticide, herbicide, wheel hoes, and seed drills for community gardens, but there was no money to buy jars.

In July, the Illinois Central RR freight house in LaSalle was stocked with canned goods. The allotment for the month included 15,125 cans of roast beef and 3,114 cans of roast mutton. Over 8,000 cans of hamburger beef made up the balance of the stockpile. Another shipment of surplus commodities arrived on Aug. 1. Six men in LaSalle had the job of repacking 40,000 pounds of dry skim milk into one-pound sacks. They packaged about 3,000 bags a day. The shipment was shared by ten counties. LaSalle County would take 15,600 sacks while Putnam County's allotment was only 1,000 bags. Marshall and Grundy Counties would each receive 1,600 of the one-pound bags. Other food expected from the federal government included butter, canned roast beef, roast veal, and hamburger.

Distribution of surplus government food in the area was based on the number of people in a family. Clients made requests to the relief agency, and nine trucks took the food to the families. The Streator and Ottawa districts had two trucks, while Marseilles, Earlville, Mendota, LaSalle, and Peru each had one truck available. The LaSalle district included Tonica, Cedar Point, Lostant, Rutland, and Wenona. Peru's area of responsibility included Utica and Deer Park.

The increasing deficit attributed to the work projects forced Washington to issue some belt-tightening measures. All single men would be removed from the relief roles as of July 31. The government asserted that there was plenty of farm work at harvest time and no need to keep these men on the dole.

Fortunately, 500 workers at Marquette Cement in Oglesby could look forward to returning to work after being furloughed for a month due to the installation of new coal pulverizing machinery. However, plant managers faced possible labor problems down the road since the returning men were organizing a local of the International Cement Workers Union of the AFL.

One WPA project had men loading this Oglesby Street Department truck at the Oglesby Coal Company. (Oglesby Library)

In early August, Co. 2601 at Starved Rock's Camp LaSalle, observed its first anniversary. To mark the occasion on Aug. 9, an all-day open house was held at the camp. The evening meal included fried chicken, mashed potatoes, candied sweet potatoes, fruit, vegetables, ice cream, and "circus water." Following dinner, a private dance with music provided by Joey Livek's orchestra was held in the pavilion at 8:30 p.m. for the men of companies 1609 and 2601 and their guests. Over 230 people attended the event.

This marker was erected at the Starved Rock visitors' center to remind the public of the work accomplished by CCC Company 2601 at Camp LaSalle.
(Photo by author)

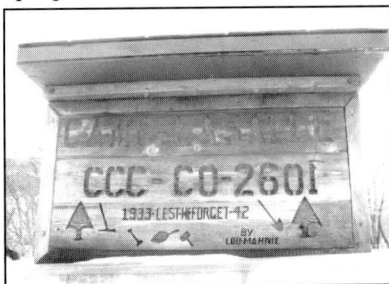

Harvest time created a temporary lull in WPA and PWA programs in Mendota in mid-August. The canning season was underway, creating an immediate demand for workers at the Inderrieden Canning Company. Thirty workers were supposed to start work at the WPA project to repair cracked sidewalks and survey water connections on August 16. The manpower shortage came as quite a shock to W. P. McMaster, administrator at the WPA office in Rockford. Commenting to a reporter he said, "You can well imagine our surprise when we found that not a man wanted a job. There were places for 15 men over a full year's time, and a similar number could work for four months at least on another project." The PWA project to construct a subway under the Burlington RR tracks already employed 50 men, and another 100 were needed. In spite of the lack of local workers, McMaster said that the WPA projects had already been funded so they would only be postponed rather than cancelled. The canning season was expected to last 6-8 weeks. After that, there would be plenty of men available for PWA and WPA work.

The story in the *Post-Tribune* caused quite a stir. After reading about the availability of work in Mendota, men came from as far away as Rockford and Peoria by car or train. Some even hitchhiked, seeking employment on the projects. They were sorely disappointed when project administrators spelled out the rules for hiring. All city projects required that workers had to be residents of Mendota for more than six months and listed on the relief rolls.

Henry, IL had gone through some tough times. On Feb. 10, 1933, its only financial institution, the First Henry National Bank (a combination of the First National Bank and the Henry National banks) closed its doors. Later in the spring, there was another economic setback. On May 5, 1933, a steel barge damaged the round pier of the swing section of the river bridge. The span had to be locked in the open position for river traffic. A free ferry service, which began on July 28, 1933, provided a temporary solution.

The old Henry Bridge with the swing center span closed was photographed in 1931.

Negotiations for a federally funded replacement bridge at Henry collapsed, so the Illinois Department of Transportation intervened. In March 1934, a contract was awarded to the Powers Thompson Construction Company of Joliet to construct the substructure. In April, each section of the old bridge was dynamited, and the wooden spans were brought to the shore to be burned. Finally, on Dec. 29, 1934, the concrete piers were complete. Construction of the steel super-structure was finished on March 6, 1935. The bridge deck was started on April 1, 1935.

A crew of about 38 men was used during construction. Some were highly skilled ironworkers, who had worked on the Golden Gate Bridge in California. Wages on the Henry bridge ranged from 75¢ to $2.00 a day.

On Aug. 15, 1935, the Henry Bridge was officially opened. The bridge was 1,703 feet in length and as much as 115 feet high. The $500,000 bridge restored the highway link between Rt. 29 in Henry with Rt. 89C to Magnolia. (Henry bridge pictures by Art Kistler – IDOT)

Just prior to the formal opening of the new bridge, two women, believed to be Mary and Emma Schultz, were waiting for the ferry to cross from Putnam County to Henry to sell produce to the grocery store. They were to be the first pedestrians to use the bridge according to the Henry *News Republican*.

In preparation for the formal dedication ceremonies on Aug. 15, the Fred Elgin Band from Peoria and the Doodledorfer Band from Peru were invited to perform at the celebration. A stage was built in Waterwork's Park for a pageant depicting the early history of Henry, Marshall, and Putnam counties. The stores in Henry had items of historical interest in their window displays. The day was filled with activities. At 10 a.m., Mayor Ford of Henry introduced several political leaders, who gave speeches praising the accomplishment. Mike Farly of Toluca cut the ribbon officially opening the bridge. Some of the spectators had attended the dedication of the original bridge. During the afternoon, 50 to 60 outboard motorboats were scheduled to participate in races along a one-mile stretch of the river. That evening, visiting dignitaries enjoyed dinner at the Henry Hotel.

One of the continuing conflicts between the Illinois Workers' Alliance and administrators of government-funded projects was the disparity of wages. On Aug. 16, 20 men from the IWA protested that the WPA project in Ottawa did not pay union scale. In Streator, where 47 men were working on sidewalk and street repairs, Mayor Elias faced the same problem but refused to shut down the projects. He cited the fact that it would be a violation of a government contract to change the wage provisions. The reasoning for the $44 per month "security wage" on PWA or WPA projects was that the government didn't want workers to feel that the jobs would be permanent. It would be better if they found other employment, where they would typically be paid union scale of $65 for common labor or $84.50 for skilled work. If the IWA had its way, projects would be jeopardized.

At the end of summer, hundreds of local men found employment. The road-grading project between Kangley and Sandy Ford was shifted from relief work to a WPA project employing two crews of 40 men each. One group started at 6:30 a.m., and another one took over at 12:30 p.m. Double-shifting resulted in shortening the three-month project to only six weeks. Another 25 men were cutting down a hill in Fall River Township south of Marseilles. Men in Ladd were blacktopping streets in their community. One project in Dalzell provided jobs for 44 men, and Spring Valley had men working on sewers, sidewalks, and streets. During August, LaSalle County reported that WPA projects made it possible to hire 152 men.

Washington was determined to clear the relief rolls by Nov. 1. That would mean even more projects funded by the federal government. Among the major works planned for the area were four National Guard armories. These would be located in Dixon, Streator, Mt. Morris, and Sycamore, IL.

Ralph Johnson of the Rockford WPA office announced expanded programs in the future. He estimated that 100 workers

126

would be needed for a variety of programs in athletics, music, drama, handicrafts, health, and first aid.

On Aug. 14, 1935, FDR signed the Social Security Act providing for unemployment and retirement benefits. (National Archives)

The NYA program at Hall H. S. paid students $6 a month to work as clerks, library assistants, stenographers, and researchers. Those on relief, who had graduated from high school and wanted to continue their education at the college level, could apply with the school for a NYA job, which paid $15 to undergraduates and $30 per month to students engaged in post-graduate work.

For other young men, there was always the CCC option. On Aug 29, another seven men from Bureau County enrolled. Edward Cassidy (Arlington), Bart Data (Ladd), Nello Piacenti (Ladd), Joe Taliana (Spring Valley), Riley Hall (Tiskilwa), Harry Noverio (LaMoille), and Edwin Kopytkiewicz (DePue) were sent to Camp Rip Mountain at Wausau, WI.

Letters to local newspapers from men who left to work at distant CCC camps gave readers a better idea of what camp life was like. The Putnam County *Record* received such a letter from Henry Westcott of Hennepin. The young man was assigned to the CCC camp in Ontonagon, MI. He was a writer for the camp newspaper, "Chiselers," and described the work of the "Hell Divers." Basically, their work involved stream improvement along the Otter River. The men were cutting trees, clearing dead wood from the streams, and breaking up unused beaver dams. "The projects were not only work, but also educational and a pleasure," Westcott wrote.

The *Post* published another letter from a CCC camp in Idaho the following month. Jake Heberling of DePue, told about the advancements made by six of the men from Bureau County who were still assigned to Camp Upper Beaver, Headquarters, Company

621. Of the original 27 Bureau County enrollees from the previous year, the six who were still there were promoted. Alva Ickes from Buda was now the senior leader, and John Downie of Dalzell was a leader. George Grotti of Seatonville and John Walker of Spring Valley became assistant leaders. John West of Wyanet was a truck driver. Heberling said he was given the responsibilities of the assistant educational leader, canteen steward, and mail clerk. He explained how Co. 621, "is manned by the down state farmers as our Chicago friends would put it." Besides the camp work, the DePue native described the local entertainment, which included a trip to the Rose Bowl parade and football game, meeting Hollywood stars at the Hoot Gibson rodeo, and watching the Cubs play the Sox in Los Angeles, which was only 45 miles from their camp. The men said they especially enjoyed reading the *Post*.

Camp Illini at Marseilles was typical of many of the CCC encampments along the I-M Canal. Hundreds of young men lived in a military-style environment. The men lived first in tents and later in barracks rising with a bugle call for revelry and following a regimen directed by the regular army.

The CCC men in Company 613 trained at Ft. Sheridan before heading to Marseilles. (Marseilles Library)

CCC accommodations at Camp Illini. (Marseilles Library)

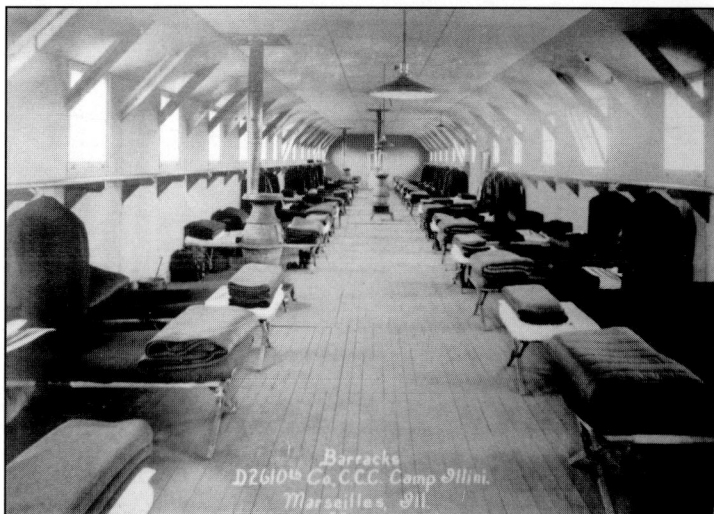

Note the potbelly stoves in the barracks for Company 2610.

Supervised by the regular Army, CCC men followed a typical military lifestyle of discipline, hard work, and low pay but without training in firearms or military tactics. (Marseilles Library)

Company 613 lived in these barracks in Camp Illini. (Marseilles Library)

After breakfast, the CCC men loaded into trucks for the ride to the I-M Canal or the state park for the day's work. (Marseilles Library)

The two CCC companies at Illini State Park decided to participate in the Marseilles Centennial on Aug 29, 1935. Twenty-six men volunteered as guards and ushers, and others took part in the Civil War pageant. A miniature shelter-house on a float in the parade was the joint effort of Companies 613 and 2610. (Marseilles Library)

Municipalities and school districts filed applications for literally hundreds of WPA and PWA projects. In addition to the usual infrastructure improvements to streets and sidewalks, there had been filings for the construction of a lodge and concession stand at Starved Rock State Park, a stadium and building addition at L-P High School, a stadium at Mendota H.S., and a municipal swimming pool in Mendota.

Another project focused on the unused Burlington RR pond in Mendota. The $37,793 application requested PWA funds to clean the pond and convert it into a small lake stocked with fish from the state hatcheries. The new recreational area would include a sandy beach around the lake and a picnic shelter.

A PWA project for an addition to L-P High School required a $248,000 bond referendum by Peru and LaSalle voters as their share of the cost.

The proposed L-P High School addition would include a new swimming pool, gym, locker rooms, and restrooms, as well as classrooms and a library. Construction was estimated to take about eight months and would initially employ about 350 local men.

A separate application for a WPA grant was filed in Washington to construct a $46,000 L-P High School stadium. The initial application was modified to include two retaining walls on the south side of the field and a 6-lane track around the football field. The stadium would have a seating capacity of 1,800. The cost was estimated at $11 per seat. Athletic equipment, showers, lockers, and a heating plant would add another $5-6 per seat. Initially, the plans called for using red brick to match the high school, but concrete was substituted in the plans to bring down the construction cost. The stadium, as proposed, would extend for 300 feet in width on the east side of the field. By using raised sections of seats, 60 percent of the spectators would be seated within the middle third of the playing field. The original architect's plans for the L-P stadium called for a massive concrete entrance on the south side. Lights would be

131

concealed behind the huge square columns giving the appearance of a cathedral-like entrance.

Future construction projects offered hope for the unemployed, but having food on the table was a more pressing need for many. In Putnam County, that need was partially addressed in late August by volunteers working under the direction of Mrs. D.R. Rawlings in the basement of the Mark School. Those on relief brought their garden produce, which included corn, beets, plums, and peaches to the school. The IERC supplied the sugar and canning supplies. Processing the food averaged 400 cans a day. Once the cans were sealed and labeled, they were placed in the stockroom for two days. Then, the folks who brought their garden produce to the facility could take home 60 cans. The only "price" for the service was the donation of one can for every five cans processed. The contributions were stocked for future relief clients or for the kindergarten class. When the IERC field representative, toured the gardens of those on relief, he commented that those in Granville and Mark were the best he had seen of the 47 locations he visited.

Hope ran high in Cherry at the end of August that the old mine, scene of the devastating fire in 1909, which claimed the lives of 259 men and boys, would reopen after being shutdown for some time. Eight men had been hired by the new owners of the Cherry Mining Company, listed as Sam Ludwig of Chicago and Holger Severdsen of Morris. A new cutting machine was in place so enough coal could be brought up to fire the boilers, which were being repaired. Reports suggested that fifty to several hundred miners would soon be at work in the first vein, once operated by the St. Paul Coal Co. However, there was no plan to enter any sections of the second vein, where the fire had taken so many lives. Optimistic predictions cited a potential output of 200-300 tons a day destined for local and Chicago markets.

Bureau County officials were just as anxious as LaSalle County in submitting WPA project applications. If approved, one $46,792 application would provide for a drainage sewer running under Sixth Street to the Borop farm. Another request called for six miles of road graveling near Tiskilwa. Yet another project for that town was an $11,000 request for a swimming pool next to the Hennepin Canal. The long-neglected exterior of the county jail was also on the list of projects. The Princeton jail had not received a coat of paint in 28 years according to the *Post-Tribune*.

Some projects were low cost items, such as repairs to the roof of Perry Memorial Hospital. Landscaping and construction of a two-car garage at the hospital carried a price tag of $2,500. The construction of a rifle range for county bank guards on the Ferris farm south of Princeton could be accomplished for $1,800. The county park needed to hire men to remove deadwood, drill a well, and construct a gravel road and some fireplaces. That project was submitted with an estimated cost of $16,551.

Lee County received approval of numerous WPA projects at the Rockford office on Sept. 6. Approximately 400 men would be taken off the relief rolls, pending approval from the Chicago office.

Because the government projects required a certain percentage of matching funds, small towns like Granville had little hope of major infrastructure improvements. A badly needed $25,000 sewer system seemed unattainable since residents would have to agree to an increase in their water bills to fund the 60 percent share ($15,000) of the cost.

While that project looked hopeless, Putnam County was successful in acquiring help from the CCC men camped in Henry. Since one of the major goals of the CCC was forestry work, 20 men went to work at the Lyle Morine farm east of Hennepin. To control hillside erosion, they constructed a number of small dams and planted 4,000 black locust and walnut trees in late October.

Besides the men working on numerous street and sanitation projects, students were hired for government programs in October. The NYA federal student aid program resulted in the hiring of 44 students at L-P-O junior college where they could earn an average wage of $15 for a typical 30-hour month.

The National Writers Project included a nationwide program to create state guidebooks. Two Illinois Valley men were selected as local WPA project supervisors. The jobs didn't pay much, but it was a source of income for a time.

Others found what they thought would be a more lucrative form of employment. Once again, the little village of Leonore was in the news in the fall of 1935. Bootlegging had not completely died out, and a few men sought to construct a corn liquor distillery on the Charles Meyers farm three miles northwest of Leonore. Acting on a tip that a large shipment of booze had left the farm on Sunday, Oct. 6, Sheriff Desper decided to wait for the truck's return. Early on Tuesday morning, Desper and his deputies approached the operation by following a little used path along the Illinois Central RR tracks. When the bootlegger's truck and an escort vehicle returned at 7:30 a.m. on Tuesday, the police made their move. Entering a large building, they found 40,000 gallons of corn mash in fermentation tanks and a small amount of the finished product. This was no small operation. It was estimated the still could turn out 500 gallons of alcohol every day. Four men were arrested: Charles Meyers, the owner of the farm; Pete Mando of Ottawa, the alleged "cooker" at the distillery; Rex Shimkort of Leonore; and Sam Vitale of LaSalle.

Six more men escaped by fleeing through a field during the raid. Desper and a deputy gave chase with the sheriff firing three times over their heads. Apparently, one of the bullets unintentionally struck one of the fleeing men in the leg. A local doctor treated a man for a gun shot wound, and called the sheriff's office to see if there had been any shooting during the encounter. The doctor hung up without giving his name. The search for the escaped men continued the next day. Desper later told the *Post-Tribune* the still was "one of the largest ever seized in northern Illinois."

Bootlegging was a dying endeavor in the Illinois Valley. Most individuals were engaged in legal – even profitable – ventures. E. E. Alger was one of those enterprising individuals in the Tri-Cities. Always looking for new opportunities, the movie theater entrepreneur decided to open yet another theater. His newest addition, the Star Theater in Peru, had several owners and different names, changing from the "Werner" to the "Riviera" and finally the "Peru". That last name was removed from the marquee when Alger opened his new Peru Theater in 1931. Before the grand opening of his newest acquisition, Alger had the old theater renovated using mainly local labor.

On Oct 26, the "Star" opened for business. Patrons bought their tickets at the sidewalk ticket booth under the illuminated marquee and crossed the carpeted foyer. The old theater had been closed five years earlier, so patrons marveled at the new interior with its red plush seating for up to 408 patrons, air conditioning, indirect lighting, and a host of other features. It was a great improvement over its predecessors, the "Nikelette," the "Princess," and the "Airdrome."

Ad for the grand opening of the Star Theater in Peru reprinted from the Oct. 25, 1935 *Post-Tribune*.

Other theater patrons were disappointed when the Rexy Theater in LaSalle suffered a major fire that gutted the theater interior in early November. Businesses located nearby were not badly damaged. Losses to at the Rexy were estimated at $16,000.

In late October, Robert Kingery, Illinois director of the Department of Public Works and Buildings, recommended a major plan for improvements at Starved Rock. The $72,000 PWA application called for the construction of a lunchroom and kitchen adjacent to the souvenir stand opposite the dance pavilion. Building material would come from dismantled exhibits at the Century of Progress exposition in Chicago. Local men would be hired to complete the walls of the lodge, the dining room, and kitchen. Plans for a boat dock would be held in abeyance until more funds were available.

WPA projects continued to be a significant source of employment for those on relief. Work on the L-P stadium was progressing slowly. Eighty-five men were at work building the retaining walls on the southwest corner.

The LaSalle sewing center at 927 First Street was a significant place of employment for a hundred women, ages 17-60. Officially known as LaSalle-Peru-Oglesby Unit No. 2640, the women worked 30 hours a week. The workers previously held a variety of jobs. These included a former music teacher, an artist, and several stenographers, but "most were ordinary housewives and mothers," according to Clara Monari, a writer for the *Post-Tribune*.

Mrs. Marie Frank, the center director, said that production was hampered by the lack of sewing machines; they had only three. Most of the stitching had to be done by hand. Some of the 41 seamstresses and six cutters would not have even had chairs had it not been for the loan of furniture by the priests of St. Valentine's Church in Peru. A public appeal was made for the loan of more sewing machines until the government allotment of 25 machines arrived. Even five additional machines would make a big difference, according to Mrs. Frank.

The women were producing a variety of products for infants and young children up to eight years old. These included "kimonos, socks, slips, dresses, and blankets." The women even took up a collection among themselves to purchase embroidery cotton and thread to trim the infant garments. Other products sent to the relief stores included aprons, bedspreads, and curtains. In November, the work focused on smock production. "If it weren't for my splendid helpers the project would not have progressed so nicely. We are

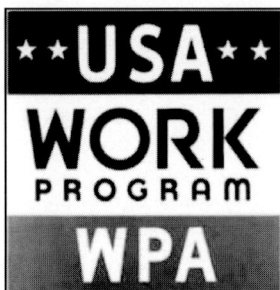

135

trying to make this a model unit in Illinois by the products being the best turned out," said Mrs. Frank. Fifty other women were employed at sewing centers in Streator and Ottawa doing similar work.

In spite of the scarcity of jobs, 68 of the 85 men working on the L-P stadium walked off the job on Nov. 23, when the local business agent came on the scene and protested the wages, which were below union scale. The men were told to check out with the time-keeper until the matter was resolved. Work was hard to find, so 15 men stayed on the job, and 70 men were back at work the following week. School officials tried to reason with the union officials that the stadium work was a government WPA contract job, and the wages could not be adjusted.

Teamsters also protested the $1 per hour WPA salary paid to truck drivers. Local business agent Lawrence Trovero was authorized to stop any trucker working for that wage. The union scale for a teamster was $1.50 per hour.

For young people, 16-25, the NYA provided supplemental funds that made it possible for students from families on relief to stay in school. The selection process gave priority to youths from large families. Students could work up to 46 hours a month and were paid one-third of the adult WPA pay schedule with a maximum of $25 per month.

Locally, some of the NYA boys worked on construction projects or in the local government commodity depot. Girls and young women were also assigned to the commodity depot or to the sewing centers. The Nov. 25 government report from Rockford stated that 148 youths from LaSalle County were employed in NYA jobs. It was a large number compared to other nearby counties. The LaSalle paper published the following figures for NYA countywide assignments: "Putnam, 10; Bureau, 3; Grundy, 4; Henry, 20, and Kendall 9."

In November, WPA jobs kept 395 men working in Hall, Selby, and Fairfield Townships. Most of the work involved improvements to streets and sewers in Spring Valley, Ladd, Cherry, Dalzell, and DePue. Others worked at Hall H. S. pouring concrete for the steps and sidewalk east of the stadium and the foundation for the two garages. Nine men were at work on the Seatonville School.

While all of these government jobs seemed to be consistently making headlines, scarcely anyone noticed the rising employment figures at Westclox. Since June 17, 1933, according to statistics in *Tick Talk,* the company magazine, Westclox had hired an additional 843 workers bringing their total employment to 2,622 at the end of 1935.

1936

BENEFITS FOR VETS & TOURISTS

The winter months saw little activity at the local CCC camps. Since Camp Illini near Marseilles had been abandoned when the company moved out, Boy Scout leaders thought it would be an excellent alternative as a summer camp to take the place of Camp Ki-Shaw-Wau near Lowell. However, they would need the help of the CCC to reconfigure the abandoned barracks into smaller units. Since the lagoon on the property was not suitable for swimming, an outdoor swimming pool was also sought by the Scout leaders. The problem was that the U.S. Department of Labor was cutting back. In fact, the normal January enrollment for the CCC in LaSalle County was simply eliminated. Still, the Scout leaders held out hope that the work would be included for a nearby CCC unit when the normal work began on April 1.

National news on January 6 drew the attention of local farmers when they read that the Supreme Court in a 6-3 decision killed the AAA. Speaking for the Court, Justice Owen Roberts said, "Regulating agricultural production is not a power of Congress." It was an "invasion of states' rights" and a tax "beyond the general welfare clause." Raising farmers' concerns even more was the Court's decision to also declare the Frazier-Lemke Bankruptcy Act unconstitutional. These setbacks would cause problems until 1938 when Congress passed the Soil Conservation Act, established the second AAA, and amended the Frazier-Lemke Bill with a three-year moratorium on foreclosures.

A few days later, military veterans, who had been seeking payment of their pensions since the beginning of the Depression, received positive news from Congress. The Patman Bill to pay the bonus passed the House 355-59. The Senate also voted its approval 76-19, but FDR vetoed the bill because of the estimated cost of $2.5 billion. However, the long-fought battle for veterans' rights could not be stopped, and the president's veto was easily overridden.

According to the terms of the new legislation, the Treasury would issue "baby bonds," valued at $50 each. The length and location of military service would determine the amount paid to each veteran, who could redeem his bonds at local post offices. Those who did not request payment immediately would collect an additional three percent annually as interest on their unredeemed bonus amounts. Although bonds were supposed to be cashable as of June 15, 1936, realistically, it was not expected that the veterans would actually receive the bonds until July 1, 1936.

The financial impact could have profound implications that summer. It was estimated that in LaSalle County veterans could receive $1.3 million. Over $700,000 might be redeemed in Bureau County. Marshall County veterans stood ready to collect over $240,000. Veterans in Lee County were entitled to about $600,000. Even Putnam County vets had earned bonuses amounting to $97,000 according to the *Post-Tribune*. However, it would be another six months before the bonus bonds arrived. In the meantime, veterans and others seeking employment had to make do with whatever jobs were available.

On Jan. 10, the 180 men and officers of CCC Co. 628 at Buffalo Rock packed their bags and boarded the train for relocation to Clarkia, ID. Their heavy equipment was sent to Ft. Sheridan. Since the CCC unit arrived in 1933, it had accomplished much. The men built two large shelters, a number of small shelters, and about 50 picnic tables. A new sewer system was installed; trails were marked; and guardrails were installed. The banks along the I-M Canal from the Fox River aqueduct to LaSalle were cleared, and the feeder canal was converted to a road stretching from St. Columba's Cemetery halfway to Dayton. The remaining roadwork would have to be completed by other units in the area. There was plenty of work for the CCC, but cutbacks were coming.

Civic improvements using a WPA grant were on the agenda of the Peru city council on Jan. 17. The beautification and general improvement of Washington Park would provide four months of work for 150 men as well as administrative personnel, such as timekeepers, foremen, and a supervisor. Of the $28,594 grant request, 92 percent of the funds would be spent on wages. The work would include leveling the land, filling gullies, reseeding, and planting 90 trees. The council also included proposals for a new road connecting the park with Shooting Park Road and leveling certain areas for a possible ice-skating rink and playground. Washington still had to approve the application.

Not all projects called for manual labor. Grace Barcus at the Barcus Studio was in charge of a WPA art education project. Anyone over 16, whether on relief or not, could participate. Thaddeus Chemelewski was named as the WPA instructor for a naturalization class in Peru. Other citizenship classes were planned for Ottawa and Streator. Money was also available for an Oglesby sewing class, which would be taught by Mrs. Margaret Nickens. In Marseilles, a WPA nursery school was scheduled to resume services.

The winter months were hard on everyone and even potentially deadly to some. Stories of hobos being killed or injured while walking the railroad tracks periodically appeared in the newspapers. Many hobos moved from town to town trying to survive, but were generally not welcomed into the community. On Jan. 8, a group of boys playing near the Rock Island viaduct in Peru spotted five hobos passed out near the waterworks. After they told the waterworks assistant engineer, Everett Strout, he called the Peru police. Police Chief Peter Walloch found the intoxicated hobos sprawled on the ground, unable to get up. "I've seen 'em drunk, but never as bad as this," he commented to a reporter. It took over an hour to haul the hobos up the steep slope and take them to the jail. The next morning, the police escorted them to the area between Oglesby and Tonica, where they were released. According to the police, had it not been for the boys' discovery, "the tramps would have become critically ill or possibly died of exposure."

A massive snowstorm covered the nation in February trapping people in subzero weather. In Saukville, WI, 55 people were stranded on a train. Food rationing was necessary in parts of Minnesota. The 140 CCC men camped in Placerville, CA were isolated. At Devil's Lake, N.D., the temperature dropped to -44°F.

Meanwhile in LaSalle, the temperature was much warmer on Feb. 14, a balmy -10° F. Robert Dingler, a Peru rural route mail carrier, reported drifts 15 feet high. "I have bucked plenty of snow drifts in my time, but never in my 23 years of experience have I seen roads blocked as they have been this year," he told a reporter from the *Post*. Joe Marchesi of Standard, the sub-district president of the UMW gave his approval for the miners to work a third Saturday in a row to mine enough coal to meet the emergency. Normally, the miners only worked a 35-hour week.

The streets of downtown Streator were passable, but the country roads were in far worse condition. (Streatorland Historical Society)

The WPA put men to work during the emergency. On Feb. 17, a group of 50 men was transferred from a WPA construction project and sent to clear the drifts from Plank Road north of Peru. The job was overwhelming, and the men gave up after an hour. One abandoned car was found buried in snow that almost covered the top of the vehicle. Other roads in northern LaSalle County remained impassible for days because there were no active WPA projects in the vicinity.

It was not until Feb. 20 that some road clearing was achieved. It took a combination of state workers and 120 WPA men, pulled from road grading projects, to clear the roads south of Peru. Even with help from local farmers, the bitter cold halted all attempts to open Plank Road and Peak's Tavern Road.

Many local WPA workers worried about the delay in receiving their wages. In fact, rumors spread that there was a riot in Oglesby. The stories were later proved to be unfounded, but the situation was tense since the men had not received vouchers for a month or longer. There were only empty promises that the vouchers would arrive soon. About 300 men in the Tri-Cities had not received their pay to cover their basic expenses for rent, heat, and food.

Even word of the arrival of a boxcar loaded with apples at the surplus commodity corporation did not bring the anticipated relief. The director of the LaSalle depot said the apples would not be distributed in LaSalle, Bureau, and Grundy counties until March.

The men just kept on working wherever WPA jobs were offered. Oglesby Mayor Frank Moyle announced the hiring of 70-80 men to spread red ash on Jones Ave. and the extension of Second Street to the state highway. The council stressed its position of only hiring Oglesby men for the $21,000 street project unless not enough men were available.

Many cities had recreation programs supported by WPA funding. In Oglesby, 100 boys, 16-20, enrolled in the intermediate WPA recreational program. Granville recreational activities took place in the WPA-remodeled mill across from the James Hynds home. In addition to a workshop, ping-pong tables were set up for use in the afternoons and evenings. Even boxing matches were planned. Ed Gensini, Richard Whitaker, Harry Wilson, and Herman Stirnes supervised the boys. Mrs. Edwin Seimers and Miss Florence Profitt were hired to coordinate activities for the girls.

The weather continued to affect the assignment of jobs. Warmer temperatures resulted in the thawing of ice and rising water on the Illinois River. This created a serious situation in Putnam County as Coffee Creek was out of its banks and within 15 inches of the top of the levee. On Feb. 28, the WPA sent 30 men to fill low places, and 150 men from Marshall County were ready to work on the levee around the Hennepin drainage district. The last time the water overflowed the levee was in 1913.

On Mar. 2, the PWA engineer-inspector along with representatives of the Decatur construction company that made the low bid for work at Starved Rock State Park visited the job site. The first project called for a new lunchroom and kitchen next to the souvenir stand. Construction materials were salvaged from the Illinois Host building (pictured) at the Century of Progress exhibition. According to the *Post-Tribune*, the contracting firm had the job of finishing the lodge and adding "a dining room, kitchen, heating plant, toilet facilities, etc." The CCC would build the nearby cabins. Money came from the PWA ($32,000) and the Illinois General Assembly ($40,000).

The Illinois deep waterway project would eventually employ hundreds of men during the summer of '36. The first project involved dredging the river between Starved Rock and Utica. That would provide jobs for 400 men for over a year. A second program, rip-rapping around Plum and Leopold Islands, located below Starved Rock dam, would provide 180 men with work for 2-3 months. The goal was to hire 90 percent of the union men on relief.

Unemployed men were hired to cover the banks of Leopold Island with rocks to prevent erosion.

Riprap was also laid out on the side of Plum Island facing the dam.

(Photos by author)

141

While news of future work programs was anxiously greeted by the unemployed, 45 workers in Mendota were already busy draining the old railroad pond into a nearby creek. Once the water level was low enough, the men could wade into the muddy bottom and try to catch the trapped fish, expected to be mostly bullheads. The fish would be released into the creek. The willow roots, large rocks, and debris at the bottom of the pond would also be removed.

The building addition at L-P High School was making steady progress in the spring when tragedy struck. On the morning of April 9, a crew was removing concrete forms from a 10-foot square footing for the building's foundation. Several men were working at the bottom of the excavation, 15 feet below the surface, when the surrounding dirt collapsed. About 40 co-workers immediately grabbed shovels to remove the tons of dirt.

Gradually, they recovered the trapped men. Ed Schlosser, 28, of Peru was buried up to his shoulders. After being taken to St. Mary's Hospital, an examination of the injured showed bruises but no broken bones. Three workers, Steve Urech of Chicago, Frank Just of Peru and Peter Campo of LaSalle were killed. Just suffered a broken neck and crushed chest. Urech also had a crushed chest. Campo had a broken neck and arm. In spite of the accident, work continued, and everything was back to normal by the afternoon.

An inquest on April 10 found that blame could not be determined. The men died from crushing injuries and suffocation. It was thought that the heavy excavating equipment caused the cave-in.

The tempo of work at the L-P projects picked up at the end of March. Two shifts were working on the high school addition. Work began at 7 a.m. and continued until noon for one crew. Then another crew went to work, not stopping until 8 p.m. The retaining walls at the south end of the stadium were showing progress, but a labor dispute on Mar. 31 temporarily brought a halt to the work. The Noonan Lumber Company had hired non-union drivers and was using its own trucks to haul material to the job site. That did not sit well with the local teamsters, who wanted a share of the work.

For the elderly, the long-awaited Social Security program got off to a slow start in LaSalle County in April. It wasn't for lack of interest. Almost 2,000 senior citizens had applied for their old age pensions at the Ottawa courthouse. That involved filling out a four-page questionnaire, which could be accomplished quickly. The real delay was due to the fact that the information had to be investigated by the LaSalle County Welfare Commission. If that body approved, the applications were sent to Springfield for a review that took 2-3 weeks before any checks were mailed.

142

For those who were not eligible for retirement and not interested in manual work, the government created other jobs. One project was the collection of information for a collection of books called "The American Guide." One of the volumes in the series was titled "Illinois: A Descriptive and Historical Guide." Over 520 researchers in Illinois gathered information on "scenic historical, colorful, unique, and recreational points of interest." For several months, Lewis Hocking, a field worker employed by the WPA's Federal Writers Project, interviewed Illinois Valley businessmen, older residents, and churchmen to collect information.

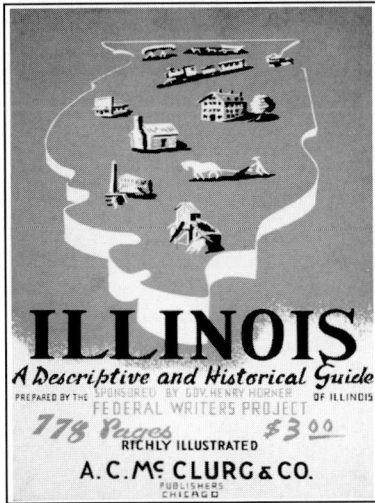

The WPA guide to Illinois included only a few photos of the Illinois Valley – Starved Rock, the Lehigh cement factory at Oglesby, Deer Park, and the I-M Canal at Channahon. The majority of the photos were of the Chicago area.

Hocking focused his research on the local history, transportation, restaurants, hotels, schools, museums, sports and recreational activities, and social and cultural centers. Portions of the report also dealt with the museum at St. Bede and the digging of the Illinois-Michigan Canal. The report also included information on the trails through Starved Rock and Buffalo Rock. The U.S. Government Printing Office had 15,000 orders for the travel guide before the book was even published.

The guide described almost every town in Illinois. Lake DePue was said to be the inspiration for William Cullen Bryant's poem, "To a Waterfowl." The Cherry miners' memorial and the annual observance of the 1909 coal mine fire were also mentioned. Princeton was cited as the location of the Owen Lovejoy Homestead, and the homes of Cyrus and John Bryant, brothers of William Cullen Bryant. Troy Grove received attention as the birthplace of "Wild Bill" Hickok for whom the town erected a monument in 1929. Researchers also found that the origins of Carson, Pirie, Scott & Company could be traced to Samuel Carson, John T. Pirie, and J. E. Scott, who operated a grocery store (now the Long Branch Saloon) in Amboy. By the end of the Civil War, their mercantile business had headquarters in Chicago and branches in Mendota and Polo. Wyanet was noted for its fish hatchery and its proximity to the Illinois-Mississippi (Hennepin) Canal. Morris was cited for its location on the I-M Canal, the nearby Mazon fossil beds, and Gebhard Woods State Park, where the WPA was improving the park facilities. The researchers only made brief remarks about Seneca and Marseilles as historic shipping points along the I-M Canal. Oglesby received recognition as "one of the largest cement-producing centers in the State," Peru's importance centered on the Peru Wheel Company, Westclox, and the "wooden swing-type bridge turned by hand."

While conducting his research in the Illinois Valley, Hocking was surprised to find that the Hegeler residence on Seventh Street in LaSalle "was built as a replica of a castle on the Rhine." (Photo by author)

Peru's 1869 bridge with its 310-foot swing span was described in the WPA Illinois guidebook as "a remarkable engineering achievement."

144

Right: Wildcat Canyon was one of the places at Starved Rock State Park pointed out in the WPA guide to Illinois. (Photo by author)
Below: This WPA poster promoted the release of the American Guide series.

AMERICAN GUIDE ★ WEEK ★

TAKE PRIDE IN YOUR COUNTRY

NOV. 10-16

STATE BY STATE
THE WPA WRITERS PROJECTS DESCRIBE AMERICA TO AMERICANS

"Through these guides to the forty-eight states, Alaska, Puerto Rico, the District of Columbia, and the principal Cities and major regions of the United States, citizens and visitors to our country now have at their finger-tips, for the first time in our history, a series of volumes that ably illustrate our national way of life, yet at the same time portray variants in local patterns of living and regional development." *Franklin D. Roosevelt.*

Hocking often focused on the economic importance of Illinois communities. As the terminus of the I-M Canal, he noted that LaSalle played an important role in maritime commerce for both canal boats and steamboats. M&H Zinc Company was noted as a principal source of revenue for LaSalle. Streator was also included for its clay products industry and glass plant. The descriptions of hundreds of Illinois towns also included Wenona, which was described as "a marketing and shipping point for soy beans and corn." Towns in Putnam County, with the exception of Hennepin, were omitted from the work. Other than a reference to being named for Father Hennepin, the book described Hennepin (pop. 312) as "of no more importance than the score of other settlements passed by the Federal Barge Line." More information was included on the burial site of Chief Senachwine.

Hocking's research included information on the boulder in Washington Park in Ottawa, marking the location of the first Lincoln-Douglas debate. A bronze plaque commemorating the event was placed there on August 21, 1908.

The Ottawa Appellate Court House, designed in the Greek Revival style, was also listed as a building of note in Ottawa in the Illinois guidebook.

The guidebook described the Reddick House in Ottawa, as "a three-storied brick limestone-trimmed building with a high front stoop." At the time, it served as the Ottawa Library. The research also included information on the Caton House, The Oakes, and the L-O-F glass plant. (Photos by author)

The Illinois guide also described the Marseilles dam and canal, constructed as part of the Illinois Waterway, making it possible for tows to avoid 2½ miles of rapids. Mention was also made of 407-acre Illini State Park and Bells Island, which separated the river from the waterway. (Photo by author)

Starved Rock Lock and Dam, the fifth major installation of the Illinois Waterway project, was also described in the WPA guidebook. This is the view from the top of Starved Rock. (Photo by author)

Small towns, such as Dalzell, took advantage of WPA funds for summer recreation programs. Under the direction of Chuck Bernabei, softball and hardball tournaments were organized. Amateur nights with singing, dancing, poetry readings, and plays were scheduled.

The Fraternity Building in Oglesby was the site of many recreational programs funded by the WPA. Concerned about the amount of federal money available, WPA workers held a public dance at the Fraternity Building to raise money to continue the summer activities. (Oglesby Library)

Spring was also the time to start planning seed distribution for those on relief so they could plant gardens. Requests came from 476 families, but the number of seed collections was limited to 399. Miss Dortha Osborn, relief administrator for LaSalle County, spelled out three factors to determine who would receive the limited supply. First requests would receive priority over those filed later. Secondly, those individuals with no other resources would be more likely to receive the seeds. Finally, priority would be given to those who had an adequate plot with better soil quality. The Peru city council had already approved a plan to allow the use of city property east of the river bridge for gardens.

Communities took special pride in the completion of major projects. One of those achievements was the completion of "The White Way," the new street lighting system extending down Walnut Street from Columbia to Portland Avenues.

Post-Tribune ad - April 29, 1936.

BIG CELEBRATION

Thursday Evening, April 30

Starts 7:30 P. M.

DEDICATING OGLESBY'S

New Street Lights

CONCERT by OGLESBY'S MUNICIPAL BAND

Speakers: Mayor Moyle
and Senator Mason

FREE STREET DANCE
EDDIE SWORDS' 10-PIECE ORCHESTRA

You're Invited To Come and Celebrate with Oglesby

The merchants represented on this page feel they are expressing the sentiment of all Oglesby in extending - - -

CONGRATULATIONS

To Mayor Moyle and Commissioners Rock, Mayers and Entwistle

—who are to be given every credit for bringing about this latest Oglesby improvement!
And here's hoping that the Mayor and Commissioners are again successful soon, in their efforts
to put thru the proposed "New EAST ROAD"!

148

At the dedication on April 30, the Oglesby municipal band entertained a crowd of about 3,000. That evening, John McCann, the general chairman of the event, was joined by Mayor Frank Moyle on the speaker's platform erected in the Union Church yard at Church and Walnut. "This new system places Oglesby in the metropolis class, and our fair city does not have to take second place with any city, said McCann. Mayor Moyle then threw the switch illuminating the length of Walnut Street.

There was mixed news for local laborers at the beginning of May 1936. Anticipation ran high at Lehigh Portland Cement when 120 men began the work necessary to restart the facility. Word finally came on May 2 that 300 men, who had been laid off in Nov. 1935, were being called back to work.

Lehigh Portland Cement Company. (Oglesby Library)

On the other hand, coal miners in Spring Valley at the No. 3 shaft got the bad news that the mine was closing for 2-3 months for repairs, remolding loading chutes, and construction of a new shop building. According to the *Post-Tribune*, they would probably not return to work until late summer. Even the employees of the Star Theater in Peru found themselves unemployed for the rest of the summer. It was hoped that the closing was only temporary.

At least the CCC men at Starved Rock had plenty to do. They had already constructed 16 cabins, and work on the lodge was continuing and not expected to be finished before the fall.

Most people were too busy to notice the arrival of a new, streamlined train at LaSalle on May 5. A crowd of about 500 were on hand as the Illinois Central's Green Diamond diesel-electric power car with two chair cars and a lounge car pulled into the depot

149

at noon. The occasion was an exhibition run from Bloomington to Freeport. Among the local business leaders on board were William Shields, LaSalle Chamber of Commerce; Joseph Caveletto, Lehigh Portland Cement; Leo Damm, Western Clock; Harry Noel and Joseph Reinhard, Alpha Portland Cement; and Stanley Smith, Marquette Cement. Commenting to a *Post-Tribune* reporter on the trip from Bloomington, Shields said, "Never have I enjoyed a ride more. The train seemingly glided through the air; vibration and road-shock is completely absent at all speeds."

On May 5, 1936, the Illinois Central's Green Diamond streamliner made a brief appearance in LaSalle before continuing its demonstration run to Freeport.

In June, the federal government finally made good its promise to pay for the bonus bonds. However, the redemption process was a little more involved than the veterans might have expected. The government calculated the amount owed to each veteran based on his military service. For domestic military service, the rate was $1 a day – up to a maximum of $500. For each day of foreign service, the amount was increased to $1.25 with a cap of $625. The total value of the bonds would be sent in multiples of $50 "baby bonds" as they were called, with a check for any balance of less than $50.

LaSalle Postmaster Mary Reardon explained the redemption procedure. Envelopes containing the bonds would be delivered on June 16 only to the addressees and would not be forwarded. If no one was home, arrangements could be made with the post office for an evening delivery. If the veteran chose, he did not have to cash the bonds immediately but could draw three percent interest on each bond after July 1937.

In order to redeem the bonds, veterans would have to go to the post office to certify the bonds with their signature. Positive identification of the veteran by postal workers or a witness accompanying the veteran to the post office was required. The local American Legion posts agreed to have representatives at the post offices to verify the identification of the veterans. H. S. Link, the American Legion service officer in Peru, said that almost 400 veterans would be receiving bonds in his city.

After certification was completed, the bonds would be forwarded to the main Chicago post office where U.S. Treasury checks would be issued and returned to the veteran, a process taking about 72 hours. At that point, veterans could cash the government checks anywhere.

Illinois Valley businesses saw the bonus bonds as an opportunity to increase sales. For the next week, the papers carried ads encouraging veterans to spend their bonus money. An example of the ads used to entice veterans was this one placed by LaSalle Buick Sales at 328 Third St. and Palmatier Motor Sales located at First and Wright Streets. It appeared in the June 17, 1936 edition of the *Post-Tribune*

THE WAR IS ON

Prices "Shot" ON OUR STOCK OF USED CARS

BONUS Offer Special

FREE GASOLINE
With Any Used Car Bought Right Now

Hey, Buddy! We're happy you are getting your Bonus and we hope you make the best of it so we suggest you invest a part of it in the car you have always wanted. Every car in our stock has been reconditioned and to make this sale doubly attractive we're going to give 50 gallons of Gasoline FREE to any Veteran buying a Car during this sale—no strings or "special conditions"—this is our Bonus Offer to give you more for your Bonus!

Come In and See These Cars

1—1935 Model 61 Buick with Trunk	1—1930 Cadillac 4-Door Sedan
1—1934 Model 47 Buick 4-Door Sedan	1—1935 Ford DeLuxe 4-Door Sedan
1—1934 Model 67 Buick 4-Door Sedan	1—1930 Ford Light Delivery Truck
1—1933 Model 96 Buick 5-Pass. Coupe	1—1930 Ford Truck with Grain Box
1—1933 Model 56 Buick Sport Coupe	1—1929 Hudson Sedan
1—1932 Model 91 Buick 5-Pass. Brm	1—1929 Hupmobile 4-Door Sedan
1—1931 Model 91 Buick, 5-Pass De Luxe Brougham	1—1926 Hupmobile 4-Door Sedan (Driven only 3,300 Miles)

Terrence Martin, the local magistrate in LaSalle, estimated that each of the 500 men who applied for the bonds would receive an average of $500 in bonds. Speaking to a reporter from the LaSalle newspaper, he said, "This new money should do much to restore some of the prosperity we've been missing these last few years." On June 15, postal carriers in LaSalle delivered 309 envelopes containing the bonds. Fifty more envelopes, each containing an average of $600 in bonds, arrived after the mailmen left on their rounds. Shortly after the LaSalle post office opened at 7 a.m., Edward Baker of West Third Street was the first to pick up his bonds. However, it was attorney Michael Faletti who was first to have his bonds certified at the LaSalle office. Jimmie Keys, a well-known local fight promoter, who served with Company C at Camp Grant from 1918 to 1919, was also among the first to receive his bonds. By noon, 30 veterans completed the 15-minute certification process. Veterans, who could not be identified by postal workers, had to return with a witness, who was known to the local postal authorities. The Peru postmaster reported that 244 registered letters were delivered to veterans. He said he would keep his facility open until 8 p.m. so they could certify their bonds.

In Oglesby, 59 letters went out to the veterans. Dr. L. Shaughnessy had the distinction of being the first WWI veteran from Oglesby to receive his bonds. Postmaster John McCann expected his mailmen to deliver bonds to about 110 veterans.

Volunteers from the Ottawa American Legion along with members of Co. C of the 129th Infantry assisted veterans with their applications. Postmaster John Hart said that about $500 on average was redeemed from each of the 160 bondholders in Ottawa.

Not only veterans but also local farmers were receiving federal benefits. Those farmers, who took advantage of the government's program to subsidize acreage designated for the soil conservation program, received checks. The national average payment was $10 per acre, but farmers in the Illinois Valley received higher payments. LaSalle County farmers were paid $13.90 for each acre sewn with a soil conservation crop. In Putnam County, payments amounted to $15 per acre. Bureau County farmers received slightly more, $15.10. Henry County farmers subscribing to the program were paid $14.60, while in Marshall County the rate was $13 per acre. Grundy County farmers did not fare as well, receiving only $12.70 per acre. Nonetheless, planting soil conservation crops seemed to be a good investment.

The Dust Bowl in the summer of '36 spread to southeastern Colorado, northeastern New Mexico, western Kansas, western Oklahoma, and northwestern Texas. North Dakota, Montana, and Wyoming were designated as emergency drought areas. The searing heat reached 105° in north central Illinois on July 6. The hottest temperature previously recorded in Ottawa was 108° on July 23, 1934. In order to cope with the high temperatures, the 42 WPA men working on the removal of interurban lines in Ottawa started work at 5 a.m. and finished their shift at 12:30 p.m. Even the *Republican-Times* changed from two editions a day to a single one "to find relief from the heat" for its employees. In LaSalle, the men working on the L-P stadium began work at 4 a.m. to beat the heat.

The weather continued to make the headlines during July. Crop losses across the country were initially estimated at $300 million, but that figure would climb along with the thermometer readings. On Wednesday, July 8, the people in North Dakota were

152

baking as the temperature soared to 120°. At the same time in Ottawa, it was only 104°.

The only good result of the rising temperatures, if indeed anything could be viewed as "good," was the government's purchase of millions of tons of meat from distressed farmers who sold off their animals because of the prolonged drought. Some of the relief meat was sent to the LaSalle commodity depot. The Illinois National Guard was assigned to aid in the distribution. In addition, a carload of fresh peas from Washington State was due to arrive in LaSalle. Relief recipients were told to stay at home to receive the food since it was perishable.

If the heat wasn't bad enough, another major problem soon confronted local farmers. Thousands of grasshoppers were devastating the crops in Groveland and Hope Townships in LaSalle County. First, they attacked the hay fields. When those crops were destroyed, the insects swarmed into the nearby corn fields. In Lostant, an entire 40-acre alfalfa field was laid waste.

The twin scourges of soaring temperatures and insect infestation continued. A new heat record was set in Ottawa on July 14 when the thermometer hit 112°. The grasshopper swarms spread through crops in Richard, Ophir, Rutland, and Dayton Townships. Farmers put out poison to try to stop the ravenous insects but had little success. Soon, Wallace Township was added to the growing list of townships that had been invaded. On July 17, the 13-day heat wave finally broke as clouds covered the area with .3" of rain, but it was only a temporary respite. More hot weather was on the way.

Through that long, hot summer, the CCC continued to work along the I-M Canal. The limestone-lined canal locks were deteriorating. Rather than quarrying more limestone, concrete walls were finished to look somewhat like the original material.

CCC workers cleaned out the rock and stone at Lock 8 and replaced the deteriorated material with concrete. (Lewis University)

153

CCC men worked in the mud at the bottom of Lock 7 and repaired the lock walls in 1936. (Lewis University)

Below: The CCC made repairs at Lock 6 at Channahon. Note the CCC tent next to the lock tender's house and the pump at the open gates to the lock. An earthen dam was built across one end of the lock to allow the CCC to pump out the water and make repairs. (Lewis University collection)

154

At Camp Marseilles in Illini State Park, Company 613 used oak logs, fieldstones, and Joliet limestone, to build several large shelters and a cabin with fireplaces. Several council fire rings, built by the CCC, still exist today. When the CCC work was completed, the park had six shelters for park visitors.

Above: The stone drinking fountain and wooden picnic tables at Marasottawa shelter at Illini State Park were replaced with a modern restroom and more durable picnic tables. (Marseilles Library)

Left: The CCC built stone fireplaces at both ends of the Marasottawa shelter.

Local stone was used to build water fountains and fireplaces. Five water fountains were constructed at Illini State Park, but they are no longer functional.

(Photos by author)

Water for drinking fountains and other facilities at Illini State Park was pumped from this well house, constructed by the CCC. Previous to this, water was piped in from Marseilles, but that plumbing would soon be removed. The facility is still operating today.

This restroom with its distinctive rock footings, log walls, and wooden shingles – now heavily covered with moss – is another structure erected by the CCC at Illini State Park.

The Pine Glen shelter at Illini State Park included a stone fireplace that was constructed in such a way that it could be used for both indoor and outdoor cooking. (Photos by author)

This is one of the CCC-built council rings found in Illini State Park. At right is the Illinois River and at center in the background is one of the two-seater shelters built at the park in the 1930's. (Photo by author)

The CCC men had time for competitive sports. Company 613 at Camp Marseilles was scheduled to compete in a track meet against Camp Thornton. The following month, a swim meet at the Starved Rock pool was on the calendar. In this photo, the un-named players hold their basketball trophy. (Marseilles Library)

Company 613 was very competitive in baseball and defeated Camp Thornton's Co. 2605 by a score of 8-5. It was the seventh straight year that the company won the championship title in the CCC league. Reorganization of the CCC resulted in the transfer of Co. 613 from Camp Marseilles to the abandoned site of Camp Illini.

CCC men from Illini State Park inspect a bridge. (Marseilles Library)

In August, the CCC men at Starved Rock were asked if they wanted to participate for two weeks in military maneuvers with Company C of the 129th Infantry. Fifteen men temporarily gave up their job of building rustic fences at Starved Rock and joined the Guard unit when it headed to Allegan, MI. Those participating in the military training returned to the state park and attended weekly drills at the armory for which they received additional compensation. The two CCC companies at Starved Rock were also notified in August that they should be prepared to fight forest fires spreading in northern Wisconsin and Michigan.

The summer heat continued to take its toll on crops raising corn futures to over $1 a bushel, the highest figure since 1930. By August, the price of corn hit $1.19 per bushel, the highest figure since November 1925. The drought also had its impact on milk production. The price for a quart of milk rose to 10¢ in Ottawa. In Streator and LaSalle, the price jumped to 12¢ a quart.

Itinerant hobos constructed flimsy shelters along the Rock Island railroad tracks and the I-M Canal. One such camp was established east of LaSalle. According to Len Keenan in his *Rockwell History*, "Hoover City" was a collection of wooden and cardboard boxes located on the south bank of the I-M towpath east of the aqueduct. Some of the hobos also lived below the Rockwell road, where the bottom road passed near the Little Vermilion aqueduct.

Shacks along the old steamboat basin in LaSalle sheltered many of the destitute hobos during the 1930's. (Phil Klabel collection)

The local police tried to keep the city free of itinerant hobos because of petty theft. In one case in August 1936, they arrested Adam Grighum, who occupied one of the shanties on the south bank of the I-M Canal. They found a stash of merchandise worth $350-$400 stolen from the Ginsberg-Khoury clothing store on First Street in LaSalle. Police assumed he had an accomplice, Jack Doyle, who lived in the shack with him, but Doyle apparently escaped capture by hopping a freight train.

Another man who had lived in a nearby shack was Carl Hansen. His body was found along the Rock Island tracks on Aug. 10. Apparently, he was struck and decapitated by the east-bound freight train. A year earlier, he had been severely injured when he fell 35 feet from a landing on the east side of the Illinois Central RR Bridge. After a time in the hospital, he returned to his hobo shack.

During the summer, the Illinois Department of Public Welfare in Springfield explained the procedures to qualify for retirement under the Social Security program. Although 123 of the 500 senior citizens who filed applications in LaSalle County were approved by the Springfield office, only 81 of them were scheduled to receive vouchers in July. The others would begin the following month. Vouchers totaling $972 would be sent to applicants in LaSalle County. The payments, ranging from $3 to $15, were actually for June but not paid until mid-July.

For the younger crowd, one of the WPA programs that involved many children and teens was the federal recreation program. The director of the WPA program in LaSalle, Joseph Delmanowski, had a registration form printed in the *Post-Tribune* calling for boys and girls to sign up for kittenball games at Hegeler Park. The boys were divided into two age groups, 6-10 and 10-15. The girls had only a single division. The WPA provided bats, baseballs, horseshoes, and volleyballs for the various activities at the park. Delmanowski asked the WPA for additional equipment including footballs, volleyball nets, checkers, and ping pong sets.

On Aug. 1, Harold Snedden, supervisor of the Oglesby program, met with an advisory committee to outline plans for fall and winter. Activities included handicraft classes, games, and ping pong at the dress factory. The Sacred Heart Church Hall would be used for tennis, ping pong, and games. Other activities, including touch football, playground ball, volleyball, horseshoe games, and an amateur night, would be held at Memorial Park. At Washington School, the WPA offered indoor baseball, boxing classes, tap dancing instruction, volleyball, and basketball.

The Oglesby summer recreational programs came to an end on Sept. 3 with a play day, which included foot races and an afternoon championship baseball game in the junior division. That evening an amateur variety show with singing and dancing was planned. Some of the handicrafts, created during the summer, were displayed in the sewing room window on Walnut Street next to the

159

Arkins Drug Store. Once the school year got under way, Snedden said there would be hikes, basketball games and other activities before and after school during the week and on Saturdays in Oglesby. Special programs were scheduled for the major holidays beginning with Halloween, with a costume parade from the Washington School to Memorial Park. Other events were planned for Thanksgiving, Christmas, and New Year's.

One of the fall WPA recreation programs in LaSalle was a soapbox derby on Oct. 3. In a previous derby, Billy Cummings had done well with his chrome-plated "Pikula Special." Also back for another try was Tony Horzen. His "Miss LaSalle" threw a wheel only 30 feet from the finish line in a previous race. Recreation director Delmanowski warned parents that the WPA would not be responsible for any injuries.

Although organizers anticipated as many as 40 entries, only 17 racers were brought to the starting line at Fifth and LaHarpe. Arnold Cassidy, Tom O'Conner, Steve Slomian, and Ed Donahue assisted Robert Kwatick, the starter. Donahue lined up the cars for each heat. Bobby Kwatick sat in his "WPA Special" hoping to win one of the numerous prizes donated by area merchants. Cummings was eliminated in the first heat when he lost control and ran into a curb. Johnny Janko won his first heat in the "Janko Phantom," but there were more races ahead.

When all the heats were completed, the finalists were announced. John Ritz in his "Green Diamond" won the senior division for boys 10-16. Tony Horzen took first in "Miss LaSalle" for the junior division championship for boys 6-10 years old. Horzen immediately challenged Ritz to one last race. The result was a tie as both boys crossed the finish line at the same time.

WPA also sponsored a number of education programs in a broad area of northern Illinois, which included Henry and LaSalle Counties. WPA paid teachers' salaries for general education classes in French, Spanish, history, civics, arithmetic, speech, drama, and music. In another program, over a thousand residents in the 13 counties making up District 1 in Illinois were taking courses in citizenship and naturalization taught by 35 teachers. Adults, some of whom were illiterate, were taking basic courses in reading, writing, spelling, geography, and social science. A third aspect of the education program focused on parenting skills, including child psychology and health. Cooking and sewing classes were also included. To improve job skills, the WPA hired individuals to teach vocational skills, such as typing, shorthand, bookkeeping, art, and other business and commercial subjects. WPA selected Marseilles as

160

one of the seven locations for the establishment of a nursery school, where children 2-5 years of age could attend an all-day program. In LaSalle County, 347 children and adults participated in the education program while in Henry County the number was 184.

School construction provided many jobs in the Depression. Marseilles H.S. was built in 1935-36. (Marseilles Lib.)

In the fall of 1936, construction work continued at L-P High School. For two weeks in September, the men covered the practice field with sod brought in from Dalzell. The concrete retaining walls around the new stadium were finally finished. In October, WPA funds were exhausted on an Oglesby road project so the men were transferred to L-P High School.

Other towns continued infrastructure improvements. With a $20,000 WPA grant, Dalzell Mayor Arthur Tonelli approved a storm sewer project that would employ 30 men for eight months. Tonica received money to pay for new sidewalks.

On Oct. 13, the WPA distributed the last food and clothing shipments to relief recipients in LaSalle, Bureau, Putnam, and Grundy Counties. Eight trucks were loaded with canned roast beef and hamburger, evaporated milk, dried peas, and flour as well as clothing and household necessities. Because WPA funds were limited, the counties would have to pick up the tab for trucking, rent, and utilities to maintain the service in the months ahead.

On Oct. 29, 1936, movie patrons in LaSalle looked forward to the reopening of the Majestic Theater after $50,000 was spent on renovation. This drawing was reprinted from the Oct. 28, 1936 edition of the *Post-Tribune*.

161

The 1936 race for the White House between FDR and Gov. Alf Landon of Kansas generated less interest than previous elections

in the Illinois Valley since neither candidate bothered to visit the area. On Oct. 31, the Republican vice presidential candidate, Frank Knox, made campaign stops at Mendota, LaSalle, and Ottawa. The crowds were small due to inclement weather.

Knox became FDR's secretary of the Navy following the election. (National Archives)

Landon (pictured at right) supported the concepts behind many New Deal programs but criticized FDR for the high cost of the Social Security program and wasteful spending that created 75 new government agencies and bureaus and boosted the national debt from $21 billion to $34 billion. In spite of the criticisms, FDR swept the election with 523-8 electoral votes. Bureau

County gave Landon the majority vote, but voters in LaSalle County gave FDR a majority. Landon lost Putnam County by only one vote.

On Sunday, Nov. 8, another special event in the area was the open house for the new Lincoln School in Spring Valley. The structure, designed with eight modern classrooms, replaced a building that was 50 years old and, according to the LaSalle paper, was in "deplorable condition." A substantial PWA grant was used to partially fund the construction of the school. After a successful referendum, the school board approved the issuance of $29,800 in bonds. Construction got underway Mar. 19, 1936. The front of the building, facing a spacious playground area, would extend for 122 feet in a north-south direction. The school was ready for classes to begin on Nov. 9.

Spring Valley's Lincoln School as it appeared in 2008. (Photo by author)

162

While the PWA and WPA projects temporarily took men off the relief rolls, it became obvious that the Social Security program would be a permanent feature of the government's plan to deal with future periods of unemployment. In order to fund the program, it was necessary to tax both the employers and employees. Businessmen in the Illinois Valley began to learn more about their role in late November when postal workers delivered 2,500 application forms, informational circulars, and instructions to 300 local businesses to assign Social Security numbers to each worker. The folders described the retirement benefits and taxes applied to wages. Once the information was completed, the Social Security Board and the Internal Revenue Service would compile the wage records of each employee beginning after Jan. 1, 1937.

Those unemployment benefits were on the minds of the 135 men, who suddenly lost their jobs at the L-P stadium project. The number of workers on that project had soared from 84, when the project started, to 235 in '36. Supervisors at the stadium determined that 100 men would be more than enough to carry on the work. The problem was that WPA funds ran out in many towns for other projects. To keep everyone busy, men had been transferred to the L-P stadium project. But now, that job site was overstaffed. There wasn't enough concrete and gravel available to keep the crew busy.

Fortunately, the concrete for the L-P stadium finally arrived, and by mid-December, the ramps leading to the stadium could be poured. With the concrete work nearly completed, there only remained the installation of 16 risers for the seats and the press box at the top of the stands. Other facilities needing completion included the ticket booths and the field house locker rooms, showers, restroom facilities, and storage rooms. In addition, the football gridiron had to be covered with sod and seats installed in the spring.

Looking forward to the holidays in 1936, nine NYA boys were assigned to help the local Boy Scouts repair and repaint donated toys, which would be distributed by the Big Hearts organization. Stella Merrick, the NYA supervisor in LaSalle County, also selected some girls to work on the toy project and to help the Elks with distribution. Baskets, magazine racks, and smoking stands were constructed as Christmas gifts at the Lincoln School.

The employment outlook brightened at the end of the year when Westclox announced plans to expand its facilities by building a 30,000 square foot addition. The expansion, expected to cost $250,000 to $300,000, would be the first major addition since 1929. Such an expansion was welcomed news, but the realization of the project would take time.

1937
CONSTRUCTION WAS EVERYWHERE

For many months, LaSalle residents could see the progress being made on the high school addition. Although a formal inspection would not be held until spring, a *Post-Tribune* reporter was given a tour of the new facility on Jan. 19. The journalist noted that although there were some things missing, such as Venetian blinds, furniture, and blackboards, the classrooms were "virtually completed." The largest room, he was told, was the combination study hall and cafeteria. It could handle 320 students, who would enter through double doors and proceed down one of two serving lines. The kitchen area, the reporter learned, was equipped with "two ranges, a stock kettle, a fruit and vegetable peeler, and a dish washer." The library, large enough to accommodate 160 students, was also nearing completion. About 1,700 lockers lined the long hallways. On the second floor, the reporter found a meeting room, large enough for 150 students. Six small conference rooms adjoined the library. The reporter also toured the girls' gym facilities. While inspecting the science rooms, he observed some subtle changes in educational methods. "Blackboard space has been reduced, and poster board space has been increased. It being held that there is no longer as much blackboard work as some years back," he noted.

A hundred NYA students from Streator and other schools participated in a book-repair project Feb. 8-15. The project involved repairing damaged books for L-P's library and other libraries in the area at no cost.

The CCC men at Starved Rock had little to do in the winter of 1937 until the water receded on 156 acres of land donated by Lehigh Cement on the east side of the Vermilion River. The plan was to create a bird sanctuary with 7-8 acres set aside as a lagoon, ranging in depth from six inches to six feet, for migrating waterfowl. A CCC-sponsored ice carnival was held in late January. The six local CCC companies had planned to hold the event in early January, but the ice was too thin. By the end of the month, it was safe enough, so the men cleared the snow off a large area of a backwater pond for ice skating.

The weather in January caused a major problem in southern Illinois along the Ohio River, which was at flood stage. The federal government estimated that it would be necessary to move 500,000 people living along the Mississippi and Ohio Rivers to higher ground. Responding to the needs of the people in that region, the garment workers at the Illinois Valley sewing centers were instructed to use all available flannel in stock to manufacture nightgowns and bloomers. Their supply of corduroy was used to manufacture trousers. The Streator, Marseilles, South Ottawa, and Peru sewing centers also turned out pajamas, sheets, and men's shorts. After the LaSalle County centers loaded a truck from the state highway department with the clothing, it headed to Marion, IL.

Fred Hunt, who was in charge of the surplus commodity depot in LaSalle, admitted that shipping thousands of clothing items to the south would cause shortages for families on relief in his area. "The need in the flood area of southern Illinois is greater than we have here, and as a result the sewing centers are cooperating with the IERC in providing relief," he explained.

Dr. A. Zukowski, president of the Tri-Cities Kiwanis Club, received a telegram from the division headquarters in Bloomington, urging the immediate shipment of clothing to Harrisburg, IL. In response, a truckload of clothing was sent that same night with the promise of additional shipments through the week. Ottawa also did its part to bring relief by loading a truck with 12 large boxes of clothing according to Mrs. Dortha Osborn, the LaSalle County representative of the IERC. John Grayhack, the assistant engineer of the highway office in Ottawa, said that the men driving the truck to Marion would stay there to assist in any way.

The local Red Cross made an urgent appeal for more funds. A quota of $2,000 was established for the Tri-Cities. "The new finances are urgently needed to alleviate the suffering of thousands upon thousands made homeless in the Ohio and Mississippi river valley," said Mrs. Bradley Turner, Chairman of the local Red Cross chapter. Within 24 hours of the notification of the emergency need, not only money but also food, clothing, and blankets poured into the local center. The Alger movie theaters in LaSalle and Peru donated $647, which was collected at their midnight shows.

Offers of aid came from many groups. Boy Scouts from 23 troops went house to house collecting food and clothing. The Boy Scouts, Girl Scouts, Women's Club, and the Kiwanis Club teamed up to pack the supplies on a truck headed to Bloomington. From there, the boxes were re-shipped to Harrisburg. The director of the WPA outdoor sanitation project also offered to direct his men to assist in the canvassing and packing.

On Jan. 30, a group of 96 young men and women from the NYA in LaSalle, Peru, and Oglesby organized a tag day to collect donations for the Red Cross. Similar tag days were held in Streator, Ottawa, and Marseilles. NYA groups also raised funds for flood relief by holding social events, such as card parties.

The CCC also responded to the growing crisis. The detachment of 15 men included Ray Levandowski of LaSalle, camp foreman at Parkman Plain; Joseph Kroll of Peru, the camp foreman of Company 2601; Frank Slimko of Peru; Ben Boyle of Ottawa; and Arthur Miller from Marseilles. Along with other men from Joliet, Pana, Benton, and Cowden, IL, they boarded five trucks and headed to Ft. Sheridan. Capt. William Kalisz, the senior officer at Camp LaSalle, was appointed chief motor transport officer for the battalion. Lt. Paul Jolley, junior officer of Company 1609, aided Kalisz. Other men from the CCC camps at Buffalo Rock, Marseilles, and Brandon-Morris would soon join the men from Camp LaSalle at Ft. Sheridan.

By the end of January, flood waters at Cairo rose to over 58 feet. The concrete seawall protected the city to a flood stage of 60 feet. As an additional precaution, over four feet of dirt was packed onto the permanent embankments. During the crisis, the CCC men from the Illinois Valley were stationed for two weeks at Little Rock, AR. Most of the men returned to their local camps by Feb. 25.

When things returned to normal, the WPA projects refocused on keeping men occupied. The pond at Second and Glen in Oglesby was flooded on Feb. 11, so that residents could enjoy ice skating. The WPA craft classes were busy building birdhouses.

The Oglesby WPA recreation program included building birdhouses as part of the crafts classes. (Oglesby Library)

Sometimes WPA job assignments had to be adjusted to deal with local conditions. For instance, Miss Celia Scapini, a typist from Oglesby, was assigned to index all of the Peru municipal ordinances. Ordinarily, a woman on relief from Peru would have been hired but no one was qualified. The tedious WPA work required additional typists and took many months to complete.

PWA and local funds were used to complete a number of elementary and high schools in the area. Contracts were let for a new school in Lostant on Dec. 10, 1935. With safety as a major consideration, no wood was used in the construction of the walls ceiling, or roof. The contractors for the H-shaped structure used bricks from Lowell for the walls. Steel was used for doors and window frames. The concrete floors were covered with grey and green asphalt tiles. A playground and athletic field with an eighth-mile track were located behind the school.

On Monday, Feb. 8, a formal dedication was held for the $80,000 Lostant School, which was built on the site of the old school. Federal funding paid for about 40 percent of the cost. An open house was held in the afternoon to allow residents to inspect the combined grade and high school facility. In the evening, Alfred H. Bell, the president of School District 400, and John Wieland, the state superintendent of schools, addressed the crowd.

The Lostant School now houses only elementary students. (Photo by author)

On Mar. 2, the *Post-Tribune* began a two-part story on the long-anticipated opening of the Bureau County courthouse. The writer of the detailed story, Mrs. Ethel Knauf, said the new structure would be the fourth courthouse for Bureau County. She described how visitors would approach the main entrance walking on a six-foot wide sidewalk up to "a flight of polished granite steps" leading to a 40-foot wide terrace "edged with a balustrade of granite with fluted polished posts at each side."

Plans for the remodeling of the Bureau County courthouse in Princeton had been revealed to the public on Mar. 27, 1936. At that time, it was expected that the exterior and interior work would be finished by the middle of December, but it was not until the spring of 1937 that the building was ready for occupancy.

The first real Bureau County courthouse built in 1845 in Princeton was described as a little "bandbox." By contrast, the 1937 building was called a "palace." The construction price of the original building was $8,764 compared to $217,000 for the new building – $119,500 was paid by the county, and the PWA provided a grant of $97,500. A small portion of the foundation of the old courthouse was used in the 1937 building.

The new Bureau County courthouse was virtually fireproof. The only wood used was in the door casings. The exterior door and window frames were fabricated from aluminum. The baseboard of the interior vestibule was lined with green Vermont marble while the walls were covered in tan marble obtained in Kasota, MN. (Photo by author)

Knauf continued her article with a virtual tour of offices from the county and circuit clerks and county treasurer to the judge's chambers and the sheriff's office and jail. She also described the courtroom and adjoining jury room, law reference library, and state's attorney offices.

Another major event was the opening of the L-P High School "annex," as the LaSalle paper referred to it. The new building housed 42 classrooms, which would be used to replace the 30 classrooms abandoned in "Old Main." The extra rooms would be used for an expanded curriculum. The new addition also provided a girls' gym, a small auditorium, band and music rooms, and a combined cafeteria and study hall.

The L-P High School annex was scheduled for occupancy in February 1937. It was estimated that the $460,000 expansion would provide enough space for over 2,000 students at the high school. (Photo by author)

Although there was no formal dedication, an open house was held on Friday, Mar. 12 from 3:00 p.m. until 5:30 p.m. and again in the evening from 7 p.m. until 10 p.m. It was estimated that 10,000 adults and children toured the facilities that day. The *Post-Tribune* reported, "Even the boiler room, reached through an underground passageway, drew hundreds who marveled at the modern efficiency of the heating facilities." Three officials from the PWA office in Chicago participated in the final inspection of the building.

WPA accomplishments also drew attention. On Mar. 10, there was an exhibition of the district's WPA crafts programs at the Hotel Faust in Rockford. Articles made in the Oglesby program included photographs from the amateur photography department, woven baskets, smoking stands, lamp stands, and beadwork. Visitors to the exhibit had special praise for a copper tapping project. Ottawa's display also had projects in weaving and photography. Granville displayed handmade lamps and other articles crafted from walnut. One of the most interesting articles from Princeton was a picture of two horses hand-burned into a wooden background.

At the end of the month, orders came from the Ft. Sheridan District Headquarters that CCC Camp LaSalle at Starved Rock, was going to be closed by Mar. 31. The CCC had occupied the camp continuously since July 15, 1934, but the remaining 155 men of Co. 2601 would be reassigned to other camps in the Sixth Corps Area.

The news came as a shock to the National Park Service (NPS), which would have to realign its construction plans. Park officials said there was enough work to keep the CCC busy for "several years." Now, the barracks, including the headquarters for the NPS, would be torn down to make room for more parking spaces. On Mar. 27, CCC equipment was loaded into a fleet of trucks and taken to Ft. Sheridan. Company 1609, which occupied Parkman Plain, was not affected by the decision.

Lone Point shelter, built by the CCC at the east end of Starved Rock State Park, still stands near the banks of the Illinois River.

Another CCC-built shelter remains at the west end of Starved Rock near the visitor's center. (Photos by author)

Rather than being reassigned, 100 of the men in Co. 2601 decided to accept discharges on Mar. 31, the last day of their enrollment. The other 55 men were scheduled to be reassigned to other companies at Marseilles, Rock Island, and Thornton. An

170

additional 38 men from other camps were transferred to Company 1609 to assist with the demolition of Camp LaSalle.

At the end of the month, William B. Foster wrote a story in the Mar. 29 edition of the *Post-Tribune* describing the history and accomplishments of Company 2601. "The new lodge and adjoining cabins compose the outstanding piece of work in which enrollees took part. The canyon bridges, of the strongest rustic construction, are regarded as the best of their type in the entire state," Foster wrote.

The cabins built by the CCC at Starved Rock State Park provided more rustic lodgings compared to the amenities of the park hotel. (Photo by author)

In addition to the CCC construction projects, Foster praised the winter ice carnival and boxing tournament and the enrollees participation in vocational, avocational, and academic courses. The highest participation was in welding, typing, shorthand, bookkeeping, and mechanical drawing courses. Also popular with the men were the hobbies, which included archery, weather studies, metal and woodworking, and art programs. Referring to the previous summer, Foster closed his article saying, "Especial interest was shown (by visitors) in the beautifully landscaped flower gardens and rock garden, all built by the enrollees."

Towns, large and small, always seemed to have sufficient resources to mark historic events. For LaMoille that came on May 31, 1937, when the city observed its Centennial. A.D. Steckel served as general chairman of the festivities. Miss Marcia Graves was chosen as Miss LaMoille. The first major event of the day was a parade at 10:30 in the morning. Other events included a ball game, concert, historical pageant, and a dance.

Mayor Orr in LaSalle continued his efforts to find federal funding for a swimming pool in Hegeler Park in LaSalle on June 18.

The WPA's portion of the cost would be $57,992 for the labor and another $6,392 for materials. The city's share would be $6,314 for labor and $52,076 in materials. The total outlay would be over $122,000. Voters agreed to a $25,000 bond issue to help pay the city's portion of the expenses. On June 25, the plan was approved by the Rockford WPA office.

Summer recreation programs were in the works at Oglesby's Memorial Park, Marquette Field, and the Sacred Heart tennis courts. The WPA-sponsored program was scheduled to begin on June 21.

Interest also grew in a plan to build a two-mile highway on the east side of Oglesby. A $92,000 grant from the WPA combined with $25,000 from LaSalle County and an additional $16,000 from the Oglesby city council appeared to be sufficient to fund the road. But, funding was just one of many steps to be taken before the new highway would be completed. The planning and construction of a major road would take years to complete.

Even though it was only mid-June, Cavalier football fans were already looking forward to the first games to be played at the new L-P stadium. In mid-June, seats were being installed. One hundred men were working in two shifts, five days a week, installing the aluminum-painted redwood planks. There was also more concrete to pour for the floors in the locker room and the ramp on the southeast corner of the stadium. In addition, the landscaping and the lighting installation were not yet finished.

During the summer of 1937, the director of the Illinois NYA released a summary of student grant distribution the previous year. He reported $1,462 was paid to help 242 students in LaSalle County. L-P High School had 35 students enrolled in the NYA program, and the L-P-O Junior College had 38 students. Each school collected $378 from NYA for monthly wages. Other area high schools participating in the NYA program included Mendota (19 students), Ottawa Township (18), Tonica (3), and St. Bede (5). The highest wage a high school student was paid was $6 a month, not much, but sufficient to pay for carfare, lunches, and incidentals. The junior college students received an average of $15 each month.

Each summer, needy families awaited supplemental federal food shipments. At the end of the month, word came that 14 carloads of potatoes were due to arrive at the commodity depot in LaSalle. Fred Hundt, head of the IERC in LaSalle, notified those on relief to come to the depot to pick up their allotment since it was simply impractical to bring the potatoes to each person's house.

Improvements in railroad transportation were also in the news. The Burlington *Zephyrs* had been speeding through Earlville, Mendota, and Princeton since 1934. Now, the Rock Island's new *Rocket* was finally ready to make a test run on July 8, 1937. Around 1 p.m., a crowd of about 100 was on hand at the Peru depot to mark the occasion. The new streamliner, pulling three cars, sped past the crowd at 70 mph. The train was only traveling from Chicago to Bureau on a test run. At 2:15 p.m., it passed through Peru again on the return trip. Those who missed the historic run had another chance to see the train the following Sunday at 8:30 a.m., when the *Rocket* traveled from Chicago to Denver.

The following month on Sept. 4, a Peoria-bound *Rocket* pulling four stainless steel cars, named the *Ottawa, Joliet, LaSalle,* and *Peoria,* stopped near the LaSalle depot. It was a public relations effort by the Rock Island RR to acquaint potential passengers with the accommodations aboard the new trains soon to be put into regular service between Chicago and Peoria. Traveling at an average speed of 80-90 mph, the train would make two round-trips every day, stopping in LaSalle each time. The 161 miles between Chicago and Peoria would be covered in little more than 2½ hours. Hundreds of local residents took the opportunity on Saturday morning to inspect the new engine and walk through the passenger cars. The next exhibition stops were at Ottawa and Joliet.

July 1937 marked the beginning of the Rock Island RR's transition from steam engines to diesel-electric streamliners. This photo, showing a Rock Island *Rocket* on the right, was taken only two years after the new train made its debut in the Illinois Valley. By that time, the *Rockets* were a common sight, running on a fixed schedule. It was one more example of how businessmen were innovating to cope with the Depression. (W. Raia)

Innovation was also on the mind of George Malone, Starved Rock's park custodian. He thought the establishment of a zoo of native animals at the state park might draw more visitors. An enclosure east of the swimming pool was already in place at Fox

173

Canyon. Its high walls, supplemented by wire mesh, would be an ideal location for the buffalo, elk, and even a bear. Apparently, the idea, suggested in late July, wasn't in the cards. He was informed on Sept. 11 that even the four raccoons and five fox he had in cages would have to be turned over for the game warden to be released.

Viewed from the rim, Fox Canyon with its steep walls at Starved Rock State Park, was briefly considered as a possible enclosure to house native animals in a zoo-like environment. (Photo by author)

Keeping the family fed seemed to be more important than visiting a zoo for the striking workers at M&H Zinc. The men had been on strike for six months, but they finally ended their walkout on July 3. Almost three weeks passed, but the roasters, acid plant, and a furnace were still not in operation. Six hundred men waited for production to resume.

The WPA's Federal Recreation program in Oglesby offered a variety of activities for children and adults. On July 30, the second annual bicycle carnival was held along with a variety of foot races including a cross-country race from East Walnut to Memorial Park. For those less athletically inclined, there was a croquet contest. Fancy and trick horseback riding rounded out the day's events. Prizes included 25 tickets to the Aida Theater.

Another celebration in Peru marked the completion of the Fourth Street paving project. The Trompeter Construction Co. won the contract, which was valued at $211,000. The main street in Peru had been paved with bricks, which were removed and replaced with a two-mile concrete roadway. Fourth Street was open to

ATTEND
PERU'S STREET
CELEBRATION
Saturday and Sunday, August 7th and 8th

We're proud to have had a part in this latest Peru accomplishment; another milestone in its progress.

TROMPETER
CONSTRUCTION CO
PERU, ILLINOIS

traffic on July 15. The curbs and sidewalks had not been finished so a formal dedication was postponed until Saturday, Aug. 7, 1937.

A two-day celebration was organized. On Saturday afternoon, there were pet, costume, and bicycle parades for the children, followed by bicycle races and a concert by the Peru grade school band. At 7 p.m. on Saturday, an accordion band presented a concert, which was followed by drill team competitions between the Peru Lady Maccabees, and the Odd Fellows from Peru and LaSalle.

The events on Sunday started at 1:30 p.m., when Mayor Hasse cut a ribbon to officially open the street. The parade started at the bridge on East Fifth Street and ended at Cross Street. Parade judges stood on the reviewing stand on the canopy of the Hotel Peru. Ribbons were presented to outstanding floats as they arrived at the hotel location. No less than eleven American Legion drum and bugle corps units from distant cities such as Cicero, Galva, Elgin, Dixon, and DeKalb marched in the parade. The Junior Corps from Kewanee also participated. Following the parade, the various Legion units participated in an exhibition drill contest. At 8 p.m., notable figures on the speakers' platform at Fourth and Peoria Streets prepared to deliver dedication speeches and convey congratulatory remarks.

More major projects were soon underway. Officials in Springfield decided that it was time to replace the old Starved Rock Hotel with a new building. Long-range plans called for the letting of bids on Sept. 10; ground breaking on Sept. 20; and completion in June 1938. In addition to the new 80-room facility, there would be a gas station on the lower level of the park and a playground for small children similar to the Enchanted Island at the 1933 Chicago World's Fair. The playground was supposed to be constructed near the dismantled CCC barracks. The hotel's west wing would be demolished, but the main floor would be used to display Indian and pioneer artifacts. The second floor would house the offices for park employees.

Enchanted Island exhibit at the 1933 World's Fair.

While these plans appeared to improve the local job situation, reductions in the WPA payroll in Illinois appeared to have the opposite effect in Marshall and Putnam Counties and other areas where the projects employed less than 150 men. Program cuts would apply to 11 of the 20 counties in the Rockford district. While LaSalle County would not be affected, Marshall County with 118 men at work on WPA projects and Putnam County with 122 men on the WPA payroll would see further job reductions. Washington's decision to cut jobs in smaller counties was based on the high cost of supervision of the smaller projects. The Rockford district in particular was targeted with reductions because of its efficiency in finding private employment for men and women.

The coal mine in Mark continued to be one of those private industry employers, but the jobs were tenuous at best. On Sept. 15, Cox announced that he would call back 350 miners in ten days. How long those jobs would last was questionable since Cox wanted to sell the Prairie State mine and move his operations to Nason, IL.

Fortunately, not all temporary jobs were based on grants through the WPA or PWA. The Illinois General Assembly finally responded to the requests of the residents in Bureau and Putnam Counties for the construction of a new bridge over the Illinois River on Route 89. It had been a long and frustrating legislative battle beginning in 1931. The bridge project appeared to be a done-deal when the Senate unanimously approved the bridge bill 116-0 on June 19, 1931, but Gov. Louis Emmerson vetoed the measure. Fortunately, his successor, Gov. Henry Horner, approved a similar bill in 1933. Bids were let in April 1934, and construction began that month.

The old Rt. 89 river bridge at Spring Valley was closed to traffic on May 25, 1934 so that dismantling could begin.
(Mautino Library)

Before construction moved ahead, rights to build a viaduct over the Rock Island railroad tracks at Route 89 had to be obtained. After much delay due to the weather, the 1,773-foot river bridge, costing a half million dollars, was completed in 1937.

Engineers had taken care to locate the center span almost 62 feet over the normal river level, allowing clearance for the tallest vessels. Even at the high water mark, there was 44 feet of clearance. The deck was 23 feet in width.

It was time to celebrate the opening of the new bridge in mid-September. To mark the beginning of the celebrations, the Spring Valley Municipal Band held concerts in Granville, Mark, and Standard on Friday, Sept. 17.

However, the more dramatic celebrations were held in Spring Valley. Beginning on Saturday afternoon, aerial bombs were fired at 1 o'clock to alert everyone that the two-day festivities had officially commenced. Next, a pet parade from Power Street down

176

through the Spring Valley business area got underway. An hour later, games and races for children were held along St. Paul Street. Boys and girls participated in the egg, hobble, wheelbarrow, and tricycle races as they competed for monetary prizes. Even the men had an opportunity to compete in a wheelbarrow race – the prize was a case of beer. In late afternoon, the crowd enjoyed a number of vaudeville and circus acts. Everyone watched in amazement as Andy Bakalar, formerly of Ringling Brothers Circus, was shot out of a canon. Musical entertainment with performances by an accordion band and a concert by the Spring Valley Municipal Band concluded the evening's festivities.

Spring Valley's Municipal Band was directed by Angelo Fontecchio (at far left). The band manager was Nate Frank (in straw hat). (Mautino Library)

The celebration events continued on Sunday morning. The all-star baseball team from Putnam County took on the all-stars of Bureau County at 10 a.m. At 11 a.m., Spring Valley alleys were filled with participants in a boccie ball tournament. Other residents went to the area north of the park to see a head-on collision between two old cars, one donated by Joseph Balestri of the Chevrolet garage and the other by Mondo Rochetto of Happy's Service Station.

The formal opening of the bridge, was held at 1:30 p.m. Judge Cornelius Hollerich served as Master of Ceremonies. State's Attorney Walter Durley Boyle headed the Putnam County delegation while Judge William Wimbiscus represented Hall Township, and Attorney Paul Perona represented Spring Valley. Other public officials from the state and surrounding municipalities were on hand to add their remarks to the official program.

A crowd estimated at 25,000 lined the streets of Spring Valley as the Spring Valley Municipal Band led the parade. It was followed by commercial floats, the fire department, and political dignitaries. Even the Chicago and Northwestern RR brought a model of one of its first locomotives for the parade.

George Condie III, son of Mr. and Mrs. George Condie Jr., of Spring Valley was the winner of the bridge naming contest. The "Spring Valley Bridge" name was the best out of 23 entries according to the contest judges, who awarded the youth the $10 first prize. Some of the other entries included Granville-Spring Valley Bridge," "Illinois Valley Bridge," "Hall-Hopkins Bridge," and "Valley View Bridge."

(Plaque photo - Art Kistler - IDOT)

The Spring Valley Bridge, which crossed the Illinois River, was the Rt. 89 link connecting Spring Valley with Putnam County. It was dedicated in 1937. (Art Kistler-IDOT)

Governor Horner gave the opening address. He said he was gratified by the praise he received for his part in the accomplishment. However, he explained, "I didn't build this bridge; it was built by the workmen, who threw the rivets, who did the steel work; by the designers; by the highway department. The bridge has been built in a community that earned the right to have a bridge, and that is how they got it,"

Judge Wimbiscus praised numerous individuals, who supported the project saying, "We now have a most modern bridge thanks to Governor Horner, the state and national administration and all the officials who aided in getting the improvement."

178

In his brief remarks, Durley Boyle, the new Putnam County state's attorney, expressed the thanks of the people of his county for the new highway. He pointed out that it brought the people closer to St. Margaret's Hospital and would serve as an outlet to Spring Valley, Peru, and LaSalle.

On Sunday evening, there were vaudeville acts and a softball game between the city councils of Spring Valley and Peru at the ABC field. At 9 p.m., a fireworks display began with skyrockets and aerial bombs fired from the No. 1 coal mine dump. The two-day celebration ended with the presentation of awards.

The next major event in the Illinois Valley was the formal dedication of the L-P stadium on Oct. 1. The high school and junior college students were dismissed at 2:30 on Friday afternoon in order to allow a public inspection of the stadium and field house from 3:00 p.m. until 5:30 p.m. At that time, visiting political officials, WPA representatives, and the board of education and their spouses enjoyed a formal dinner in the high school cafeteria.

Before the kickoff, representatives of the American Legion posts in LaSalle, Peru, and Oglesby held a flag-raising ceremony while the band played the national anthem. The band wore the new military-style uniforms, which were tailored in dark blue serge with gold stripes running down the trousers. The caps were trimmed with gold braid with an eagle emblem topped with the L-P letters in gold on the visor. The evening's performance began with the band, led by Drum Major Jacqueline Hand, marching on to the field and playing "Pride of the Illini." At halftime, the Cavalier band formed an "S" for the visiting Joliet H. S. Steelmen and played the Joliet school song. Then, the band marched to the L-P section; formed the letters "L-P"; and played the "Red and Green" school song. Later in the evening, both bands joined in a half-hour concert before the dedication speeches got underway.

On Sept. 4, about 3,000 patrons paid 25¢ admission to the "The Last Round-up," a concert sponsored by the Tri-Cities Kiwanis Club, to help purchase 100 uniforms for L-P band, band master, and drum major. Wearing her new white serge uniform trimmed in gold and her 17-pound feathered hat, Drum Major Jacqueline Hand, led the Cavalier Band at the dedication performance. (1938 L-P yearbook)

179

Mike Bender, the *Post-Tribune* sports editor, described the L-P football game viewed by a crowd estimated at nearly 6,000. "Not only because the victory came with the dedication was it especially welcome, but the fact that it marked the return of the Red and Green to winning ways in the Big Seven conference was cause for jubilation and celebration "down town" in both LaSalle and Peru until late into the night," Bender wrote. "It was the first LaSalle-Peru victory in the conference after dropping seven in a row." Of special note in the 26-12 win was an interception by fullback George Zevnik, who sprinted for 25 yards for a touchdown, the second one for the L-P team in the last four minutes of play. It was a fitting end to the dedication game.

The 1937 L-P football team was the first varsity squad to play in the new stadium. First row: Wesley Tregoning, Lester Joop, Mike Kasap, Gilbert Amos, Louis Orlandini, Tom Briddick, Francis Krolak; Second row: Grazio Berritini, Avio Zuccarini, Charles Walters, Stan Krystofek, Bob Gens, Sam Renis, Bob Donnelly; Third row: Kinczewski, Gene Gore, Robert Goering, William Ebener, Don Walters, Elmer Engel, Emil Ulanowski, Emil Soneski; Fourth row: Julius Spriet, Ed Jesiolowski, Larry Schaefer, Ed Flannery, Henry Stanfield, Dean Donoho, George Zevnik.
(1938 L-P yearbook)

Although the L-P stadium was essentially complete, there was still $40,000 in expenditures for landscaping and a concrete ramp to replace wooden steps. Coatings still had to be applied to the roofs of the field house, ticket booths, and toilet facilities. There would be plenty of work for the fall and winter months.

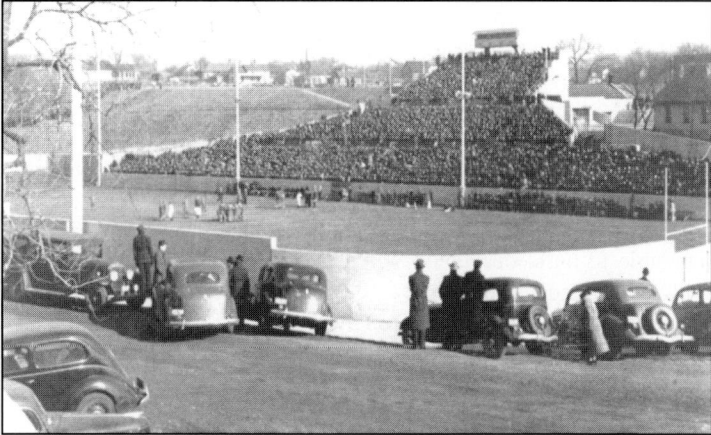

Howard Fellows Stadium, which took two years to construct with an outlay of over $300,000, was dedicated on Oct. 1, 1937. The crowd of about 6,000 fans watched L-P defeat Joliet 26-12. Photo circa 1938. (Oglesby Library)

The unemployed and underemployed read encouraging news in October. In Mark, the Prairie State mine was hoisting enough coal to sustain a payroll for 200 men. LaSalle was awaiting action on its application for a $72,000 PWA grant for the Jackson school and gym, and Spring Valley officials were seeking a WPA grant for a community center.

However, some individuals weren't satisfied with the meager wages paid to laborers on government jobs. Once again, bootlegging seemed to provide a more financially rewarding enterprise. The business was becoming profitable again as the demand for illegal alcohol drove prices up to $15 for a five-gallon can of moonshine. On Thursday, Oct. 14, federal agents made a raid at 122 E. Eleventh Street, the home of Leo Vitale, who had allegedly boasted that no one could find his still. Vitale was out on bail, having been connected with a booze-running operation and operating a still in a wooded area near Leonore the previous year. The agents found a 250-gallon mash vat accessible through a well-concealed trap door in the basement. They also discovered, a five-gallon can of sugar alcohol, and 20 empty five-gallon tins. Vitale was charged with possession and concealment of an unregistered still and untaxed alcohol.

A few days later, a less dramatic raid was conducted at 1460 Fourth Street in LaSalle, the residence of Mrs. Esther Kracen, located east of the Illinois Central tracks. The authorities acted on a tip from Miss Darlene Ristau of Troy Grove, who bought a half pint

181

from Kracen and took it to the police as evidence of the illegal operation. During the raid, the police found a five-gallon can half full of moonshine. Apparently, Kracen was selling liquor for 10¢ a half pint to the hobos living near the tracks. Since Kracen could not pay the $500 bail, she was confined in the Ottawa jail.

Washington continued to curtail WPA projects that fall, but there was still $10,000 available locally for the rural sanitation program. That was the government's way of saying money was available to build out-houses for poor farmers. Actually, there was quite a demand for the labor-intensive jobs. A farmer, who would supply the wood, could apply to have a WPA crew come to his farm to construct a "sanitation facility." Over 500 out-houses had already been constructed by the WPA in LaSalle County. Of those, 60 were built in Naplate.

In November, the CCC company at Starved Rock began work on a 46-foot bridge crossing one arm of Tonti Canyon. The connections in the concrete arches would be inserted in lubricated sockets in the concrete abutments. Then, the center section would be poured to form the key. It was a unique design, less expensive to manufacture, and faster to erect than other types. Rising 150' above the canyon bottom, the bridge would be visible from Highway 7A.

Pictured is one of the bridges crossing the creek whose waters flow from waterfalls in LaSalle Canyon and Tonti Canyon. Although the decking is relatively new, the stone abutments are the original work of the CCC.

182

A small stream of water flows over the rim of Tonti Canyon in the spring of 2008. (Photo by author)

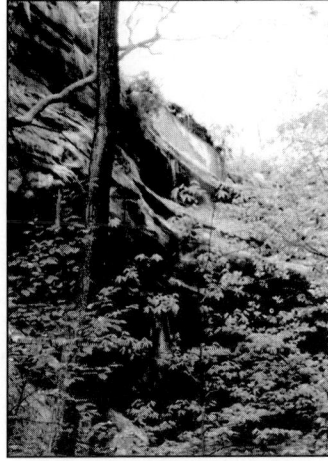

Work at Starved Rock kept men busy. On Nov. 4, bids were requested for the 48-room Starved Rock Hotel, which would be connected to the Lodge on the bluff. Rooms would be equipped with a tub and shower and steam heat. An elevator was included in the three-story design. The 16 cabins on the proposed site were moved by the CCC to the campgrounds west of the south entry road to make room for the hotel. The Department of Public Works and Buildings planned to modernize the cabins spending about $700 on each one to make them more attractive for occupancy.

This is one of the cabins moved by the CCC to make room for the new hotel at Starved Rock State Park. (Photo by author)

Most of the local CCC enrollees were never assigned to the Illinois Valley state parks or I-M Canal restoration. Phil Baratta, who joined the CCC with Ed Brate, Leo Miklavcic, and others from the LaSalle-Peru-Oglesby area wrote to the LaSalle paper telling about life with at Camp Echo, WI. Their meals, he said, included a lot of deer meat. Some of the men had been fighting forest fires in northern Wisconsin where 1,500 acres had been destroyed. The other excitement in camp came when their officers shot a bear at the door of the camp kitchen.

The advent of winter weather meant it was time to issue cold weather clothing to the 170 enrollees at Parkman Plain at Starved Rock. Outfitted with new flannel underwear and shirts, wool socks and coats, heavy shoes, a heavy cap and leather or wool-lined mittens, the men were expected to go out to work as long as the temperatures remained above 10°. The men could look forward to five-day leaves during the holidays.

In Oglesby, 40 men on the WPA crew began work on the highway on the east side of town. Working a single shift from 8 a.m. until 3 in the afternoon, their first job was to clear trees and brush at the western approach to the highway. City trucks took the men to the job site. Some of the oak trees in the path of the road were cut into lumber for fence posts along the right-of-way. This type of work would occupy the men for the next two months.

It was hoped that the December weather would be cold enough to flood a 100' x 300' area in Peru's Central Park to provide an ice skating rink, but it was still relatively warm. The WPA men experimented with flooding the new tennis courts at Washington Park, but until the temperatures dropped to freezing, the plans for ice-skating had to be delayed.

In December, two Putnam County villages decided to improve their infrastructure by applying for WPA grants. Mark filed an application for $6,174 to hire 17 laborers and a few supervisory personnel to pour some badly needed sidewalks, and to build a 24-foot wide bridge over the Hennepin Street creek. Standard applied for a $6,254 storm sewer project. If approved, 12 common laborers along with a tile layer, a foreman, and a timekeeper could be hired.

Marjorie Smythe, NYA supervisor for Putnam County, announced a job registration day on Dec. 8, for unemployed workers who had not registered with the national employment service or the state office in LaSalle. Registration would take place at the IERC-NYA-WPA office in Granville and the Hennepin courthouse.

For months, various charitable groups in the Illinois Valley had been collecting funds, clothes, and toys for the less fortunate so that by Christmas gift baskets could again be distributed. Many toys had been dropped off at the *Post-Tribune*. Toys needing repairs were first sent to the Campbell School, where the youngsters in the manual training class and a group of NYA boys would recondition the toys. The Knights of Columbus donated the use of their hall's upper floor to store and wrap toys for the Big Hearts program in LaSalle. Both Boy Scouts and NYA students would participate in the distribution of the toys and other gifts on Christmas Eve.

The Elks distributed 110 food baskets to needy families in LaSalle, Peru, Oglesby, Utica, and Dalzell the day before Christmas. Each basket contained 16 or more items – enough for a complete Christmas dinner. The American Legion and Auxiliary distributed baskets with toys, food, and clothing to 30 homes of needy war veterans. The Auxiliary also brought six baskets to widows of veterans with children so that no child would go without a toy on Christmas morning.

The Big Hearts sponsors later reported that the gift-giving was the most successful since the organization began in 1929. A thousand children had turned out for the annual movies at the Majestic Theater. After the movies, they each received a bag of candy, an orange, and an apple. Toys were taken to a like number of children at their homes. In addition to the cash contributions amounting to $155, Mrs. J. H. Sharpe of 1608 St. Vincent, LaSalle provided a bushel of canned goods, which the managers of the Big Hearts organization divided between the LaSalle-Peru hospitals. Another gift, a used radio donated by Mrs. Anton Grzybowski of 1622 LaHarpe, was given to a LaSalle patient in the tuberculosis sanitarium in Ottawa.

One bit of bad news at the end of the year was the announcement in Washington that there would be dramatic cuts in the CCC program. Although the January enrollment was fast approaching, only 28 young men, 17-23 years old, coming from families with limited income would be accepted for the LaSalle County quota. That compared to the 43 men, who were accepted in LaSalle County during the previous enrollment period. The national CCC budget was cut from $350 million to $226 million. Enrollees would be limited to 275,000 nationwide, a reduction of 75,000, and 104 camps could be closed. There was no news on whether those decisions would affect the companies in the Illinois Valley.

WPA and PWA jobs were still available. On New Year's Eve 1937, the LaSalle paper printed architect's plans for the new Washington School. The proposed school would need voter approval in a $35,000 bond referendum in addition to the $100,000 already authorized. Voter approval was needed on Jan. 1, 1938 in order to obtain a $99,000 PWA grant.

This architect's drawing for Peru's Washington School appeared in the Dec. 31, 1937 edition of the LaSalle *Daily Post-Tribune*.

1938
FOCUS ON SCHOOLS AND PARKS

At the beginning of January, stories about new schools dominated the local news. Some school boards were just beginning the process of obtaining federal matching funds, while other schools were already under construction or ready for dedication ceremonies.

On Jan 6, 1938, the architect's drawing for the Jackson School in LaSalle was published in the LaSalle *Post-Tribune*. On Oct. 21, 1936, the first steps were taken to secure funding for the construction. Bids would be opened on Feb. 23, and construction was scheduled to begin on March 15.

The NYA reported in January that 59 students at L-P High School and L-P-O Junior College had collectively earned $625. Twenty-seven students at the high school were employed in typing and clerical positions. Thirty-two junior college students were earning extra money engaged in such jobs as playing piano for the girls' gym classes or assisting in the science labs, cafeteria, or the library.

In Streator, 35 women were employed at the WPA sewing center on East Main. The women performed specialized duties: 19 worked at the sewing machines; 4 were cutters; 2 sewed on buttons; while other women worked at the button hole machine and the press. They used an average of 125 yards of cloth a day. All of the material was purchased from local stores, contributing $250-$350 a month to the local economy. In addition, the women earned $44 for 130 hours of work each month. Once a month, the clothing they manufactured was divided among the needy families in the district. That included everything from pajamas to work clothes.

There were still many individuals without any employment. The labor statistics indicated 3,354 workers were totally unemployed in LaSalle County. Streator had one of the highest unemployment situations with 778 individuals unable to find any work. In Bureau County, the number of unemployed in January stood at 860, and in Putnam County, the figure was 178. Others were able to find part-time jobs or worked on a government-sponsored project and were classified as underemployed.

Sometimes projects were cancelled because of the lack of qualified applicants. One such program was the plan to train a minimum of 15 women for household service. In a *Post-Tribune* interview on Jan. 22, the WPA district supervisor of women's and professional projects said, "WPA is a medium ready to step in and help distressed communities, but we can't do this unless people are certified to us for employment." The supervisor explained that only seven women in LaSalle County were certified, possibly because only one person in a family was eligible, and many men were already working on WPA projects.

She cited other projects, such as the women working at the sewing center in Peru and the program that hired workers to prepare and serve school lunches to underprivileged children. "There are many likely projects if we could get together with LaSalle County, but until certifications are made by the township supervisors, nothing can be done," she explained to the reporter.

The weather again played a role in providing temporary jobs. The 2.48" rainfall between 4 p.m. on Sunday and 9:30 a.m. on Monday, January 23 was described as the worst since 1904. The gauge at Shippingsport Bridge indicated an increase from 8 feet to 18 feet in the Illinois River on Monday, Jan 23.

The area most affected was a 10-mile stretch in Bureau County between Tiskilwa and Bureau, where the water of the Hennepin Canal overflowed the banks. Fifty WPA workers were immediately reassigned to road repairs, joining over 200 other workers as they tried to repair large sections of a gravel road. Some sections of the Rock Island tracks were reportedly under six feet of water. During the rapid rise in the water level, a coal car was purposely left on the tracks hoping to stabilize the ballast, but the current was so strong it flipped the fully loaded car on its side, dumping tons of coal into a farm field. Because of the washouts, trains had to be rerouted to Rockford to reach Chicago. It was estimated that 7,500 acres were under water. Livestock drowned, and people were marooned in farmhouses. To make matters worse, the temperature was predicted to drop to 10°F.

The rising waters also affected the Hennepin area. On Jan. 27, WPA men were sent to the Coffee Creek levee near Hennepin to clear the debris brought in by the heavy rains.

In February, the WPA assigned 48 men to projects at Peru's Washington, Centennial, and Sunset Parks. Federal authorities also approved a $92,000 library project for LaSalle and Bureau counties.

Needy individuals would be hired to work in public libraries and school libraries, organizing and indexing files, typing, repairing magazines, and similar work connected with maintaining library functions. The government assured regular employees that they would not be replaced with the less costly WPA workers.

CCC work in the state parks and along the I-M Canal continued during the winter months, but there was also time for some fun. Seventeen of the men entered the Golden Gloves boxing competition held at Streator H.S. The men from Camp Illini, Company 613 at Marseilles, had high hopes when they entered the ring for the two days of competition in mid-February.

One of the NYA's more original programs was a plan discussed in Sterling on Mar. 5 by Mrs. Stella Merrick, director of NYA for LaSalle, Marshall, and Putnam counties, and Miss Betty Raymond, director in Bureau and Stark counties. They thought that sky highway markers (huge painted signs on the ground) would be a great navigational aid for pilots flying over the region. NYA could furnish the labor to paint the signs if local communities and civic groups would supply the paint and other materials. Their goal was to get the project underway by April 1, but it would take a little longer than expected. Funding was eventually found to paint 25 signs in six counties. Five-man teams from NYA would be assigned to the jobs. If local men were not available in the counties where the signs were to be painted, the NYA would draw on applicants from Somonauk.

Some of the proposed signs included ones for the hanger at the old LaSalle-Peru Airport, the Hunter-Duncan lumberyard in Oglesby, and the Burl George implement store in Spring Valley. The sign on the Standard Oil building in Ladd would simply be repainted. Other communities requesting signs included Toluca, Wenona, Hennepin, Lacon, Henry, Streator, and Ottawa.

Another NYA project involved painting street names on curbs. It would provide a small income for 42 adults and 23 students. A similar program in Wenona provided jobs for 30 project workers and 52 students. Some NYA students in Putnam County were busy improving a road leading to Mark.

Utica had been waiting for about a year to have a WPA application approved. Finally, at the end of March, Walter Bosselman, the village clerk, reported that the $5,840 grant from Washington had been approved for "clearing brush, excavating and widening the channel of Clark's Run Creek."

After a number of rejections, LaSalle's Mayor Orr realized his plans for a WPA-funded swimming pool for Hegeler Park would have to be changed. The city council submitted a scaled down version of the plan. By reducing the size of the pool from 60' x 265' to 60' x 200', the anticipated cost dropped to $100,000 instead of the original estimate of $125,000-130,000. However, WPA returned the application in June specifying the need for additional funds from the city to cover its share, $34,693. LaSalle voters had only authorized $25,000 in bonds in 1936.

In mid-April a number of smaller towns applied for federal funding. The Ladd school board hoped to rehabilitate the old school at a cost of $30,000. Dalzell wanted to build a $16,000 recreation hall annex to their school. Cherry was interested in the construction of a four-mile farm-to-market road. Of the $17,000 cost, it was hoped that the government would fund $11,567. Gravel for the road improvement would be obtained from Western Sand and Gravel in Spring Valley. Standard's school board president, Joseph Marchesi, led the effort to replace the 1903 school building with a new three-room structure with an attached auditorium. The village would have to pay $8,000 to match the WPA contribution of $25,000.

On April 27, 1938, WPA workers were digging a trench on Cherry Street for a new water main in Cherry, IL. (Photo submitted by Nellie Giacomelli)

The plans for a new gym at Hall H. S. had been delayed for a year because the board missed a deadline for government approval. Just as the school board was ready to advance the $70,000 project on its own, the federal government unexpectedly approved the original request for a gym and pool.

189

In order to promote the nation's struggling airmail service and observe the 20th anniversary of airmail service, the USPS designated May 15-21, 1938 as National Air-Mail Week. A new 6¢ stamp (pictured) was issued on May 14. Locally, plans were set into motion to have an airplane make a landing at Starved Rock State Park to pick up the mail. To accomplish that, a landing strip had to be cleared and leveled by CCC Co. 1609. The spot chosen was a 3/4-mile strip west of the parking area at Starved Rock. A unique cachet was imprinted on envelopes for the occasion.

On May 19, the official day for the 1,700 one-day-only flights, heavy rains had made the landing field soft and slippery. Rather than take a chance on an accident, Ellis Friedrich of Peoria flew an amphibious plane to the state park, landed in the Illinois River, and taxied to the shore, where a large crowd was waiting. After picking up the mail pouches, he flew them back to Peoria and then on to Chicago where he landed in Lake Michigan near Seventh Street. Dr. Sidney Walker, who was to have piloted the original aircraft, said the situation showed clear evidence for the need of a suitable landing field in LaSalle County.

On May 19, one of those historic first-day letters was flown from Starved Rock to Peoria. From there, it may have been flown to Chicago and returned to Maurice Sheehy in Utica by way of the Rock Island RR. (Author's collection)

The CCC men at Starved Rock were involved in several training programs in 1938. Dr. Donald Ries, the park naturalist, was interested in developing a natural history museum and a naturalist guide service, using some of the men from Co. 1609 trained as tour guides. In addition, Lt. H. F. Traua, company commander, organized a physical fitness program for the 205 enrollees, in accordance with a directive from Maj. Gen. H. A. Drum, Sixth Corps commander. Academic and vocational training were also stressed. While there was no illiteracy in the camp, 23 boys lacked eighth grade diplomas. Fifteen of those boys eventually received their certificates.

190

Summer relief food supplements were soon arriving at the LaSalle commodity depot. The warehouse already had received two boxcars loaded with Arizona grapefruit, and a like amount of cabbage and celery. A carload of California prunes had also been unloaded. The depot also held supplies of Arkansas rice, Michigan navy beans, Wisconsin peas, Arizona grapefruit juice, and Idaho potato flour. Eight more carloads of food, including tomatoes from Texas, were on the way. Families of four or more on relief could pick up half a bushel of tomatoes when they arrived.

At the time, there were 3,500 families on relief in LaSalle, Bureau, Putnam, and Grundy Counties. In addition to those families who were eligible to receive surplus commodities, senior citizens and mothers on pensions were also qualified. The food was purchased by the Federal Surplus Commodity Corporation to maintain market prices.

During the Depression, it was the federal government's policy to establish one major public building in each congressional district each year. It was decided that a new $70,000 post office in Oglesby would be the main project for 1938. A parcel of land, 165 feet long and two blocks deep across from the Washington School, was selected for the construction site.

There were also plans to improve the I-M Canal between Ottawa and LaSalle to keep local WPA assignees busy during the winter months. The ambitious goals called for building a second gravel-surfaced towpath on the south side of the canal, rebuilding weakened canal walls, reconditioning the locks, dredging silt and debris from the channel, building landings and parking areas, and constructing 30-40 fire pits and 50 picnic tables. Once the canal was cleaned and filled with water from the Du Page River, the waterway would be stocked with fish supplied by the Illinois Department of Conservation. This type of work was already underway in Du Page and Grundy Counties. Everything depended on the approval of the $200,000 application. An estimated 2,000 laborers would have jobs for a year or longer if Washington approved the plan in its entirety.

Applications were prepared for many projects, but they all had to be evaluated in Rockford. In some cases, months would pass before any news on the status of a project was received. In the summer of 1938, one WPA grant was approved to build a gym at Mendota H. S. However, the request for a PWA grant of $75,000 to build the Jackson School with a gym in LaSalle was rejected. In spite of the disappointment, the LaSalle school board decided to go ahead with the project by holding an $88,000 bond referendum.

191

Work continued in Oglesby to open the new road on the east side of town. Weather problems and the shifting of crews to other WPA projects delayed construction. (Highway photos from Oglesby Library)

WPA workers were grading the Ed Hand Highway in June 1938.

WPA workers in Streator lined up for this photo in front of the Owens-Illinois Glass plant in 1938. (Streatorland Historical Society)

One of the major events youngsters always looked forward to during the Depression was a day at the circus. However, the children were going to be very disappointed in the summer of 1938. In spite of all the publicity, the Cole Brothers Circus wasn't coming to LaSalle. Instead, it was headed back to Indiana.

The circus, featuring Clyde Beatty, the famous wild animal trainer, was playing in Bloomington, IL. After the last show on Wednesday, Aug. 3, the circus train was scheduled to be attached to an Illinois Central engine for the trip to LaSalle. Everything seemed fine at 2 a.m., when the last of the circus personnel went to bed. However, at 4 a.m., the 30 circus cars were uncoupled from the IC engine and coupled to a Nickel Plate engine. Then, it headed back to their winter quarters in Rochester, IN.

This ad was placed in the LaSalle *Post-Tribune* on Aug. 3. The Yellow Cab Company in LaSalle offered circus discount rates. Five could ride in a taxi to the circus for the price of one. The LaSalle-Peru bus lines would only charge 10¢ for the ride from First and Gooding Streets down to Joliet Street to the circus tent that was supposed to be located on the Bapst farm on north St. Vincent Ave.

NOW the LARGEST CIRCUS in the WORLD!

LA SALLE NORTH ST. VINCENT AVE.

TOMORROW

REAL OLD-FASHIONED STREET PARADE AT 11 A.M.

COLE BROS. CIRCUS *with*

CLYDE BEATTY World's Greatest Wild Animal Trainer!

THE GREAT FLORENZO

SOMERSAULTING AUTOMOBILE

HUNDREDS OF INTERNATIONALLY FAMOUS CIRCUS STARS

the FINEST SHOW ON EARTH *presenting*

18,000 Marvels—1,100 People—400 Arenic Stars—Army of Clowns
Mammoth Menagerie—4 Herds of Elephants—500 Horses—27 Tents,
3 Railroad Trains of Wonders!

TWO PERFORMANCES DAILY AT **2:00** and **8:00 pm** **POPULAR PRICES**
DOORS OPEN AT 1:00 PM AND 7:00 PM

Children Under 12 Yrs., MAT. ONLY 25¢

Reserved Seat Sale Tomorrow at CLANCY'S DRUG STORE, 441 First St., La Salle.

Calls flooded the *Post-Tribune* office trying to find out why the circus train wasn't coming. Everyone was looking forward to the parade and shows. Many had not attended the Tom Mix Circus in Peru the previous week because they wanted to see the bigger Cole Brothers Circus. Tony Bapst had already taken down fencing to allow the heavy circus equipment to access his property. Local businesses had contracted to deliver food and supplies. A feed store had already delivered three tons of hay to the Bapst farm for the circus animals.

For hundreds of youngsters, it was a major disappointment. The son of Leo Boyle of Ottawa broke into tears when his father told him that he wasn't going to be able to attend his first circus.

193

A few days later, it was learned that the circus owners had run into financial problems while in Bloomington and had to cut personnel. The performers and other personnel had tried to keep the financially ailing company afloat by not demanding their salaries for some time. The owners explained their predicament citing a 21-day period of constant rains that kept audiences away.

The local children could at least look forward to the new swimming pool at Hegeler Park in LaSalle. The WPA grant for $49,245 was finally approved. Mayor Orr said, "When we are finished with Hegeler Park, there will not be a better spot for recreation in a city of LaSalle's size." In addition to the pool complex, there would be lighted tennis courts, baseball diamonds with bleachers, and fireplaces for cookouts. What the children didn't know was that the pool would not be opened until 1940.

Business was a little slow for Westclox, one of the major employers in the Tri-Cities. Over 3,400 employees were working a 40-hour workweek in spite of a 50 percent decline in orders. To stimulate business, the company introduced two new products for the coming holiday season. Westclox managers hoped with the nationwide debut of the new clocks on Sept. 10, 1938, production would rise to 70 or even 80 percent of capacity.

The new travalarm with its sliding front cover (at right) was the smallest alarm clock manufactured at Westclox. The table clock (at far right) was finished in ivory with a green background and could be used with a perpetual calendar easel. Photos from the *Post-Tribune*.

While many were looking to the future and new jobs, others were reviving local history by planning the dedication of a marker at the old site of Ft. Wilbourn, one of the significant locations in the Black Hawk War. The Illini Chapter of the Daughters of the American Revolution decided it would be appropriate to erect a monument to mark the location of the fort, which was used as a training camp, hospital, recruiting site, supply depot, and refuge for settlers during the conflict. Of additional historic note was the fact that Abraham Lincoln came to the fort to enlist as a private in Jacob Early's company.

The dedication ceremony took place on a bluff south of LaSalle overlooking the river on Sept. 15, 1938. Participants in the unveiling of the bronze plaque were David Reynolds Sims and Louise Sims, great grandchildren of James Reynolds, who was born in the fort in June 1832. Also attending the event was Miss Addie Cora Cary of Troy Grove. She was a daughter of George Cary, who was born in the fort when the Cary family took refuge during the war. Nineteen civilians and one volunteer soldier from LaSalle County were killed during the Black Hawk War.

The boulder with the Ft. Wilbourn dedication plaque was originally located on the bluff overlooking the Illinois River at LaSalle, but it was moved and is now located on the IVCC campus. (Photo by author)

There was little time for ceremonies for desperate families seeking jobs during the Depression. Just as one project ended, some of the unemployed were lucky enough to find new employment. Plans were in the works at the Rockford WPA office to employ 744 men for a year. The pay varied from 40¢ to 65¢ an hour depending on the particular township where the work was done. Workers in LaSalle and Peru Townships were paid the highest rate in the county. Over $700,000 was available for road improvements in LaSalle County. Rural road improvements in Bureau County were eligible for up to $200,000. The local townships would be required to pay 35 percent of the cost.

A variation of the NYA program, which typically involved part-time work for students living at home, was the Resident Training Program in the Young Men's Athletic (YMA) Club House on Second and Peoria Streets in Peru. (Photo by author)

195

In Peru, 36 boys enrolled in the NYA and resided at the YMA Club. They worked up to 70 hours a month and were paid 35½¢ an hour, a total of $24.85. From that amount, $20 was deducted to pay for the rent, utilities, and food. The remaining $4.85 was paid to the boys so they could cover incidental expenses. While living together, they worked on a variety of projects and also attended L-P High School or the junior college. Some of the initial jobs included building open fireplaces in the city parks and rip-rapping the banks of creeks. One of their first projects was building pheasant and quail pens for the LaSalle and Oglesby-Cedar Point Sportsmen's Club.

Foreign-born residents were encouraged to take tuition-free, citizenship classes at the Jefferson, Grant, Washington, and Campbell schools. Starting on Sept. 22, Mrs. Millera Mason of LaSalle would serve as the WPA instructor for the evening classes.

In Spring Valley, the fall of 1938 marked the beginning of the work on the Hall H.S. gym. The PWA grant for $55,000 coupled with a $70,000 expenditure by the school board would fund a new gym and a 1,200-seat auditorium.

Improvements and repairs were badly needed to restore the I-M Canal corridor. In September, the federal government authorized a WPA program costing $255,000 to restore the canal for recreational use, a concept that had been discussed for years. This would be the first major attempt to carry out that goal. Locally, the stretch between Ottawa and LaSalle was targeted for improvements including the installation of 15 picnic tables and 30 fireplaces. The men would also plant 10,000 trees, restore 10 log bridges, paint the canal aqueducts at Ottawa and LaSalle, build 3 rustic boat landings, and riprap 3,000 yards of the canal banks.

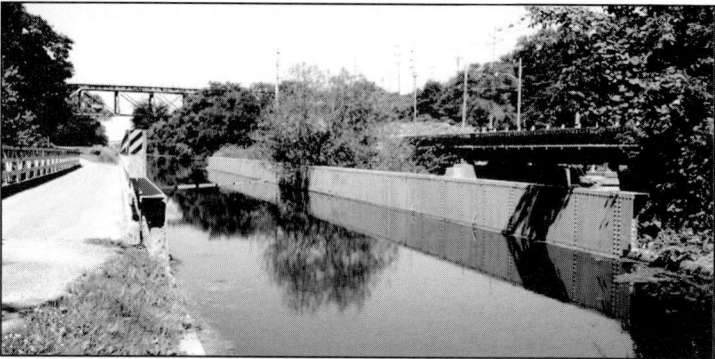

WPA workers were assigned to repaint the steel aqueduct for the I-M Canal at LaSalle. (Photo by author)

Thirty men began work on the canal at Ottawa while 100 men were working at LaSalle. Working in two alternating weekly shifts, they repaired and widened the 16-mile towpath between the cities. The men worked from 8 a.m. til noon, when they had a half hour break. They typically worked seven hours a day Monday through Friday but only six hours on Saturdays.

Other CCC improvements to the canal were taking place further to the east. By mid-October, 50 CCC workers were busy rebuilding the Morris aqueduct, a job that was expected to take 3-4 months.

The CCC built this stone arch bridge to support the Nettle Creek aqueduct of the I-M Canal at Morris. (Photo by author)

A spillway at the arch bridge carries excess water from the I-M Canal aqueduct into Nettle Creek. In order to stabilize the arch bridge, concrete repairs, appearing as stonework at far right, were made. (Photo by author)

197

Near the I-M Canal at Morris, the CCC built a caretaker's house for Gebhard Woods State Park. The garage was originally detached from the house.

The Brandon-Morris CCC men built rustic shelters with stone fireplaces at Gebhard Woods State Park.

(Photos by author)

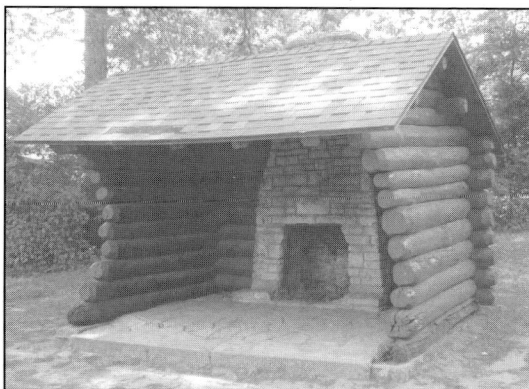

One of the CCC-built stone fireplaces at Gebhard Woods is located close to the parking area and campsites.

A blue heron flying over the waters of the I-M Canal illustrates how the goal of returning the corridor to a natural habitat was achieved.

The CCC built both wooden and stone shelters at Gebhard Woods.

Below: The CCC constructed spillways to maintain a consistent water level in the I-M Canal. The excess water flowing over the stonework creates a gentle waterfall feeding one of the fishing ponds located in Gebhard Woods. (Photos by author)

199

CCC barracks were built in McKinley Woods. (Lewis University collection)

CCC men drained water from the I-M Canal at McKinley Woods. (Lewis University collection)

A footbridge was built to cross the I-M Canal in McKinley Woods to access a trail leading to the Illinois River. Although the bridge decking is new, the rock abutments date from the 1930's. (Photo by author)

This was one of the shelters constructed by the CCC at McKinley Woods. A stairway on the opposite side of the shelter leads down to the I-M canal.

Right - This shelter, built by the CCC in McKinley Woods, overlooks the Illinois River.
Below - This stone overlook on the Illinois River at McKinley Woods was a result of the work in the Depression. (Photos by author)

While the CCC and WPA were kept busy along the I-M Canal and in the state parks, other men were building schools. The Jackson School at Sixth and Bucklin Streets in LaSalle was designed by architect Louis Gerding. The virtually fireproof building was constructed of reinforced concrete with a pastel brick exterior. According to the *Post*, "The rotunda on the axis of the main entrance has a large compass in color in the linoleum tile floor and a monogram 'J' as a center feature."

Jackson School was completed in 1938. A unique design feature included the three-inch rounded brick and stone corners of the building, coping, and sills. The east and west facades were finished with glass brick to illuminate the interior stairs and main corridor. (Photo by author)

A dedication ceremony was held at the Jackson School on Nov. 6. The program began with a half hour concert by the L-P High School band. Following the raising of Old Glory by the Boy Scouts, the superintendent of L-P High School gave the main speech.

School construction was a major goal during the Depression. In Putnam County, voters approved a $20,000 bond issue to build a gym for the Hennepin school. The PWA grant for $18,000 only waited for approval in Washington. The school board in Peru decided to add a balcony to the gym for the Washington School. This would provide 350 additional seats. A similar number of pupils could be seated on the main floor.

On Nov. 14, the NYA resident program in Peru suffered a setback when it was discovered that two bird pens had been torn open, and 50 half-grown quail chicks were missing. A noisy outcry of the birds chirping was heard at 4 a.m. It was not until 6 a.m., when one of the NYA boys spotted some of the chicks in the lawn across the street and notified Lester Reid, the resident manager.

About half of the birds were found huddled together at a nearby house. Authorities were mystified trying to determine who or what had ripped open the cages.

In spite of the unpleasantness, the boys continued building pens for additional quail chicks they would acquire from the Illinois Department of Conservation. They also built game feeders from old nail kegs. Some of these would be set out on nearby farms.

A few days later, there was another attack on the quail pens, resulting in 23 dead birds and 20 missing birds. Some speculated that someone had broken into the cages and used a sharp instrument to cut the canvas covering the tops of the cages. Indeed, there was troubling evidence to support such speculation.

On the same day the first attack occurred, there was a break-in at the Hopkins H.S. in Granville. Several artifacts including two German rifles, two German pistols, and a bayonet were among the artifacts stolen from the school's museum. Police gave chase to two young men who fled in a car, which crashed in Peru during the pursuit. The uninjured boys abandoned the museum artifacts and escaped capture by hopping an eastbound Rock Island freight train to Chicago, where one of the suspects was later arrested.

When Putnam County Sheriff Lawrence Ellena questioned the boy, he learned that the accused teenager was Leonard Zraniak, 16, who was on probation and living at the Edward Kelsey residence in Granville. While attending the high school, the boy said he saw the numerous artifacts in the museum cases. Zraniak left Granville and returned to Chicago, where he conspired with another youngster to steal a car from the Manhatten Brewing Co. They drove to Granville, and robbed the school museum with the intent of selling the war souvenirs in Chicago. Zraniak confessed to the Hopkins' theft but denied any connection with the attack on the NYA quail project.

The items on display in the Hopkins School museum included a variety of historic artifacts including WWI weapons. Note - The boys pictured were not the ones involved with the theft. (Putnam County Hist. Soc.)

The incident at the Peru NYA center was soon resolved. Shortly after the second attack on the quails in Peru, word was received about a similar incident at another NYA facility in southern Illinois. In that case, the attacker was determined to be a dog. That seemed to solve the Peru mystery. The rips in the canvas-covered pens were not caused by a bayonet but rather by one or more dogs. To help the Peru boys salvage their work, the Department of conservations sent another 500 chicks to Peru.

While the NYA boys kept busy, the 200 young men at the CCC camp at Starved Rock faced the possible reassignment of their company since the local unions continued to protest the infringement on jobs that should belong to skilled union workers. Specifically, the union disputed the right of the CCC to be building a bathroom addition at the cabins, laying water mains and sewer lines, and constructing a footbridge across Fox Canyon. Charles Casey, the assistant director of the Illinois Department of Public Works and Buildings, defended the work of Company 1609 saying, "This is the first time I am told that there has ever been any objection to CCC boys doing this work and it has been going on all over the country." At a meeting with the union leaders, he pointed out that the department had always tried to be on favorable terms with the unions and had spent $200,000-$300,000 on projects that benefited union men. Most of that money went for wages. Discouraged, he left the meeting explaining to the press that there seemed to be little room for compromise on the part of the union.

Charles Reynolds, a native of LaSalle and an enrollee in Company 613 in Marseilles, wrote to the *Post-Tribune* expressing his feelings about the dispute with the union. "As to myself," Reynolds wrote, "I am a strict union man and always have been, but they must take into consideration that they are benefiting by the (CCC) company being there. They have done some very notable work in the park and in the vicinity of LaSalle. So please do your utmost to keep (Company 1609) there."

CCC men working at Starved Rock. (Lewis University)

204

In November, local PWA projects were going smoothly. L. J. McHugh, the resident engineer at the PWA's centralized headquarters in the Masonic building in Peru, outlined eight major projects in the area. These included the new school in Peru and the Peru sewage treatment project, grade school construction in Tiskilwa and Standard, gym construction in Mendota and Spring Valley, the sewer project in Marseilles, and the hospital addition in Princeton.

In spite of December's cold weather, public works projects continued. In Spring Valley, a two-inch water line was finished between First and Dakota Streets from Cornelia to Powers Streets. Next, the WPA men installed a six-inch water main in Webster Park as far as the Northwestern RR tracks. The year-long work at the Ed Hand Highway in Oglesby would soon be seen by all movie-goers. Mr. Alger promised to show a film clip featuring 18 scenes of the construction in all of his theaters at no cost.

Right: Another public works project was the Marseilles post office.
(Marseilles Library)
Below: Avery E. Johnson was hired in 1938 to paint a mural titled "Industrial Marseilles," over the entrance to the postmaster's office. The U.S. Treasury Dept. Section of Painting and Sculpture paid Johnson $550. Other nearby locations of Depression art, funded by the government, are found in post offices in Oglesby, Peoria, Chillicothe, Dwight, and Sandwich. (Photo by author)

The WPA also continued to emphasize work on the I-M Canal by assigning 175 men to the LaSalle section at Split Rock. They concentrated on clearing brush and widening the towpath. Every 300 feet a turnout was constructed so that cars would be able to travel east and west from LaSalle to Split Rock. In December, the men laid down a layer of shale on the towpath as far as Utica. The south side of the canal at Split Rock was to be turned into a picnic area with a parking lot, picnic tables, and fire pits.

Looking west, the I-M canal and towpath cut through Split Rock in this 2008 photo.
(Photo by author)

Although the original work of the WPA at Split Rock can no longer be seen, the new shelter, bench, and information boards provide a welcomed stop for hikers on the towpath.

In 2003, the Split Rock site was redeveloped by Jeremy Wasilewski of Ottawa to attain his Eagle Scout status. Those involved in the project were (1st row) Gail Lowman, Tiffany Wasilewski, Jackie Wasilewski, (2nd row) Josh Lowman, Jeremy Wasilewski, Kyle Lowman, Trevor Lowman; (3rd row) Joe VeZain, Linda Wasilewski, John Burns, Emil Crouch, and Mike Wasilewski.

(Photos supplied by Jeremy Wasilewski)

WPA projects competed for manpower. Forty men working on the canal were reassigned to the LaSalle swimming pool project in Hegeler Park. To replace them, 40 men were taken off the Ed Hand Highway project in Oglesby and assigned to the canal project. At Hegeler Park, the inauguration of excavation for the pool project began at 8 a.m. on Monday, Dec. 12. City engineer Larry McGonigal turned the first spade of dirt, and then Charles Buckwald and John Entwistle, two of the WPA men, filled a wheelbarrow with dirt. Soon, the entire crew was busy at the excavation. The work would continue with crews of about two dozen men, each working four 7-hour days and one 6-hour day. At the end of the week, another crew was brought in; they would alternate each week. Additional WPA men were needed as night watchmen, foremen, and timekeepers. With this system of keeping men employed only two weeks each month, the wages were low, and families had to stretch the meager finances to the limit.

Working to collect money, toys, and candy for many weeks, the Big Hearts program held its tenth annual party at the LaSalle Theater. On Christmas Eve, approximately 1,000 children began forming a line from Marquette and First Streets to the theater at 9 a.m. When the doors opened at 9:30, they raced in to find seats. Toddlers sat in the laps of their older siblings through the movie, after which all of the children lined up to receive a pound of candy, a Jonathan apple, and a California orange.

Much credit for the success of the program was given to the NYA, Boy Scouts, and other volunteers, who repaired, wrapped, and tagged toys, which were stored temporarily in the *Post-Tribune* plant until space was found in the Masonic building. Among the NYA workers, Edith Karlosky and Florence Barzstaitis had spent many hours dressing dolls as presents. The boys included Adolph Loebach, Edmund Kierczywski, Peter Shurman, Edward Croissant, Frank Kozar, Edward Zebron, Robert Facer, Roy and Ray Grant, and Frank Tomazin. All of these NYA assignees took part in working with union truckers to distribute toys on Christmas Eve.

Many needy families in Oglesby enjoyed a traditional Christmas dinner thanks to the city council's distribution of 30 food baskets. If there were children in the family, toys were included. The Oglesby Junior Women also contributed 10 food baskets. The Oglesby Union Church gathered the food donations made at the previous week's church service and took the baskets to the poor. The Marquette and Lehigh Cement companies also gave food baskets to the families of needy employees.

At the end of the year, talk of the reassignment of CCC Company 1609 from Starved Rock did not slow the activities at the state park. There was plenty of work to do during the winter months. One of the major programs was to install handrails and repair or replace the steps leading to the top of Starved Rock to remove any hazards. Both stone and concrete were considered as building materials for the steps. There was a temporary lull in the construction of the concrete bridges over the Fox and Tonti Canyons because of the freezing weather, but improvements to trails and walkways around the lodge were still in progress. The CCC would also be occupied working on the parking lots adjacent to the lodge.

Above: The main entrance to Starved Rock Lodge. (Oglesby Library)

Right: This bronze plaque mounted at the entrance of Starved Rock Lodge reminds visitors of the contributions of the CCC.

THIS BUILDING STANDS AS A TRIBUTE TO THE WORK OF THE YOUNG AMERICANS OF THE CIVILIAN CONSERVATION CORPS 1933 — 1939 WHO ADVANCED THE DEVELOPMENT OF OUR STATE PARK SYSTEM A FULL DECADE

The massive fireplace in the Great Hall lounge at Starved Rock Lodge was built by the CCC men using 250 tons of limestone brought from Lemont. The CCC used white oak to construct the furniture.

The Starved Rock dining room was designed to seat 200 patrons. The room was finished with an oak floor, knotty pine walls, rustic lighting fixtures with flame-tinted bulbs, and a 12-foot wide fireplace. (Oglesby Library photos)

It was hoped that the new Starved Rock hotel would be completed by the beginning of 1939. Local workers were busy putting the finishing touches on the 48 rooms with their knotty pine walls and rustic lighting. In the three-story structure, laborers were painting, installing an elevator, laying carpeting and linoleum, finishing the plumbing, and installing a telephone in each room.

The hotel was designed to be operated year-round instead of only in the summer as the old hotel operated. There was even talk of installing a ski-jump to encourage winter sports.

A. Smith and Company was the winning bidder on the contract for the new $80,000 Starved Rock Hotel adjoining the lodge. This photo of the rear of the building, with rooms overlooking the Illinois River, was used in advertising by the Illinois Division of Parks. (Oglesby Library)

One of the shelters was built at Starved Rock State Park near Wildcat Canyon. (Oglesby Library)

This shelter was built at Starved Rock State Park near the cabins along Fox Canyon. (Photo by author)

Government contracts were also negotiated for the construction of armories throughout the country. Two facilities were built locally during the late 1930's, one in Streator and another in Dixon.

Plans for the Streator armory were drawn up in December 1937. The $204,000 building, constructed by the WPA, was adorned with large stone eagles at the entrance. WPA had assigned 140 men to work on the structure in May 1938. It was completed that year and is still in use today.

The Dixon armory was built about the same time as the Streator facility and appears much the same today as it did when it opened. (Photos by author)

211

1939
PUBLIC WORKS NEAR COMPLETION

Many of the long-term government-supported projects were well underway in 1939. WPA workers were cleaning up the I-M Canal. A dredge had been sent from Grafton, IL to Buffalo Rock so an eight-foot channel could be cleared near Locks 11 and 12. Repairs were completed at Lock 12, but more work was needed at Locks 11, 13, and 14. The Nettle Creek aqueduct at Morris was finished, and locks at Marseilles were being rebuilt. New schools and school additions were nearing completion in a number of towns. Construction of a new bridge in Hennepin would be completed by the summer. The local domestic outlook was positive.

CCC repairs to Lock 11 are evident in this 2005 photo. The original limestone blocks are located at the left while newer concrete replacement blocks are to the right. (Photo by author)

CCC men at right inspect Lock 10 at Marseilles. (Marseilles Library)

International events claimed the headlines in January as Mussolini prepared his country for military action, and Hitler was on the move in Czechoslovakia. War clouds threatened Europe again, but the politicians in Washington cautioned against any involvement. There were still many problems to solve domestically to revive the economy. The need persisted for federal jobs with the CCC, NYA, WPA, and PWA. However, Washington wasn't willing to support every project suggested by local governments. Plans using federal funds for a municipal building in Peru were rejected. The restoration of the Illinois-Mississippi (Hennepin) Canal was determined to be too expensive. The chief of the Army engineers estimated it would cost $30 million to make the canal usable for commercial maritime traffic, but he recommended that the government retain the federal right-of-way in case of changes in the future.

Another disheartening situation was the likely closure of the Prairie State mine. Cox failed to pay off a $30,000 mortgage. It would languish until Dec. 5, 1941 when the Union Coal Co. bought the property, which still had an estimated 100 years of coal mining potential. There was even talk of drilling for oil on the property.

At the end of January, the NYA reported on local funding. L-P-O Junior College would be eligible for a grant totaling $2,430, an amount sufficient to provide jobs for 18 students. St. Bede received a grant of $405, enough to fund the work of three students.

Ten of the NYA assignees had spent the winter months building 500 birdhouses in the basement of the Lincoln School in Peru. The birdhouses were built as a habitat project for the Oglesby-Cedar Point Sportsmen's Club.

Although it was still winter, it was not too early to plan for summer gardens. The NYA residence director in Peru advised the 36 boys living at the YMA building they would be raising vegetables for their meals on a 15 to 20-acre plot. Some of the produce would be shipped to the girls' NYA resident center in Rockford. Any extra produce, such as tomatoes, beans, and peas, would be canned. Other vegetables, especially dried beans, potatoes, and onions, would be stored for the following winter. When the boys were not occupied with work on the garden, they would attend classes.

The residence center concept seemed to be beneficial. Boys came to Peru from many counties in northern Illinois. During the winter of '39, they worked on the skating rink in Central Park and rip-rapped the creek banks in Centennial Park. For some of the boys, it was a temporary job. Six boys found private employment, and five others returned to their homes for various reasons.

213

Local school construction continued to provide many jobs. On Nov 30, 1937, a contract for $150 was offered to tear down the old school in Standard.

Children at the old Standard School were assigned to other buildings until a new school was completed. (Putnam County Historical Society)

On Feb. 6, 1939, the new Standard School was ready for the return of the students. (Putnam County Hist. Society)

Another New Deal program in the Illinois Valley was the Federal Theater Project. The L-P-O Junior College sponsored "Prologue To Glory," a play about a year in the life of Abraham Lincoln when he lived in New Salem. There was only a one-night performance of the two-act play. A crowd, estimated at 600, filled Matthiessen Auditorium on Tuesday, Feb 7, 1939 to see Lyle Hagen's portrayal of "Honest Abe," Other notable members of the 35-member cast were Fannie Allen in the role of Miss Ann Mayes Rutledge and Dallas Tyler as Grandma Rutledge.

STAGE PLAY - 35 PEOPLE
Road Production

STURDY, PULSATING, DRAMA

PROLOGUE TO GLORY
by E. P. CONKLE

The Romance of the Young Lincoln

A 4-STAR STAGE HIT
Greatest Love Story in American History

Matthiessen Memorial Auditorium

TUESDAY, FEB. 7
8 P. M.

Auspices
La Salle-Peru-Oglesby
JUNIOR COLLEGE
Adults 50c   Students 25c

On Feb. 26, 1939, an informal open house was held to mark the completion of Peru's Washington School. Beginning at 10 a.m., thousands of visitors, greeted by patrol boys located at the main entrance and in the corridors, inspected the facilities as well as student projects.

The Washington School in Peru was ready for occupancy in January 1939, but the open house was not held until February. (Photo by author)

Local construction projects numbered in the hundreds during 1939. Many towns, such as Tonica, had street paving underway. WPA men in Dalzell had already laid down miles of concrete sidewalks and were in the process of blacktopping 1½ miles of roads. LaMoille applied for a grant to build a high school gym. In Hennepin, the state had completed about half of the work on the bridge spanning Putnam County and Bureau County at Route 71. Work on the Starved Rock Hotel was almost completed.

WPA men made a startling discovery as they cleared the area around Split Rock. While excavating near the east side of the sandstone formation on Wednesday, Mar. 22, they found a skeleton. The bones, which were virtually intact except for the ribs, were determined to be those of a male, over six feet tall. Carefully removing the remains so they could be sent to the University of Illinois for analysis, speculation ran high that the WPA men might have unearthed Chassagouac, a chief of the Illinois Indians some 200 years ago. It was known that the burial site was located somewhere near Utica.

The government continued to provide jobs for young men. The CCC recruited young men in April although the occupation of Starved Rock by Company 1609 was about to end. The 62 enrollees from LaSalle County and the 6 boys from Grundy County would be

215

heading to one of two locations in Wisconsin, Camp Highland or Camp Horeb. The NYA boys in Peru would be occupied during the coming summer with a landscaping project at Hall H.S. In return for their work, they would receive training in auto mechanics and wood shop courses.

Right: The Ed Hand Road project in Oglesby continued into 1939. Progress was documented in this photo taken on April 22, 1939. (Oglesby Library)

Below: The PWA project at Hall H. S., which cost over $129,000, had begun with groundbreaking on Sept. 19, 1938. The dedication took place in April 1939.

PWA workers built the Hall H.S. gym, auditorium, and pool. On Dec. 8, 1939, the dedication basketball game was played before an overflow crowd of 800 fans. Unfortunately, Hall lost to LP 41-21. The Class of 2000 added the sign over the east entrance. (Photo by author)

The formal dedication of the auditorium-gym-pool addition at Hall H.S. was held April 28, 1939. After the speeches and performances by the band and glee club in the 1,100-seat auditorium, the public was invited to an open house. The auditorium and gym were finished, but the swimming pool was a few weeks from completion. During the ceremonies, Andrew Savio, president of the Hall Township Older Boys Association, was scheduled to present an electronic scoreboard to Coach Richard Nesti. The Spring Valley Municipal Band was on the program to present a half hour concert. The evening's activities concluded with a dance in the gym with music provided by Billy Waite's Orchestra.

About the same time as the Hall dedication, over 200 representatives of the Illinois State Employment Service met at L-P High School for a briefing on the policies and procedures to qualify for Social Security pensions and unemployment relief.

The pension program, funded by a one percent deduction in wages, would provide monthly payments to recipients over age 65, beginning after Jan. 1, 1942. Social Security numbers were assigned and accounts established for 43 million workers nationwide. The requirements to participate in the pension program included having earned at least $2,000, a work record indicating one day of employment in five different calendar years since 1936, and being retired from covered occupations. Those who did not qualify for monthly payments would receive a one-time cash payment. For those who met the stipulations, pension checks would be based on a complex formula that set the minimum payment at $10 and the maximum at $85.

For the previous two years, about 30,000 businesses made payments to a federal treasury fund, which was to be used only for the payment of unemployment benefits. The fund was expected to reach $160 billion by July 1939. Unemployment compensation for those who lost their jobs through no fault of their own would begin on July 1, 1939. The weekly payments would be approximately half of a week's full-time wages. After a waiting period of three weeks, a worker was eligible to collect benefits for 16 weeks out of 52 weeks. There was a long list of disqualifying factors to receive benefits including being fired for misconduct, leaving without a good cause, or refusing work.

Social Security was a complex program. Not every job was covered. Small businesses with less than eight employees could opt out of the program. Teachers, agricultural workers, priests, ministers and similar religious employees, as well as government employees, workers for charitable organizations, and domestic servants did not qualify. Coal miners, who had been ordered to go on strike May 4, presented a special problem. Some mines naturally shut down during the slack season. It would ultimately remain for the director of the Department of Labor in each state to determine who qualified for unemployment benefits.

217

As work on the I-M Canal continued in July 1939, the WPA workers found a variety of artifacts, many of which dated from the time when the canal was in operation. Included in the finds were a typical four-armed anchor used by the boats, a number of pistols, a rifle barrel, handmade nails, the base of a kerosene lamp, clay-pipe bowls, an ice hook, a hand pick, hatchet heads, false teeth, and even human skulls. The relics, with the exception of the skulls, were put on display in the WPA headquarters in Ottawa.

The WPA assistant superintendent of the project, James Bennett, reported that 51 percent of the canal work was completed and estimated that the entire dredging and repair work would be completed by the summer of 1940. The CCC enrollees worked mainly on the locks while the WPA cleared the towpath and constructed turnouts for cars. New canal gates, constructed of white pine, stained with creosote, were being installed at LaSalle Lock 14 (pictured), Utica Lock 13, Ottawa Lock 11, Marseilles Lock 10, and Channahon Lock 8. Spillway gates were also under construction. The area around Lock 12 was provided with restrooms, picnic tables, benches, and fireplaces. Fine gravel paths wound 2½ miles to Buffalo Rock State Park. The WPA landscaped around the lock tender's house at LaSalle and applied red ash to the roadway.

According to Hedley Berger of Ottawa, the superintendent of the LaSalle to Ottawa restoration work, Split Rock was expected to become a beauty spot. "When the Split Rock development is finished, the big rock will stand out like a diamond," he told a LaSalle reporter. The credit for the work went to the 301 WPA assignees and the 600 CCC enrollees. Berger also pointed out that hundreds of visitors enjoyed the view of the lotus beds, which were in full bloom with their yellow flowers floating in the canal.

A major labor confrontation developed for WPA men in July when the federal government changed the WPA work rules to cut costs. The number of hours of required work increased to 130 hours per month, but the pay remained the same. At that time, the monthly pay was as follows: common laborers - $55.20; semi-skilled workers - $66; skilled - $85.20; and professionals, such as doctors and lawyers - $90.

Another unacceptable aspect of the law was a mandatory 30-day furlough for any WPA worker who had been on the job for 18 months or more. That would apply to 650,000 workers. Howard Hunter, deputy director of the federal WPA, commented on the furloughs. "Few of those people will get back on WPA. We've got a million people, certified and waiting for places on WPA," he said.

The effects were immediate and widespread. On July 8, 100,000 WPA assignees participated in a nationwide walkout. Locally, 500 men left their jobs in LaSalle County. In Peru, 53 men working on the Seventh Street project walked off the job en mass as a protest. Work on Peoria Street was also disrupted. WPA men at the Hegeler Park pool and the I-M Canal, who had been working 67 hours a month at an hourly rate of 44¢ - 65¢ saw their wages drop to 34¢ per hour. Five hundred men in Streator refused to work, forcing the closure of all WPA projects, except at the sewing center in that city. A mass meeting scheduled by the Illinois Workers Alliance – not to be confused with the Workers Alliance of America, a communist group – was scheduled to meet in Ottawa.

The response to the job action was predictable. President Roosevelt said, "You cannot strike against the government." Federal and regional WPA managers warned workers if they failed to report to work within five days, they would be fired. LaSalle Police Chief Peter Walloch said he was "prepared to cope with any emergency which may arise."

Desperate men could ill afford the luxury of a strike. Most men decided to go back to work. In Peru, 57 of the 99 men working on the street projects returned by the end of the week. The president of the local WPA organization said, "Men on both the swimming pool and canal projects are one hundred percent against a strike."

After the weeklong strike, and no willingness to compromise on the part of FDR and the Congress, more of the disgruntled men went back to work. However, some men were adamant in their opposition and were subsequently discharged. Nationwide, over 32,000 men were fired for failing to report to work after five days. In Illinois, the number was 8,623.

The federal government's plan was to cut costs by trimming over 300,000 WPA jobs by August 1, 1939. The less expensive Social Security unemployment compensation would provide minimal income to the unemployed.

On July 24, Robert Jones of 425 Wright Street in LaSalle, who had been unemployed for 11 weeks, was the first man in the Tri-Cities to receive his Social Security pay-order. Under the new system, unemployed workers had to wait almost a month – a two-week mandatory waiting period, another week to process the paperwork, and a few more days – to get the money from the Department of Labor in Chicago. Jones did all that and finally received his first check for $15. His application was one of 1,391 filed in LaSalle since July 1, 1939.

By August 1, about $9,000 in pay-orders arrived at the LaSalle office. Most of the pay-order cards varied from $13 to $14. Unemployed workers could collect anywhere from $7 to $16 a week for 16 weeks.

The negative reaction generated by the 130-hour monthly work requirement was tempered somewhat when the government announced pay increases in August for WPA workers still on the job. Common laborers in cities with a population over 5,000 would see their salaries rise from $44 a month to $48.10. The wages in communities of less than 5,000 would only move up from $40 a month to $42. Generally, each skill level had an increase. Semi-skilled wages went from $50 to $57.20. Skilled workers went from $63 to $74.10. Professionals employed by the WPA had the biggest increase. Wages would rise from $59 to $76.70. The only workers not getting a raise and actually taking a cut in pay were the women at the sewing centers. Their pay dropped from $44 to $42.90.

In August, the NYA held an essay contest in each county in the Rockford district. The theme of the writing was moneymaking projects. More than 1,200 entries were submitted in the district.

In Putnam County, four McNabb boys, Don Loesch, 16; Ken Grasser, 16; Vernon Johnson, 19; and Wilbur Johnson, 14; submitted a paper on their wood shop, where they made chairs, tables, stools, and poultry pens. They described how they used part of their profits to buy 300 chicks, some ducklings, and feed. After they raised and sold the fowl, they used the profits to expand their woodworking business. Their essay won first place. The prizes included a $300 check from the NYA district office and a Bible from the Women's Christian Temperance Union.

Bureau County's first place winner was Elvera Curran (Spring Valley). Maxine Pistono (Ladd) was second. Milton F. Searle (rural Princeton) was third, and Hugh Ulrich (Spring Valley) was fourth. Frank Baracani (Spring Valley), Manuel Lee Allen (Princeton), and Lillian Rauh (DePue) received honorable mentions.

Fifteen of the top 100 county entries were selected for district competition. The McNabb boys again came in first. The other finalists were Baracani 4th, Earl Chambers, (Lacon) 6th, Wayne Hodgeson, (Peru) 10th, Searle 11th, Ulrich 13th, John Dubach (Ottawa) 15th. Since all of the 15 winners were boys, two special awards were presented in a girls-only competition. Helen Barnett (Rochelle) and Margaret King (Dixon) were selected as the winners. The cash award was only part of the rewards at the district level. Each individual was offered a permanent job, a scholarship, and merchandise prizes.

A week later, Mayor Orr of LaSalle acknowledged the hard work of the WPA crews working on the Hegeler pool. Fifty WPA workers gathered for a picnic at Mitchell's Grove located north of LaSalle. Orr criticized the general public for describing WPA workers as "shovel leaners" and "idlers." "My experience with you has shown you to be fine, industrious, co-operative workmen and you deserve the highest commendation for what you have done for the community in which you live," said Orr. The mayor also praised Fred (Teddy) Blakely, superintendent of both the pool project and the Rockwell Road rail removal project.

Although the pool complex was still incomplete due to changes in the bathhouse design, the pool was filled with 400,000 gallons on Aug. 11. "It was too tempting," said Emil Bejster, who, along with another NYA assignee at the pool, Tony Lijewski, jumped into the water fully clothed. The pool was still not open to the public.

Just as Peru, LaSalle, and other towns in the Illinois Valley took time to remember significant events and people in their history so did McNabb. On Sunday, Aug. 20, 1939, a memorial service was held to mark the 100th anniversary of the death of Benjamin Lundy, a noted abolitionist of the 1830's. At the Friends Cemetery in McNabb, a crowd, estimated at 600, enjoyed the singing of The Exclusive Sharps and Flats, a 46-member choral society from the Chicago Urban League. Mrs. Katie L. Griffith, 80, from Henry, who was Lundy's granddaughter, and Miss Margaret Parrett of Normal, Lundy's great, great granddaughter, unveiled a monument to Lundy's memory.

The John Swaney School Alumni and the Society of Friends placed this marker near Lundy's grave at in McNabb.

221

In September, news was generally upbeat. Work continued on the Ladd school and the Dalzell gym. Twelve more NYA assignees were reporting to the YMA building in Peru, bringing the total to 40. The Libby-Owens glass plant in Ottawa was hiring again. Most significantly, the resumption of coal mining in the Tri-Cities accounted for the removal of 400-500 men from the relief rolls and government jobs.

However, those stories were offset by bad news. The PWA was overwhelmed with over 5,000 grant applications with a total value of over $766 million. Grants for a new city hall in Peru and Henry were now unlikely. The PWA returned applications for water works improvements in Varna and Princeton; the waste disposal plants in Spring Valley, Oglesby, Bureau and Ottawa; school projects in Sparland, LaMoille, and Princeton; and a stadium in Streator. Another $36,000 was needed to complete the Hegeler Park swimming pool. Unemployment continued to be a problem in Spring Valley and Streator. CCC administrators were tired of the complaints from local labor unions about the competition from the CCC. Oct. 9 was set as the date for the 200-man CCC company to pack up and leave Starved Rock State Park and move to Danville, IL.

In spite of the disappointments, there were many projects still underway. One project in particular was coming to an exciting conclusion, the opening of the Hennepin Bridge at Route 71.

The $700,000 Hennepin Bridge on Rt. 71 was built under the direction of the Illinois Department of Public Works and Buildings. Average employment during construction was about 100 men. At left, workers pour concrete for the Hennepin Bridge. (Putnam County Historical Society)

Work started on the Hennepin Bridge Sept. 21, 1936 and was completed in September 1939. (Art Kistler – IDOT)

222

The Hennepin Bridge, measuring 2,414 feet long, had a 44-foot clearance at the extreme high water mark. Note the ferryboat located in the foreground. (Putnam County Historical Society)

A two-day celebration to mark the completion of the bridge began on Saturday, Sept. 16, with a softball tournament followed by a talent show and dance in the evening. Concession stands, rides, and games were located in the Hennepin park.

Sunday's events began with a pet and hobby parade. Miss Ellen Ellena won the $5 first place award with her model of the courthouse. Mary Alice and Edward Paxson took second place ($3) with a model of the old ferry. At noon, the softball tournament ended with a victory for DePue over Henry 6-1. The DePue team won $12 as tournament champs. In an exhibition soccer game, the Dalzell Star Models beat the Mark Okays 2-1.

The big event of the day was the 1 p.m. official crossing of the bridge from Bureau County to Putnam County. Three

HENNEPIN

CORDIALLY INVITES YOU TO ATTEND THE

BRIDGE DEDICATION

All Day Sunday,—September 17th

Featuring at 4:30 P.M.

INTERNATIONAL NAUTICAL STUNT TERM

Direct from Winter Haven, Fla. Famous for their disregard for laws of gravity and safety. Featured in movie shorts as "The Hydra-Maniacs." The greatest attraction ever shown on the river.

DEDICATION CEREMONIES

2 P.M. to 4:30 P.M. Sunday.

Sunday Program from 9:30 A.M. to 10:30 P.M.

Saturday Program from 3 P.M. to 12 M.

AMATEUR CONTEST, SUNDAY, 7 to 9 P.M.

Hennepin children, whose families had lived in the area for many generations, assisted in the ribbon-cutting ceremony. Tommy Dore, 8, portrayed Uncle Sam, and Sharon Hamm, representing the state of Illinois, held a white, silk ribbon. Patsy Jones, 4, cast as Little Miss Illinois, stepped forward holding a gold and white pillow with the scissors for the ribbon-cutting ceremony. F. Lynden Smith, director of the Illinois Department of Public Works, cut the ribbon, and the Senachwine Band played "America." Then, the parade of dignitaries, floats, fire department units, and bands began crossing the bridge into Hennepin. The crowd gathered at the courthouse to hear the speakers. Attorney Durley Boyle acted as master of ceremonies as federal, state, and local politicians made speeches on the courthouse steps for 2½ hours!

The village and county were celebrating not only the completion of the bridge but also the centennial of the Putnam County courthouse. Many improvements were undertaken in 1934-35, using a PWA grant. The cupola was removed; the basement was refinished; plumbing and electrical improvements were made; the exterior and interior were redecorated; and all of the original furnishings were refinished and returned for use in the courthouse.

The Putnam County courthouse in Hennepin.
(Photo by author)

Attention shifted to the riverfront at 4:30 p.m. on Sunday. The Hydro-Maniacs, a nautical stunt team from Winter Haven, FL, began their program, which included aquaplaning, boat races, and water skiing. A LaSalle girl, Betty Beaumont, was asked to participate in the show when one member of the troupe was unable to appear. The day's events closed with a band concert, singing, an amateur show, and fireworks.

During the summer and fall of 1939, the NYA boys living in the YMA building were always busy. They released 95 quails and were raising another 96 birds. On Monday through Friday, eleven boys worked in the Peru parks. Five others were involved with clerical work and as lab assistants at Hygienic Institute. The NYA boys enrolled at L-P High School worked as assistants in the art department, mechanical drawing department, wood shop, and metal shop. Four young men at the L-P-O Junior College supervised the social room. Others worked in the city clerk's office and the surplus commodity depot. On Saturdays, the boys painted the airplane marker signs in LaSalle, Bureau, and Putnam Counties. These wooden signs had letters measuring 2 feet wide and 10-20 feet high. There were painted first with an aluminum-colored paint and then with a coat of yellow paint. On Sept. 23, one of the signs was placed on the roof of the Granville bank. Others were planned for buildings in Bureau, Hennepin, Spring Valley, Princeton, Ottawa, and Streator.

224

John Strell Jr., director of the LaSalle recreation program, had high praise for the 14 NYA assignees who worked on the ball diamonds and tennis courts, maintained the playground equipment, and cleaned the parks. The boys included Felix and Emile Bejster, Roy and Ray Brandt, Ray and Walter Lijewski, Anton Cubohowski, Clifford Irwin, Joe Gordon, Pete Pacetti, Francis Kowalski, Ira Stevens, Pete Kolonosky, Ray Koskosky, and Roy Wozniak.

In November, the Peru NYA residence program was selected to be one of the twelve Illinois sites for an aircraft ground mechanics program. Although the Chicago, Lockport, Marion, and East St. Louis sites received complete airplanes for training from the U.S. Air Corps, the Peru facility was scheduled to receive only an aircraft engine for training purposes. Only a few small cities were selected to participate in the mechanics program. In addition, the boys could take related courses in metal and electrical shop, navigation, geography, meteorology, math, radio communications, drafting, and blueprint reading. However, there would be no flight training. Only young men 18-25, whose families were on relief could qualify for the program. While visiting the Peru NYA facility, the assistant state NYA director said, "This course will train youths in a field which should provide then with employment opportunities in airplane factories." He emphasized that it was not connected with the U.S. Army.

Another NYA project was the numbering of Rural Electrification Administration (REA) utility poles in Bureau and LaSalle Counties. The boys would attach aluminum identification plates to the electric poles in a 30-40 mile area south of Starved Rock. The REA program was established in 40 states, and over 50,000 poles had already been marked. NYA boys nationwide were responsible for 95 percent of the work, which was designed to help electrical maintenance crews quickly identify downed power lines.

Other young men continued to work on the I-M Canal. Speaking at a meeting of the LaSalle Sportsmen's Club on Nov. 13, Hedley Breger of Ottawa, distinguished between the work of the CCC and the WPA on the canal. He pointed out that the WPA men worked primarily on rebuilding the towpath and constructing turnouts for cars as well as dredging the canal and constructing shelters. The CCC and National Park Service on the other hand, focused on the hydraulic structures, the locks, aqueducts, and spillways. He was especially proud of the work completed by the WPA at Split Rock, where "there is a picnic and parking area, a scenic refuge from the rush of world affairs." He went on to predict that it would "match the Lock 12 area in natural beauty."

225

The work of the CCC included improvements by Co. 612 at Camp Chicago-Lemont. This bronze statue, "The Worker," was erected in 2001 by the Willow Springs Historical Society near the intersection of Archer Ave. and Willow Springs Road to "commemorate the spirit and dedication of the young men who served in the Civilian Conservation Corps from April 1933 to July 1942." (Photo by author)

While the demand for CCC enrollees continued, the staff at the Peru sewing center had been reduced over the years. In 1935, as many as 50 women found WPA jobs there, but the mandatory furlough for those who had been there over 18 months was having an impact. In November, the employees numbered only 20 women, who were unable to find private employment. Working 130 hours each month, they made trousers for men, cotton dresses for women, and flannel sleepers for children.

The numbers on relief were gradually declining. Many qualified for benefits under Social Security's old age assistance and unemployment provisions and were no longer eligible for state relief.

While on a tour of northern Illinois on Nov. 30, Charles Miner, the State WPA director, cited Dalzell for its accomplishments achieved through WPA grants. He noted that the Dalzell coal mine had been closed for 15 years; car wheels sank up to their hubs on the main streets; and the village had little tax money. "Today nine miles of sidewalk and four miles of black top road with a gravel base are installed," he said. He also noted the WPA installation of a sewage system and the rehabilitation of the school's gym.

At the meeting, Dalzell Mayor Tonelli also pointed out how the improvements had the indirect affect of raising pride in home ownership in Dalzell. "Homes which not so long ago brought only $350 today are being sold at upwards of $2,000." Residents were repainting and re-roofing their houses. He even noted that after the sidewalks were finished, parents bought 200 pairs of roller skates for their children.

While the exterior of the Dalzell School and gym remained unchanged, WPA funds made it possible to raise the gym floor. The current Dalzell gym interior looks like those in other area schools, but a visit to the storage room below the gym reveals the original wooden basketball court of the old gym. (Photo by author)

On Dec. 23, months of work collecting funds and refurbishing old toys ended for local NYA assignees and Boy Scouts. A thousand children filled the LaSalle Theater on Dec. 23 to watch "Penrod and Sam," a children's film in which a couple of junior G-men try to capture bank robbers. Each child received the customary bag of candy and fruit and went home, hoping to receive one of the toys being distributed. Local groups and companies also remembered the needy with baskets of food.

As the year closed, the Grant school in LaSalle, which was abandoned by the LaSalle school board for educational purposes in the fall of 1939, became the focus of plans for a new recreation center. On Dec. 29, the school board ordered the removal of desks and other equipment so that Streel could begin working with the NYA and WPA authorities for the use of the empty rooms. Vernon Grandegeorge, area supervisor of the NYA, brought hand tools to the building and asked Streel to make out a requisition for power tools for the building's handicrafts program. Those taking shop classes as well as the general public would be invited to use the facility. The opening of the community center was planned for Jan. 15, 1940.

227

1940
LOOMING WAR CLOUDS

The New Deal's REA held a ceremony on Jan 18 at the Starved Rock electrical substation to mark the completion of 35 miles of REA electrical transmission lines. Sixty-nine customers in four townships in LaSalle County: Deer Park, South Ottawa, Fall River, and Grand Ridge, would now benefit from the improvements.

WPA-funded school construction continued. In the fall of 1938, the school year was extended in Ladd so that the traditional course of studies could be completed a month earlier to allow construction to begin on an addition funded by a WPA grant. The old wooden school, dating from 1890, was demolished. In March 1939, all of the students were crowded into the brick building. By November 1939, the WPA workers were ready to re-plaster cracks in the old building but soon discovered that the walls were in such bad shape that large sections would have to be torn out and new lath would have to be installed. The new addition, started in 1939, was essentially finished by March 1940, but about $6,000 was still needed for finishing work.

The $35,000 school addition in Ladd provided for four new classrooms and a gym in the basement. (Photo contributed by Jim Piacenti.)

Although the CCC had left Starved Rock, other companies continued their work constructing the towpath, bathrooms, shelters, bridges, and parking areas from Ottawa to Buffalo Rock. A few more shelters were planned for the portion of the canal from Utica to LaSalle. Lock 12 restoration was complete, and the CCC continued repairs at Lock 11. The crew would then move to Lock 13 west of Utica. The final local project was the work at Lock 14 at LaSalle. While the CCC worked on the locks, the WPA men, soon expected to number 700, would be mainly assigned to canal work in Will and Grundy counties.

In spite of that positive news, the job situation was still a significant problem. The April 1, 1940 report on LaSalle County unemployment indicated 1,900 men and women could not find jobs. More bad news was reported on April 6. The WPA was cutting jobs again. This time, 4,300 men, about 1/3 of the WPA jobs in the Rockford district, were to be dropped during the next three months. To make matters worse, the Oglesby application for a waste disposal plant was rejected. It also looked like the NYA resident center in Peru would close on June 30. If that happened, 40 students would be left without a place to live and without an income.

The uncertain times were reflected in the latest movie in early April at the Majestic Theater. The "Grapes of Wrath" may not have painted a realistic view of the Illinois Valley, but it reminded folks of the challenges of the past that might still lie ahead. Ad from the April 5, 1940 LaSalle *Post-Tribune.*

MAJESTIC

4 BIG DAYS **Starting SUNDAY**

DARRYL F. ZANUCK'S **THE**
GRAPES OF WRATH
by John Steinbeck

Fortunately, work in progress at the I-M Canal would resume on April 25 because $200,000 had been authorized at the federal level. The project, employing 450 men, had been suspended for six months.

That spring, WPA assignees were "busy as beavers" working on Starved Rock landscaping the area where the old hotel, annex, and custodian's residence had stood until being razed during the winter of 1939. Congressional cutbacks had reduced the local WPA numbers from 400 to 132 on the parkway project. The WPA crew was next scheduled to work on the seawall at Starved Rock.

During the first week of May, problems continued with the financing of the Hegeler pool. First, the city council voted for an ordinance authorizing $26,000 instead of $25,000 in bonds. Another vote was required. The following week, someone failed to notice an error on the referendum ballots as they were being printed. The ballot specified a referendum for $25,0000 instead of $25,000. Mayor Orr said, "It's been a nightmare for me since (the pool project) started." Instead of canceling the referendum, Orr allowed the vote to be taken with some of the misprinted ballots being used. Even though the LaSalle voters approved the bond issue 9-1, legal opinions over the misprinted ballots swayed the mayor to determine a new vote would have to be taken on June 25. Frustrated with the invalid referendum, Orr recommended using tax anticipation warrants for $25,000 until a new referendum was held. Fortunately, two bond companies in Chicago offered to buy the bonds based on the city's high credit rating. So work on the pool continued.

Progress was also being made to finish the bridge over the Vermilion River in Oglesby. A bid of $72 million was accepted by the state on May 10.

The government did not fund every construction project. Only days after the LaSalle pool bonds were sold, Oglesby residents were thrilled with the announcement that Bertha K. Evans, a major stockholder in Marquette Cement from Libertyville, donated money for the construction of a community center. The facility would be named for Theodore G. Dickinson, founder of Dickinson Cement and later, Marquette Cement Manufacturing. The $90,000 Dickinson House would include bowling alleys, a swimming pool, and reading rooms on the first floor and room in the lower level for crafts projects. Groundbreaking took place on May 18. One of the speakers, Ray Williams, business representative for the cement workers union, said, "It will help take care of one of our greatest problems – unemployment – for in its construction the labor of many men who would otherwise be idle will be employed." The gold-plated shovel used at the ceremony was given to Postmaster John McCann for a similar ceremony for the new Oglesby post office.

WPA promoted the achievements of its numerous projects during the week of May 20-25. The theme was "This Work Pays for Your Community." The Grant Recreation Center in LaSalle and the Oglesby recreation rooms included displays of clothing manufactured by the sewing center, maps of a land-use survey, a display on the effects of hearing and vision problems for children, and a variety of arts and crafts projects.

While there were many opportunities for young men in the NYA and CCC, some of the young ladies from the Illinois Valley chose to live in the Rockford NYA residence facility, where they took a six-month program in business skills. On May 17, the girls were awarded diplomas at the Metropolitan Business College. Rita Ferrari of Spring Valley, Frances Underwood of Ottawa, Ruby Thompson of Ladd, and Frances Ross of Walnut were among the 15 girls receiving award certificates for completing the NYA courses.

Spring events also included the opening of the new Coca Cola bottling plant in Peru managed by Al J. Hebel and Andrew Hebel. Construction had begun April 1, 1939, and the plant was in operation as of Dec. 1, 1939. However, an open house was postponed until May 23 so that visitors could see how 5,100 Coke bottles were filled every hour. Everyone who visited the plant that day was given a free bottle of Coke.

In June, the Sampsel Time Control Company began operations in Spring Valley. At the June 17 dedication of the $28,000 plant, 3,000 industrialists and manufacturers visited the facility. Little did anyone anticipate the factory would play an important role in manufacturing of torpedo fuses during WWII.

Several small towns had celebrations during the summer of 1940. Ladd observed its Semi-Centennial Celebration at the end of June. The five-day affair began with music by Bannon's Accordion Band and a dance. Torchlight parades, games for the children, and concerts filled the schedule of events. The *Post* reported that 10,000 people jammed the village streets for the celebration. Mr. and Mrs. D. K. Talbot, Mrs. and Mrs. William Kramer and Mr. and Mrs. William Morgan, all village pioneers, were on hand for a mile-long parade. A display of fireworks on the final evening concluded the festivities.

Dalzell held its Homecoming on July 18-21. In addition to a carnival, baseball games, and boccie ball tournaments, the village brought in the Caren Scotch Highlander Bagpipe Band from Miami.

Granville also held a celebration during July 26-28. In addition to the usual carnival rides, water fights, airplane and jalopy rides, the village held a dedication of its new street lights. Dr. Germano, the celebration chairman, introduced I. F. Stonier, the president of the businessmen's association, who thanked the WPA and NYA men for their work on the project. The celebration included the crowning of Shirle Harker, the "Queen of Light."

The village of Mark held a homecoming Aug. 31-Sept. 2. Carnival rides, boxing matches, plane rides, and entertainment by Dezutti's Orchestra were scheduled for the festival. The coal mine dump served as a focal point during the celebration. Ace Hillard's Circus of Death, featuring 32 daredevil car stunts, was the big draw for the crowd. On the final day of the celebration, a car was hauled to the top of the old coal dump, and Hillard drove the car down the 600-foot slope without injury.

In spite of all the festivities and a sense of completion of major construction projects, the news of the Nazi's military advances through Norway and Eastern Europe, and the persistent Luftwaffe attacks on England could not be simply ignored. The American response to those belligerent actions by Germany was reflected in subtle changes in government programs. Calls for a draft and military preparedness increasingly filled the front pages of local newspapers.

On July 2, the Illinois Aeronautics Board selected LaSalle as one of the 36 potential sites for a seaplane base. The NYA assignees could use materials costing LaSalle only $150 to construct and place a floating dock in the water to moor seaplanes.

New WPA directives focused on three areas of military preparedness for the Illinois Valley: canning of surplus food for the armed forces; production of war garments, hospital uniforms, mattresses, and sheets at the sewing centers; and instruction in first aid. Statewide, the WPA began construction of an airfield at Carbondale, and other military facilities at Camp Grant, Ft. Sheridan, and Chanute Field at Rantoul.

Washington rescinded its plan to close the NYA residence center in Peru. Instead, the federal government leased the building to train 75 men in woodworking and radio technology. A similar number of women would be taught home economics skills.

The possibility of war also had an impact on the local schools. Nationwide, there was more emphasis on training for national defense industries. A special summer program was offered at L-P High School to men 18 and older with aptitudes in machine shop, sheet metal welding, auto and aircraft mechanics, forging, and drafting. Initially, only twelve men enrolled, and it was thought the program would be canceled. However, when the deadline for enrollment arrived in mid-July, over 300 men had applied. Of that number, 125 were accepted. The classes were divided into day and night classes, but because there were so many men involved and facilities were so limited, the day classes were split into two, three-hour sections running from 9 a.m. to 12 noon and 1 p.m. to 4 p.m. Since the federal authorities insisted that each class run a minimum of six hours each day, half of the enrollees were sent home hoping to resume their studies after the first class completed training.

The Hennepin Canal, once viewed as too expensive to operate, suddenly took on possible military significance as a critical link connecting Chicago by way of the Illinois Waterway with industries on the Mississippi River. Because of the raging battles in Europe and lack of overseas orders, only eight grain barges had used the canal during the spring and early summer. However, International Harvester in Chicago used eleven barges to ship steel to its Farmall tractor factory. Anticipating a spreading war and potential need for the canal, the federal government decided to appropriate $175,000 to operate and maintain the canal for 1940-41.

More local men signed up for the Citizens Military Training Camp (CMTC) at Ft. Sheridan. The July enrollees in the month-long program included William Dugdale, Charles Gillman, Robert

232

Zacher, and Mason Knudston (all from Peru), Lewis Ebener (Oglesby), Art Edgcomb (Utica), and Harold Schmitt (Mendota).

Meanwhile, Congress debated the merits of a military draft. There were 2,346 men eligible for the draft in the Tri-Cities.

The New Deal programs continued in the Illinois Valley with some changes. CCC enrollees were still being accepted for work in northern Illinois and Wisconsin rather than Camp Illini in Marseilles or Camp Brandon in Morris. CCC quotas – 130 in LaSalle County and 22 in Grundy County – were becoming difficult to fill since better paying jobs were available. Pay for NYA participants was changed to a flat rate of $18.50 for 56-74 hours. NYA supervisors received $24.72 a month. At Starved Rock, WPA men were assigned to work on the backfill for the privately contracted 1,100-foot seawall. Eighty-eight WPA men were employed on Peru's storm and sewer projects and in city parks, and by August, the LaSalle swimming pool was finally completed.

Construction of the brick bathhouse for the LaSalle pool began on June 17, 1940. A ticket booth was located at the entrance to the brick structure. To provide extended hours, six, 35-foot light poles were installed around the pool. (Photos by author)

Recent improvements at the LaSalle pool appear in this 2008 photo.

Hundreds of children had already enjoyed the 45'x 45' wading pool in mid-August, but the official dedication ceremonies did not take place until Labor Day, Sept. 2, 1940. To set the tone for the afternoon dedication, the Peru band began with John Phillip Sousa's "Stars and Stripes Forever." John Bartloszewski, chairman

233

of the playgrounds commission, continued with his dedication speech. The L-P High School band and St. Hyacinth's Boy Scouts drum and bugle corps provided musical entertainment. A crowd, estimated at 5,000, came to see national and international diving and swimming stars from the Chicago Towers Club. Headliners included Olympic backstroke champion Adolph Kiefer and Otto Jaretz, the "world's fastest swimmer," who held the records for both indoor and outdoor speed in the national 100-yard competition.

The prospect of American involvement in a second world war was becoming a more significant concern. Already there was news that submarines, built in Wisconsin, would be coming down the Illinois River. The federal government anticipated that more military and civilian pilots would be needed so a special course in aeronautics was offered at L-P High School. Betty Benckendorf, a petite, 5'3" graduate from Ottawa H.S., was the only female in a group of ten selected for flight training. Within two weeks, the 19 year old soloed at the LaSalle airport and was certified as a pilot.

The emphasis on military preparedness was seen first hand near the Matthiessen School when the 121st Field Artillery used the school grounds for a two-day bivouac on Oct. 19-20. Five batteries of the National Guard unit with 500 men and 72 vehicles were on their way to Alexandria, LA for maneuvers.

The war was intensifying. Italian planes pounded British positions in Alexandria, Egypt while the British were bombing Dunkirk, France, the likely jumping off port for the Nazi invasion of England. Meanwhile, draft information forms were sent across the U.S. to prepare for the first peacetime, military conscription. In anticipation of the registration process, Mayor Orr directed the WPA garment center to be vacated to make room for the local draft board.

The possibility of America's involvement in the war would soon change job descriptions from digging ditches for sewers to building tanks, planes, and ships. The young men in the CCC, who had been putting out forest fires, might soon wear a different uniform and face a different kind of fire.

In September, the presidential race between FDR and Wendell Wilkie (pictured) included whistle-stop campaigning in the Illinois Valley by the challenger. Wilkie's train took him to Joliet, where 8,000 supporters cheered him. In Morris, 5,000 people greeted the challenger. Even bigger crowds of 10,000 came out in Ottawa and LaSalle to see the man, who was trying to prevent FDR from being elected to a third term.

At each stop, his speech focused on the same issues. "If I am elected, I shall never send an American boy to fight in any European war. Our American people will get jobs not spinach," he promised. Although Wilkie criticized FDR for the lack of job creation, the number of families on relief in LaSalle County had been in steady decline – 195 in 1938, 169 in 1939, and 147 in 1940.

While Wilkie had significant support among the rural population, he was not able to capture a majority of the urban vote. The Nov. 5 election returns showed that the contender received a majority vote in LaSalle, Putnam, and Bureau counties, but nationwide, Wilkie failed to win enough electoral votes (449-82) to unseat the incumbent president.

The New Deal programs continued. Construction began on the LaMoille grade school gym in the spring of 1940. A formal dedication of the $30,000 building was held Oct. 22, 1940. About 500 residents attended the program, which began with musical presentations by the LaMoille H. S. band, the girls' chorus, and Miss Reba Brown, the school's music teacher, who performed a violin solo. Dr. Frank Jensen, superintendent of L-P High School was the principal speaker. The first major event after the dedication was a presentation of "Tom Sawyer" by the grade school on Oct. 25.

The LaMoille school gym was constructed in 1940 with a distinctive exterior of tan building tiles.

(Photos by author)

The recreational area at Lake Mendota, started in 1936, was completed after many years. The federal government contributed $25,449, and the city added $12,344 to pay for rip-rapping the lake banks, and building

spillways, restrooms, a dam, a bridge, and landscaping. (Photo by author)

235

On Oct. 31, the cornerstone of the Oglesby post office was set in position. John McCann, serving as master of ceremonies, introduced Governor John Stelle and Mayor Frank Moyle. The Oglesby municipal band played a number of songs. Part of the ceremony included the insertion of a copper box holding historical documents, such as the L-P-O phone book, the dedication program, J. R. Bent's history of Oglesby, and the list of draft registrants published in the *Post.*

The Oglesby post office was nearing completion on Nov. 30, 1940. The building was unique in that the walls were all poured concrete. (Oglesby Library)

The high cost of the public works projects compelled the federal authorities to issue new mandates. WPA workers were told they would have to take full-time or part-time jobs at prevailing wages if private employment was offered to them.

There was little apparent change in the local WPA projects. Concrete piers under the Illinois Zinc Co.'s WWI acid plant were dynamited since the piers were on the city's sewer property. Sixty-two men began work on Utica's interceptor sewer project, and more men were assigned to work on the I-M Canal – 160 from LaSalle and Ottawa and 40 from Morris.

The CCC authorities decided on a plan to make sure enrollees would leave their assignments with money in their pockets to help them make the transition to private jobs. As of Jan. 1, the junior enrollees would receive $8 in cash. A $7 monthly deduction would be deposited to a special account so they would have $42 to buy clothes and incidentals when they left the corps. The allottees received only $15 instead of $25. Leaders and assistant leaders also had $7 deductions applied to their salaries of $45 and $36 respectively. Their allottees also received reduced payments.

The year ended with the 13th annual Big Hearts party for over 1,000 children at the LaSalle Theater. After watching Bing Crosby in "Star Maker," over a half ton of candy and cases of apples and oranges were passed out to the kids. Much thanks was given to the NYA boys and girls, the Boy Scouts, who had repaired toys and the Urbanowski Department Store, which donated 24 dolls.

236

1941
FINAL PROJECTS

In January, the CCC again announced a call for enrollment, at Camp Illini near Marseilles or the Central Life Building in Ottawa, but quotas were seldom filled. Those who completed a six-month program sometimes joined the Army reserves and were assigned to the position of subalternate, an administrative position at the camps. Regular Army officers were being called to active duty.

To mark the official opening of the Oglesby post office in January, a special cachet, drawn by Francis Aimone of Oglesby, was stamped on all first-day letters. A special postmark was also used.

On Friday, Jan. 31, the finishing touches were added to the Oglesby post office. An open house on was held Feb. 1-2, 1941. (Oglesby Library)

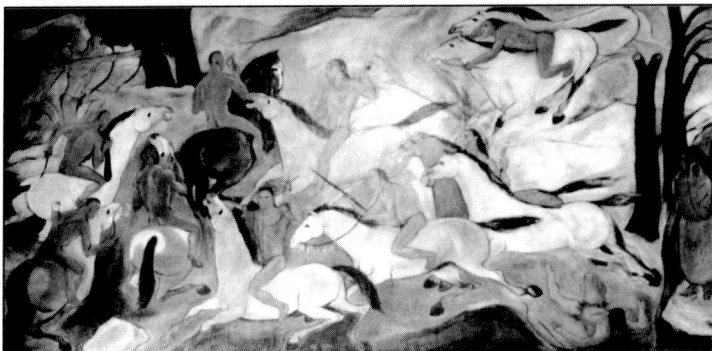

On Feb. 28, Fay E. Davis, was offered a commission to paint a mural in the Oglesby post office lobby. The U.S. Treasury Section of Fine Arts paid $700 for her work titled, "Illini and Pottawatomie Struggle at Starved Rock." She completed the mural in 1942. (Photo by author)

237

One of the last schools built during the Depression was the Rockwell School, designed in 1939 by Louis Gerding of Ottawa. It was dedicated on Feb. 7, 1941. One teacher was in charge of 24 pupils in grades 1-8. Today, the building is a private residence.

The federal government estimated 20-30 percent of all children were undernourished. One local response to that situation was the hot lunch program at the grade school in Granville. Lunches were available for 5¢, if a child could afford it. Otherwise, it was free. WPA assignees served nutritious lunches consisting of IERC surplus commodities. Menus might include macaroni or rice with cheese or tomato soup with homemade noodles. Included with the entrée might be buttered rutabaga, peas, carrots, prunes, peaches or baked beans. Children brought their own plates, cups, knives, and forks. Empty milk bottles were placed in area businesses to collect additional funds for the Granville program.

The Oglesby First National Bank opened in February in the renovated facilities of the former Oglesby State Bank. It was a major improvement for the city's residents, who in many cases had moved their savings to LaSalle. The federal government insured accounts of national banks up to $5,000 so it came as no surprise that within five minutes of the bank's opening that $10,000 was deposited.

WPA projects in LaSalle were almost finished, leaving about 100 men without jobs. The LaSalle WPA Workers' Organization called for increased quotas of men working on the canal and the Oglesby road project. Peru, Mendota, Ottawa, and Streator still had work. In Oglesby, the city's WPA recreation program was curtailed; so activities were moved to the Lorenzatti Building on Walnut St.

In spite of all the New Deal programs to create jobs, there were still a number of hobos found in the area. One fellow known only as "Dutch," who was over 70, had roamed the Illinois Valley since the beginning of the Depression in '29. He had lived with a companion in one of the hobo "jungles" east of the Ladd roundhouse. On Feb. 18, a Milwaukee RR agent found his body lying faced down along the tracks not far from the depot. It was felt that Dutch died of natural causes although his advanced age, coupled with exposure to the sub-zero temperatures, may have contributed to his demise. He had no positive identification. He was just one of many homeless men, who tried to survive the best he could.

In the closing days of the Depression, many men still relied on WPA projects for work, such as graveling and blacktopping roads, constructing bridges, pouring concrete sidewalks, digging drainage ditches, laying storm and sanitary sewers, installing water lines and fire hydrants, and building pump houses, water storage tanks, and a variety of county buildings. The area's play schools provided for the socialization of children ages 5-6. Teens and young adults continued to enjoy the variety of recreation programs, such as craft classes and athletic activities offered in most cities. An example of the emphasis on offering a variety of social outlets was the opening of Dickinson House in Oglesby.

On June 27, 1941, the Dickinson House in Oglesby was dedicated. A thousand people used the bowling alleys the first year, and over 37,000 people enjoyed the swimming pool during that time. Thousands of others used the reading room and vocational facilities.

The rear of the Dickinson House faced a large open field. Marquette Cement Co. donated the 12-acre tract. (Photos by author)

One of the longest-running local projects during the Depression was the work on Oglesby's east side road, which started when the first dirt was moved on Dec. 1, 1937. Progress was slow, and work was suspended when federal funds were exhausted. Workers were simply shifted to other WPA projects. On Jan. 30, 1941, WPA workers from LaSalle were re-assigned to work on the approaches to the Vermilion River Bridge.

The road project was finally completed in 1941. At 2:30 p.m., on Oct. 19, Mayor Frank Moyle of Oglesby and Mayor D. J. Cahill of Utica cut silver ribbons, one at the end of the Burlington Bridge and the other at the end of the Vermilion River Bridge, to symbolize the opening of the link between the two cities. The two mayors then shook hands before a crowd of 1,200. The ceremonies continued with speeches by public officials interspersed with music by the Oglesby Municipal Band.

Work was temporarily suspended on the concrete decking for the bridge over the Vermilion River until the spring of 1941. (IDOT)

The Ed Hand Highway, stretching 9/10 of a mile, created an entrance to the east side of Oglesby and a shortcut to the state parks. (Art Kistler – IDOT)

The bombing of Pearl Harbor by Japan on Dec. 7, 1941 created work opportunities in war plants for millions of Americans. Others were called to serve in the Armed Forces. From that date forward, the influx of massive amounts of federal dollars for military projects marked a gradual end to the Depression. One by one, the PWA, WPA, CCC, NYA, and other jobs programs were phased out. Now, those who struggled through the hardships of those times faced a new chapter in their lives, WWII.

Today, the improvements in schools, sidewalks, bridges, roads, and state parks are taken for granted. Few remember the sacrifices of those who lived through the Great Depression.